Man and Work
in Society

Man and Work in Society

A Report on the Symposium
held on the occasion of
the 50th Anniversary of
the original Hawthorne Studies,
Oakbrook, Illinois, November 10-13, 1974

Edited by

Eugene Louis Cass

and

Frederick G. Zimmer

Members, Headquarters Staff
Western Electric Company

VNR **VAN NOSTRAND REINHOLD COMPANY**
NEW YORK   CINCINNATI   TORONTO   LONDON   MELBOURNE

658.3
M 266z

Van Nostrand Reinhold Company Regional Offices:
New York   Cincinnati   Chicago   Milbrae   Dallas

Van Nostrand Reinhold Company International Offices:
London   Toronto   Melbourne

Copyright © 1975 by Western Electric Company, Incorporated

Library of Congress Catalog Card Number: 75-26866
ISBN: 0-442-29359-3

Manufactured in the United States of America

Published by Van Nostrand Reinhold Company
450 West 33rd Street, New York, N.Y. 10001

Published simultaneously in Canada by Van Nostrand Reinhold Ltd.

15 14 13 12 11 10 9 8 7 6 5 4 3 2 1

Library of Congress Cataloging in Publication Data
Main entry under title:

Man and work in society.

    Sponsored by Harvard University Graduate School of
Business Administration and Western Electric.
    Includes bibliographies and index.
    1. Personnel management—Congresses. 2. Psy-
chology, Industrial—Congresses. I. Cass, Eugene
Louis. II. Zimmer, Frederick G. III. Harvard
University. Graduate School of Business Administra-
tion. IV. Western Electric Company.
HF5549.M299   658.8   75-26866
ISBN 0-442-29359-3

Contributors

Henry M. Boettinger
  Director of Corporate Planning
  American Telephone and Telegraph Company

Dr. Marvin D. Dunnette
  University of Minnesota

Dr. Fred E. Fiedler
  University of Washington

Dr. Robert M. Guion
  Bowling Green State University

Dr. J. Richard Hackman
  Yale University

Dr. Howard W. Johnson
  Chairman of the Corporation
  Massachusetts Institute of Technology

Dr. Robert L. Kahn
  University of Michigan

Dr. Edward E. Lawler III
  University of Michigan

Dr. Paul Lawrence
  Harvard University

Dr. Harold J. Leavitt
  Stanford University

Dr. Harry Levinson
Levinson Institute

Dr. Jay W. Lorsch
Harvard University

Dr. Alfred J. Marrow
The Harwood Company

Dr. Alan A. McLean, M.D.
New York Hospital–Cornell Medical Center

Dr. W. Walter Menninger, M.D.
Menninger Foundation

Wyllys Rheingrover
General Manager, Hawthorne Works
Western Electric Company

Dr. Edgar H. Schein
Massachusetts Institute of Technology

Dr. Victor H. Vroom
Yale University

Dr. Richard E. Walton
Harvard University

FOREWORD

One of the prevailing characteristics of Western Electric and the Bell System is a deep and continuing preoccupation with the future. This is reflected in long-range planning, which must anticipate the communication needs of the public five, ten, and twenty-five years from now. To have things ready at the time they are needed requires that work be started and risks be taken years before a new service goes into operation.

With that kind of orientation, it requires something of special significance and magnitude to cause Western Electric people to look backward in time and to consider at length work that was accomplished in earlier years. This book suggests something of the pervasive importance of what was done and what was learned at Western Electric's Hawthorne Works beginning fifty years ago.

The Hawthorne Studies were a pioneer effort by the late F. J. Roethlisberger of Harvard and W. J. Dickson of Western Electric to investigate human behavior in one limited, but extremely important domain—the world of work. They began this exploration in an area where there were few, if any, paths to follow. However, they left a trail that became part of the basic knowledge of human behavior in the work place for the hundreds of students who followed them. The Hawthorne Studies came to be regarded as one of the important headwaters of modern sociological and industrial psychological knowledge.

In that sense, the Hawthorne Studies will never be concluded because the questions they began raising in 1924 concern the human nature of individuals and groups—easily the most dynamic factor that must be taken into account in any modern industrial operation. It was in recognition of the stimulus this research provided to continued study and debate that the Harvard University Graduate School of Business Administration and Western Electric once more joined their efforts by cosponsoring a symposium in November 1974 to commemorate the

50th anniversary of the Hawthorne Studies and to rekindle the enthusiasm to learn that carried those original studies so far.

The chapters included in this volume represent the thinking of a group of contemporary experts as they view some selected topics which, while rooted in the Hawthorne Studies, continue to have implications for today and for the future. They contributed much to the success of the symposium. Especially noteworthy for this contribution is George F. F. Lombard, Senior Associate Dean of the Harvard University Graduate School of Business Administration, and many members of the faculty. We have been privileged and honored to be associated with Dean Lombard in cosponsoring this symposium with Harvard.

To the many others who helped make the symposium a success—including our own employees, both at Hawthorne and at corporate headquarters in New York—I extend my sincere thanks.

D. E. Procknow
President
Western Electric Company

PREFACE

Anyone who has had the opportunity to review in detail the research represented in the Hawthorne Studies cannot help but be awed by the depth and scope of these efforts. To have the opportunity to actually see and look through the original records is a still more awesome experience. Therein is contained the story of systematic inquiry. In viewing these records one must be impressed by the meticulous documentation, the attempts at scientific rigor in an area most difficult to approach in this manner, and the openness of the spirit of inquisitiveness and inquiry which followed many paths, some to broad highways of scientific investigation and others merely to blind alleys. It would appear that just about every lead was followed and just about every possibility explored in the attempt to assure that as many of the relevant questions as possible would be asked.

Because of the vast scope of these research studies, the interpretations, comments and even criticisms related to them cover a wide range. One is reminded of the fable of the blind men and the elephant, each interpreting and describing what he "saw" based upon where and how he made contact, Truly, the Hawthorne Studies have "something in them for everyone."

As the proposal for commemorating the 50th anniversary of the start of these studies in some appropriate way germinated, and the idea of a symposium began to take form, the difficult task of selecting topics for inclusion loomed up. The problem was eased somewhat by a decision to design the symposium to commemorate the Hawthorne Studies and to honor the people who were a part of them—but not to relive the past. The feeling grew that the true value of these classical efforts derived not so much from their place in history but from the implications they have for now and the future.

This is the nature of classics. Their value does not rest with the studies and writings of historians, but with the impact they can have on the thinking and

actions of contemporary and future scholars and practitioners. The Hawthorne
Studies meet this description of a "classic" to the fullest.

From this philosophical base, there evolved three criteria which served as
guiding principles for topic selection:

1. Topics were sought which had some rooting in the original studies by
   virtue of their being a focus of major research efforts or a major topic of
   explanation and interpretation.
2. Topics were sought which would have present-day interest and impact,
   and would therefore permit an analysis of trends and progress from the
   time of the original studies to the present.
3. Topics were sought which would have implications out into the future
   since it is only in terms of the future that plans and adjustments can be
   made.

Even the rigorous application of these criteria did not reduce the number of
possible topics sufficiently to meet the time and attention-span limitations for a
symposium of reasonable duration. The final reduction was accomplished by a
process some might consider arbitrary, but which those involved prefer to feel
was based upon a judgment of the contemporary and future importance of the
topics.

To a considerable degree, the selection of the topics dictated the selection of
the topic speakers. Each selected topic became the subject for a panel of two
speakers. The search for panelists focused on those who had worked and written
extensively in the topic area, and who therefore could be expected to be in a
position to discuss the current state of knowledge, the obstacles to application
and what the future might hold.

In addition, the attempt was made to bring together two speakers for each
topical area who might be expected to differ in their perspective, and thus
would represent different points of view. Obviously, there are many names
that could be associated with each of the panel topics and difficult selections
had to be made among many potential contributors. With the knowledge that
not everyone who could make a worthy contribution would be asked to participate, the selection was made with the full confidence that those selected were
capable of such a contribution.

The papers prepared by the panelists in each area constitute the major portion
of this volume. Also included because of their contribution to the tone, insights
and philosophy of the symposium are the addresses of Mr. Henry M. Boettinger,
Director of Corporate Planning, American Telephone and Telegraph Company,
the keynote speaker; Dr. Howard W. Johnson, Chairman of the Corporation,
Massachusetts Institute of Technology, the banquet speaker; and Wyllys Rheingrover, general manager of Western Electric's Hawthorne Works.

Shortly before his death, William J. Dickson, retired from Western Electric and
one of the authors of *Management and the Worker*, had the opportunity to hear

of the plans for the commemorative symposium. Bill, whose interest in the entire area of people at work never waned, listened to these plans with increasing enthusiasm and finally made the following statement, "Fritz (referring to his co-author, the late Professor Fritz Roethlisberger of Harvard University) always said it would take at least a generation before these studies will be fully understood and appreciated." Let this be that generation!

Paul J. Patinka
Symposium Program Coordinator

Contents

PART I

Unique or Similar—How De We Live With Individual Differences?

The Hawthorne Studies demonstrated—as many studies before them and since have—the unique characteristics of people—the commonly acknowledged thought that people are different. Yet, there is continued evidence that as a convenience to organizing human institutions, particularly the work place, this idea of "individual differences" is frequently overlooked. Why isn't this concept better applied? How can it be?

This issue is covered here from two orientations. The first is the traditional approach of looking at how people differ and how those differences get translated into the performance of work. The second approach looks at how different people relate to organizations.

1

THE HAWTHORNE TYPE — AMONG OTHERS

Robert M. Guion
Bowling Green State University

INTRODUCTION

As practically everyone knows, the Hawthorne Studies were about the most important and influential pieces of scientific research ever done on the psychology of work. They have had a direct line of descent, in which research on employee attitudes begat research on work motivation, which begat interest in leadership, which begat studies of the impact of the organization's social structure on the work group, which ultimately begat the branch on the right-hand side of the hyphen in the field of Industrial–Organizational Psychology. What kind of genealogy might the left-hand side have had if as much attention had been given to the matter of individuality in interpreting the Hawthorne studies as was given to group processes?

The left-hand side has functioned these fifty years on a heritage predating Hawthorne. It's ancestry, which might be characterized as E. K. Strong out of Walter Dill Scott by Alfred Binet, has been dominated by measurement. Interest in attitudes and job satisfaction was stimulated by the Hawthorne results, but the response was scale development.

My comments come from this heritage. It tells me that my role is to contribute to scientific knowledge through research using reliable tools for measurement. It assumes that a firmly-grounded science of human work will help managers be more effective. And it insists that the science has no firm ground if it ignores the fact of individual differences.

In one sense, the topic of individual differences is irrelevant to recollections of the Hawthorne studies. The general tenor of *Management and The Worker* (Roethlisberger and Dickson, 1939) is indicated pretty well in the index where the entry for "Individual" tells you also to see "Social Organization."

3

In a different sense, the fact of individual differences permeates the Hawthorne studies from beginning to end. Individual production records are presented in *Management and the Worker*, not mere summaries. Attitudes are represented through extensive individual quotations. And the principal action program resulting from the research was one of individual counseling.

In still a third sense, the Hawthorne investigators made the same intuitive compromise regarding individual differences that characterizes most psychological research. They studied a limited, three-dimensional "type" of person for whom their results would generalize. The "Hawthorne type" was experienced, willing, and cooperative. There are other types. There might be people who are experienced, willing, and uncooperative; or experienced, unwilling, and uncooperative; or inexperienced, willing, and cooperative; etc. (see Figure 1).

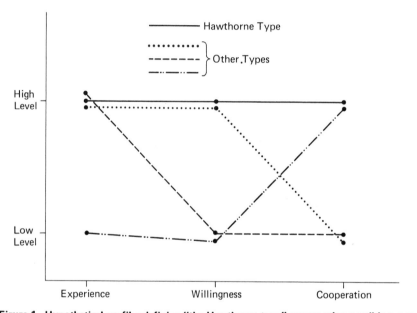

Figure 1. Hypothetical profiles defining "the Hawthorne type" among other possible types.

These are not contradictory interpretations. They simply represent three different frames of reference from which to view individual differences, and I should like to consider each of them as they relate to contemporary personnel research.

THE MEANING OF INDIVIDUAL DIFFERENCES

The Measurement Perspective

The most common criticism of the measurement specialist is that he tends to think of an individual as a bundle of traits. He may be concerned with physical traits: some people are taller than others, some darker than others, some stronger than others, etc. He may be concerned with traits of personality or character: some people are friendlier than others, some more anxious than others, and some in one sense or another more honest than others. He may be (and probably is) concerned with traits of intellect: some people are generally smarter than others, some may comprehend more words than others, or some may be able to educe more symbolic relationships than others. The study of individual differences from the measurement perspective has been extremely analytic. The result is that human behavior can be described by choosing from a list of traits rivaling in length the old lists of instincts.

Despite all these elements, the measurement specialist is actually interested in individual differences only along a specific dimension or set of dimensions. He implicitly assumes that his subjects are all alike on dimensions for which he has no interest. It is paradoxical that the branch of psychology called individual differences is rarely concerned with individuality. Rather, its concern is with individual differences among people only along the dimensions of the investigator's interests.

This is not necessarily bad. If we try to predict performance by adding more than a few variables, we will introduce more error than solid prediction. It is entirely appropriate to focus on the most salient variables, those that account for the most variance in the performance we try to predict. Thus, intellectual traits will be used for the prediction of academic achievement, while character traits may be more salient in the prediction of emotional stability under social stress. Neither intellect nor character would help identify people who can endure muscular and skeletal stress in situations requiring unusual posture for prolonged periods.

In short, the scientist picks variables with great care; one does not attempt to deal with all possible sources of variance simultaneously. Scientific advance is usually based on relatively simple functional relationships. For example, laws related to the volume of a gas consider temperature and pressure but ignore the physical and chemical properties of the container in which the gas is housed. It is fair to ask whether measurement specialists are as adept in selecting their variables.

Some think not. In summarizing a symposium on learning and individual differences at the University of Pittsburgh (Gagné, 1967), Melton emphasized the importance of individual differences in the experimental study of learning, but the individual differences with which he and the conference were concerned were not static traits. Rather, Melton demanded that hypotheses be formulated in terms of the process constructs of contemporary theories of learning and performance, i.e., differences in the way people handle the task at hand, as opposed to characteristics that describe people independently of special settings or problems. A somewhat similar point of view was expressed by Tyler (1965) when she said that the study of individual differences should be "basically a psychology of development rather than of measurement. Its graphic symbol would be not the normal curve but the growth curve" (p. 507). The idea was cemented by Underwood (1974) with his insistence that the fact of individual differences in processes that determine responses to a stimulus are the "crucible" in learning theory.

What can a measurement specialist offer for describing individual differences in terms of process variables? Answers, unfortunately, are rare and generally nebulous. Some answers may result from information about cognitive styles or strategies for coping with tasks. At a very elementary level, we recognize different test-taking strategies such as guessing on every multiple-choice item as opposed to answering only those items where the correct answer is known with some minimal degree of certainty.

At a more sophisticated level, some factor-analytic research has identified process variables. Certainly, the original Thurstone research (1944) on perception dealt with processes. A major landmark in the use of factor analysis to study process variables is the work by Fleishman and Hempel (1955) showing the changes in the factor structure of a task over a period of successive trials.

At a different level is the synthesis suggested by Royce (1973) in which individuality is defined in terms of cognitive styles, affective styles, and epistemic (knowledge-seeking) styles inferred from patterns of factor scores on more traditional traits.

I am not at all sure that any clean distinction can be made between a "process" such as solving problems by following formal rules and a "trait" such as intellectual compulsiveness. But there is a point to the confusion. The measurement specialist may find greater utility in identifying situationally-specific processes or approaches to tasks, and measuring the effectiveness or consistency of their use, than in relying on a standard catalog of traits.

The Ideographic Perspective

It is convenient to distinguish "nomothetic" from "ideographic" research. The approach of the measurement specialist has been nomothetic; i.e., a search for universal generalizations. On the various dimensions identified through factor analysis, for example, it has been implicitly assumed that everyone can be described as falling somewhere along the continuum defined by each factor. Further, the implicit assumption has been that these highly generalizable factors would enter the equations of equally universal functional relationships with other variables. One measurement specialist (Cronbach, 1974) has recently questioned the wisdom of trying to reduce human behavior to a set of nomothetic laws.

The alternative, ideographic research, is the attempt to explain in depth the behavior of the single case. Ideographic research generally treats individuals as unique and attempts to understand their total individuality. It permits generalizations since observations in one single case are sometimes repeated in others and the generalizations are built upon similarities from case to case.

In intention and interpretation, the flavor of the Hawthorne studies is certainly nomothetic. Experiments were performed and conclusions reached in the spirit of authoring universal generalizations. Yet the method of research was in many respects ideographic.

The most prominent form of ideographic research in psychology has been the case history method. In a world where the term, "Harvard-case-method" is as much one word as "damYankee," it is not surprising that this particular bit of Harvard history is heavily larded with caselike quotations and records of individual performance. We are told more than we may want to know about the home life and general value systems of individual employees.

A Skinnerian approach is an alternative form of ideographic research. It is, of course, quite different. It is heavily endowed with numbers, the most important of which is the base rate of response before the experiment begins. This, certainly, was a characteristic of the Hawthorne Studies.

Despite all this, the Hawthorne studies can hardly be said to be preoccupied with the total individuality of their subjects. You will look in vain for a heading "Individuality" in the index of *Management and The Worker*. Under the heading "Individual" you will find a reference to the various titles people might have and you will be referred to a paragraph headed, "The Individual" near the back on page 554 and to another paragraph of five lines on page 556. Then you will be told to see also "Social Organization."

That paragraph on "The Individual" is especially instructive. Its principal point is that an individual comes to a work situation largely shaped by social experiences in his family and cultural and community history. Individuality, if seriously entertained by Roethlisberger and Dickson, implies that different people have had different social group experiences. The total emphasis is on the individual in the Gestalt of a social organization.

I think it is high time social scientists recognize more widely that the Hawthorne Studies demonstrated other things as well as the influence of a social group. One person has. Parsons (1974) has convincingly argued that the so-called "Hawthorne effect" is explainable in terms of the consequences of performance. Specifically, the production curves of each individual worker show effects which can be interpreted as the results of both reward and information feedback resulting in turn from performance. These individual performance curves may be explained in terms of goal setting (Locke, 1968) or in terms of operant conditioning (Skinner, 1953). These explanations are, of course, nomethetic generalizations, but they are generalizations inferred from the consistencies of the performance curves of individual subjects.

Ideographic research seems to be the ideal; it permits scientific generalization without forgetting individuality; in fact, it may permit a science of individuality

(Allport, 1961). Even so, its practicality can be questioned. The study of one person in depth takes a great deal of time, and there are a great many people in most organizations.

The Typological Perspective

"Type" is a four-letter word, and psychologists generally have disapproved of its use. Along with other such words, however, it is being used increasingly by respectable people. Tyler (1965), for example, has argued that typologies based on developmental processes would be immensely useful. Paul Lawrence, in this symposium, speaks of a "Herzberg type." The trend is welcome since the idea of typologies is a useful compromise between a misguided search for universal truths about all workers, at all levels, in all jobs, and the impractical ideal of tailoring all management programs for every unique person. The idea has been implicit in most research but needs to be pulled out of hiding and made systematic.

Tryon and Bailey (1970) have shown one method. They identified fifteen intellectual types. The typology started with the intercorrelations among scores on twenty-four ability tests. A cluster analysis yielded four clusters or basic kinds of intellectual ability. Four-point profiles were then computed for each subject, and the subjects were grouped into the fifteen types on the basis of profile similarities. With the same method, they developed typologies in personality and urban ecology problems.

Landy (1972) used an extension of the method to classify occupations. Profiles on three semantic-differential dimensions were used to classify people into one of fourteen types. Frequency patterns of types in nine occupational groups were then used to develop a matrix of occupational similarities. A linkage analysis of this matrix identified three occupational clusters and two isolate occupations. Landy argued that it may be better "to cluster occupations on the basis of perceptions of job incumbents than on the basis of role demands of job descriptions" (p. 116). His recommendation is that such a classification system may well serve as a moderator for research related to work motivation and job satisfaction.

Before going any further, we must admit the frailty of the moderator concept (Abrahams and Alf, 1972a, 1972b; Dunnette, 1972; Velicer, 1972a, 1972b). After more than a decade of research, it offers no glowing promise. Before dismissing the moderator concept as a will-o'-the-wisp, one should heed well the mild words of Ghiselli (1972), pointing out that he has never failed to obtain a moderator, although no one else has been as successful. Then he says, "No one has made much of the fact that most of the moderators I have used have been developed from an item analysis of that curious instrument, the forced-choice inventory" (p. 270). He goes on, rather apologetically, to say that responses to such inventories are not "pure" and that, therefore, his moderators may be open to question.

I offer a different interpretation of his unique success. For one thing, the forced-choice inventory involves a process, choice. For another, it is but one of a possible array of methods for scoring characteristics ipsatively. Profile analysis is another ipsative procedure. It appears, therefore, worthwhile to investigate the moderating effect of types based upon profiles of process variables.

One will not find explicit typologies in *Management and The Worker*. As I have suggested, most nomothetic research, including the Hawthorne Studies, implicitly follows a typological perspective. There is an implicit typology in defining a population from which a research sample is drawn, and that may be more important to science than the moderating effect of ad hoc typing. The implicit "type" defines the limits of the generalizations drawn. In their final comments, Roethlisberger and Dickson make the point that the program they describe "has been shaped to meet the needs of a particular situation. For that reason it works especially well in that situation. For the same reason it is doubtful if it could be applied equally successfully anywhere or everywhere in that specific form" (p. 604).

Their limits of generalization are defined as the specific organization studied. But the limits could also be applied to the kinds of people sampled. Briefly, the Hawthorne subjects could be classified as "reasonable people." Can the results be generalized to unreasonable people? One's answer is irrelevant to my major point that some systematic method of defining characteristics of groups of research subjects will also provide us with a means for defining the extent to which research findings may or may not hold true. The findings about social organization may generalize to reasonable people, but we may question the validity of these generalizations when applied to the uncooperative "rugged individualist."

Whether seeking moderators or defining limits, the hard problem is how one goes about determining a classification system for individuals. The typing so far described is based on profiles of dimensions identified by factor or cluster analysis. It could be much more complex. Royce (1973) has suggested a fairly elaborate process involving at least five levels of potential factor analyses and permitting some types to be based on cognitive structure, some on epistemic styles, some on value hierarchies, and others on emotional patterns. Combinations of all of the possible classifications provides a foundation for a scientific concept of individuality. The complexity seems to be essential.

Sokal (1974) has done a great deal to clarify my thinking about classification techniques. One does not, he argues, establish a classification system by looking for the one unique characteristic uniform to all elements within a classification: "Although cows can be described as animals with four legs that give milk, a cow that only has three legs and does not give milk will still be recognized as a cow. Conversely, there are other animals with four legs that give milk that are not cows." (p. 1117).

The attempt to find a single property or set of properties uniform within a class is described as nomothetic classification. Sokal advocates polythetic classification in which the groups of individuals or objects share a large proportion of designated properties even though they may not necessarily be alike in any one characteristic. Most moderator variables in the psychological literature are nomothetic typologies. The difficulty with a nomothetic classification is that it is not widely applicable. It may be optimal in one case without generalizing to others. A polythetic classification might not be optimal in any given situation, but it will be workable in many.

INDIVIDUAL DIFFERENCES IN FUTURE RESEARCH

Now, let us look to future research. I shall discuss, emphasizing typologies, what I see as directions for the use of concepts of individuality and individual differences in four different areas.

Employee Selection and Promotion

Employee selection is too often identified with employment testing. I will use the term "test," but I mean it to refer to any procedure for assessing a candidate for employment or promotion. It is used here simply as a handy abbreviation for a wide variety of predictor variables.

For that entire variety, the most serious problem is validity generalization. We are still, after nearly three-quarters of a century, stuck with the concept of situational validity. Consider the histograms of Figure 2, provided by Ghiselli (1966), where reported validity coefficients may range from substantial negative values to quite high positive values. Can we look at them and make any great claims for generalizable validity? I think not.

To account for such a range in validities we draw either a blank or pure speculation. Perhaps many of these studies were technically incompetent, the incompetence resulting either in deflation or inflation of "true" validity. Perhaps different conditions obtained in the different settings represented by the different studies; the validity statement may generalize only to certain kinds of conditions. But we have no idea what those conditions are.

Consider another example of our rather disturbing ignorance. For the better part of a decade, we have been immersed in the problems of equal employment opportunity, testing, and differential prediction by racial group. With the publication of the analysis by Schmidt, Berner, and Hunter (1973), some people have claimed that the whole concept of differential prediction is dead. This is nonsense. There are many forms of measurement and many bases for subgrouping not considered in that analysis such as personality tests, biographical data, or other types of predictors; men versus women; Spanish-speaking versus

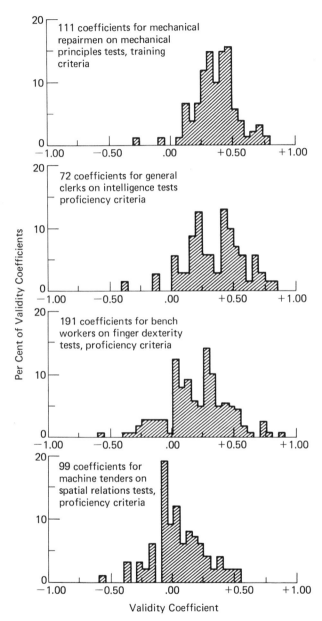

Figure 2. Ranges of obtained validity coefficients in four combinations of jobs, predictors, and criteria (from Ghiselli, 1966).

English-speaking. These are static, nomothetic, legal entities, not psychological processes. If we follow the argument for polythetic classification, and if we follow the argument that individual differences are expressed more vitally in terms of situational processes than in terms of static traits, it becomes obvious that we have not yet begun to investigate psychologically useful moderators for differential prediction equations.

Attitudes and Motivation

It is convenient to classify several contemporary theories of motivation under one of two broad headings: those emphasizing the drive concept and those concerned with expectancy and value. Lip service is given individual differences in both.

Logan (1971) offers a contemporary formulation of drive or incentive theory. In it, behavior depends on drive, incentive, and of these, only prior habit is indispensable. Only under the most carefully controlled laboratory conditions can individual differences in habit strength be reduced to a trivial level. In any application of incentive theories to work, the fact of individual differences in work habits is a major determinant of individual differences in work responses. Moreover, there must be, in Logan's formula, equally strong individual differences in the learned values or "emotionally significant events" that have been part of each individual's unique background determining incentive associations.

An apparently different approach to understanding human motivation is reported by Atkinson and Birch (1970). According to this view, the tendency to carry out a certain activity is a function of both "instigating forces" (those increasing the action tendency) and "consumatory forces" (those decreasing the action tendency). "Instigating forces" may be simple sensory stimulation, but they are more commonly the product of the strength of a particular motive, the value of an appropriate incentive, and the subjective expectation that the action will lead to the incentive. The theory assumes wide individual differences in all three components.

Most contemporary research on work motivation is based on expectancy theories (e.g., Vroom, 1964; Porter and Lawler, 1968). These theories, too, emphasize individual differences: differences in prior reward contingencies and in perceptions of prior rewards, in attitudes, and in the abilities with which particular motivated behavior may be carried out. Despite such theoretical significance, however, much research on work motivation is carried on as if the fact of individual differences were indeed a trivial, well-controlled source of variation in performance or effort.

If individual differences are ignored, it is because they are so pervasive in human affairs that there doesn't seem to be much one can do about them. In laboratory research, one can breed a generation of rats with similar genetic properties, rear them in an antiseptic, controlled environment, provide common histories of reinforcements, and then treat any remaining differences between animals as relatively minor influences on behavior, which, indeed, they are. The psychologist attempting to understand the motivation to carry out one's assigned tasks, day in and day out, after vacation periods, fights with the spouse, or mortgage payments, is not so fortunate. One has only to read the records of the interviews reported in *Management and The Worker* to realize the real-life severity of the uncontrolled events in the personal histories of ordinary men and women.

In spite of the problems, some investigators recognize individual differences. Turney (1974) classified subjects as rational or as irrational and successfully moderated the effect of the expectancy–value interaction. Evans (1974) demonstrated a similar moderating effect using the concept of locus of control. These are nomothetic classifications, but surely a polythetic classification could be developed on the basis of several related processes, including such variables as planning styles or time perspective along with rationality, locus of control, and others.

Work style is being investigated in a project we have underway in two Western Electric plants. Using the rating scales developed by Williams and Seiler (1973) and our own motivational scales (Landy and Guion, 1970), we expect to define performance and motivational types among engineers. These types will be compared in membership with types based on process variables, for convenience identified as four bipolar dimensions of work style: contemplative versus active, solitary versus group oriented, steady versus erratic, and independent versus submissive. What we have in mind are differences in the ways people approach tasks. Some people, for example, approach tasks in isolation. They want to go into a room, close the door, and think without interruption about the characteristics of the task that faces them. In contrast, others would be likely to call a meeting.

Training and Development

Training, at all levels, is important to any organizational enterprise, and the study of individual differences may have several contributions to make. Anderson (Gagné, 1967) has advocated the use of factor–analytic techniques to provide taxonomic task analysis, very much as Fleishman (1974) has done. In another context, he looks to the measurement of individual differences as a diagnostic tool for evaluating flaws in a training program. If verbal comprehension is highly correlated with achievement in an essentially nonverbal job, that correlation tells you something about the necessity for simplifying the verbal communications used in training.

It seems worthwhile to study the interactions between individual differences in traits or processes and methods of training. For example, the choice between programed and conventional training may depend on such distinctions among people as an analytic versus a global approach to tasks, or tendencies toward introversion or extroversion, or anxiety levels. Cronbach (1974) has ably pointed out that the search for interactions takes one into a Hall of Mirrors where there are always further interactions, such as those with situational or task variables.

Even though important interactions may become much more complex, the simple trait-method interactions have proven useful in many situations. The most serious problem in such research, according to Cronbach has been inconsistency of results. But this is to be expected in nomothetic classifications (such as a high–low dichotomy on some trait). A polythetic type should yield more consistent generality.

The notion of a polythetic type seems also relevant to the whole concept of career development. I have never been happy with the concept of the early identification of management potential because it seems to freeze people through self-fulfilling prophecies. Nevertheless, systematic career counseling is a good idea, and I would like to see it done with a good deal of attention to individual differences. Perhaps, as one possible example, people might be classified into two interest types: (1) the "type" of person who tends to focus on one long range goal at a time and to organize his behavior in deliberate attempts to achieve that goal, and (2) the "type" of person who tends to have more amorphous goals, pursuing a wide variety of interests as opportunities present themselves. If such a classification could be made reliably, then people who are less dominated by long-range goals might be appropriately placed in management development tracks leading to the role of organizational generalist, whereas those who are more focused in their goal setting would be most appropriately placed in professional or technical tracks (cf. Albright & Glennon, 1961). I offer this hypothesis with no particular conviction. Rather, I offer it as an antidote to the poisonous view that organizational plans for career development can be applied uniformly throughout an organization.

Environmental Design

I would be remiss, considering some of the controversies in which I have found myself, if I did not say something about individual differences and the whole concept of environmental design. I have already expressed my dissatisfaction, and subsequently my awakened interest, in the notion of "perceived organizational climate" (Guion, 1973, 1974). It is obvious that we are talking about individual differences in perception (more accurately, in cognition) when we use that expression. What may be less obvious is that one's understanding of the organizational climate may be largely a function of prior patterns of reward and punishment, prior patterns of emotional stimulation, or prior patterns of external events leading to the formation of subjective expectancies. I am deliberately choosing these terms because I have already used them in connection with concepts of motivation. What I am suggesting, then, is that different understandings of the climate of an organization may be characteristic of different polythetic motivational types.

I especially regret that the study of possibly more important environmental variables seems to be abandoned for the convenience of questionnaires. Perhaps Industrial and Organizational psychology should take another look at the initial problem of the Hawthorne studies: the effect of physical conditions of work on productivity and satisfaction. Illumination studies would probably have been killed by the fluorescent light if the Hawthorne Studies hadn't done it first; so also with rest periods, now so firmly enshrined in the bargaining process that research data would have little impact on them in any event. Other areas of environmental characteristics have not been studied and may have an impact on the way people work, their effectiveness, and their intrinsic reward. One example is the recent interest in the design of office settings. I have gone into some new offices where the far wall is way off yonder and the intervening space has been broken up into little cubicles arranged in a mazelike pattern between potted plants, presumably providing both privacy and easy interpersonal communication. Even though these seem contradictory I have been assured that workers in these settings enjoy both. The assurance has come less from empirical investigation than from anecdotes.*

It is time for more serious research on the effects of the area of individual working space, patterns of traffic flow, or the physical, visual, or auditory barriers between adjacent desks. Such research would be improved by considering individual differences in preferences in these matters. I am not referring to the mere question, "Do you like this?" Rather, I am suggesting that there are individual differences in the affective processes through which people respond to various kinds of physical arrangements, in the cognitive processes used in various modes of communication, and in the psychomotor processes accompanying privacy or companionable conditions.

CONCLUDING COMMENT

I have thoroughly enjoyed the foregoing flights of fancy. Neither the Hawthorne Studies nor more recent research has imposed any serious constraints on them. I can indulge in my fantasies about the research rewards that can be obtained through the use of a polythetic typology of individual differences in functional processes for the very simple reason that there are no data to contra-

---

*Survey of literature reported in an unpublished manuscript.

dict me. What has been done in typological research has been based on the measurement of static traits, and it has been encouraging. By developing the appropriate kind of profiles of traits we can, with relatively simple and straightforward numerical manipulation, develop reasonably discrete patterns and, except for a few isolates who really do not fit into any class because of their uncommon individuality, we can do a fairly good job of putting people into numerical abstractions or pigeon holes. Since I see ideographic research as an impractical ideal, anything that moves toward it is moving in the right direction. Classification moves toward it, but without loss of the benefit of nomothetic research. If there is to be any value to the behavioral sciences, we must seek generalizations applicable across at least some groups of people. And here the basic question is, "What are the limits within which a generalization will fit?"

There is no question in the field of psychology more urgently needing an answer. Consider that plague of the employment psychologist, the fact of situational validities. Surely we can develop some generalizable principles concerning the types of human characteristics useful in the performance of specific types of human tasks, and surely we must define the limits within which those statements of principle can apply.

Here is the real value of a typological approach. By establishing a system of functional typologies, we can provide a reasonably parsimonious handle for at least the human portion of the limits on the generalizability of a proposition. (A taxonomy of situations and a taxonomy of environments will be needed to handle the rest of the problem but these are beyond the topic at hand.)

This is not, I think, a pipe dream. The basic analytic technology is available. In the next fifty years, psychologists need to study the uniformities in human behavior. They must identify the basic psychological processes of perception, cognition, epistomology, value formation, and physical functioning. A start has been made (cf. Gagné, 1967; Royce, 1973; Underwood, 1974). In a relatively short period of scientific history, taxonomies could be developed directly applicable to the task of defining the limits of many of the generalizations about human functioning in organizations.

But a word of warning is in order. From a purely technical perspective, there is a serious obstacle to the development of such taxonomies, the problem of sample size. Landy (1969) had 171 subjects which were not enough to fill the cells of his 15×13 matrix of types. In the typologies with 1436 cases, we had barely enough to establish the original classifications and there were no cases left to "cross-validate" our results.

In short, a typological analysis is an exceedingly big research effort. It will not be done by individual scientists in isolated individual settings. It can be done only through a very large scale, industry-wide effort, and that effort will be as much an innovation in the application of science to the problems of human work as the Hawthorne Studies were fifty years ago. In the last fifty years, I can think of only one concreted research program sponsored by an American industry that can rival in duration and imagination the Hawthorne Studies (Bray, Campbell, & Grant, 1974). If important typologies are to be developed, a research program is needed that will dwarf the magnitude of the Hawthorne Studies themselves. I think it is time for others, and I think they would pay.

REFERENCES

Abrahams, N. M., and Alf, E., Jr. Pratfalls in moderator research. *Journal of Applied Psychology*. 1972 (a), **56**: 245–251.

Abrahams, N. M., and Alf, E., Jr. Reply to Dunnette's "Comments on Abrahams and Alf's 'Pratfalls in moderator research.'" *Journal of Applied Psychology*. 1972 (b), **56**: 257–261.

Albright, L. E., and Glennon, J. R. Personal history correlates of physical scientists' career aspirations. *Journal of Applied Psychology*. 1961, **45**: 281–284.

Allport, G. W. *Pattern and growth in Personality*. New York: Holt, Rinehart, & Winston. 1961.

Atkinson, J. W., and Birch, D. *The Dynamics of Action*. New York: Wiley. 1970.

Bray, D. W., Campbell, R. J., and Grant, D. L. *Formative Years in Business: A Long-term AT&T Study of Managerial Lives*. New York: Wiley. 1974.

Cronbach, L. J. Beyond the two disciplines of scientific psychology. Address to American Psychological Association, New Orleans, September, 1974.

Dunnette, M. D. Comments on Abrahams and Alf's "Pratfalls in moderator research." *Journal of Applied Psychology*. 1972, **56**: 252–256.

Evans, M. G. Extensions of a Path-goal Theory of Motivation. *Journal of Applied Psychology*. 1974, **59**: 172–178.

Fleishman, E. A. Toward a taxonomy of human performance. Address to American Psychological Association, New Orleans, August, 1974.

Fleishman, E. A., and Hempel, W. E. The relation between abilities and improvement with practice in a visual discrimination reaction task. *Journal of Experimental Psychology*. 1955, **49**: 301–312.

Gagné, R. M., ed. *Learning and Individual Differences*. Columbus, Ohio: Merrill. 1967.

Ghiselli, E. E. *The Validity of Occupational Aptitude Tests*. New York: Wiley. 1966.

Ghiselli, E. E. Comment on the use of moderator variables. *Journal of Applied Psychology*. 1972, **56**: 270.

Guion, R. M. A note on organizational climate. *Organizational Behavior and Human Performance*. 1973, **9**: 120–125.

Guion, R. M. Open a new window: Validities and values in psychological measurement. *American Psychologist*. 1974, **29**: 287–296.

Landy, F. J. A typological approach to the relationship between the motivation to work and job satisfaction. Unpublished doctoral dissertation, Bowling Green State University, 1969.

Landy, F. J. A procedure for occupational clustering. *Organizational Behavior and Human Performance*. 1972, 109–117.

Landy, F. J., & Guion, R. M. Development of scales for the measurement of work motivation. *Organization Behavior and Human Performance*. 1970, **5**: 93–103.

Locke, E. A. Toward a theory of task motivation and incentives. *Organizational Behavior and Human Performance*. 1968, **3**: 157–189.

Logan, F. A.   Incentive Theory, Reinforcement and Education. In Glaser, R. (ed.) *The Nature of Reinforcement*. New York: Academic Press. 1971.

Parsons, H. M.   What happened at Hawthorne? *Science*. 1974, 183: 922–932.

Porter, L. W., and Lawler, E. E., III. *Managerial Attitudes and Performance*. Homewood, Ill.: Irwin. 1968.

Roethlisberger, F. J., and Dickson, W. J. *Management and the Worker*. Cambridge, Mass.: Harvard University Press. 1939.

Royce, J. R., Epistemic styles, individuality, and world-view. Address at University of Pittsburgh NATO Advanced Study Institute on Information Sciences Conference at Aberystwyth, Wales, United Kingdom, August, 12–24, 1973.

Schmidt, F. L., Berner, J. G., and Hunter, J. E. Racial differences in validity of employment tests: reality or illusion? *Journal of Applied Psychology*. 1973, 58: 5–9.

Skinner, B. F. *Science and Human Behavior*. New York: Macmillan. 1953.

Sokal, R. R. Classification: purposes, principles, progress, prospects. *Science*. 1974, 185: 1115–1123.

Thurstone, L. L. A factorial study of perception. *Psychometric Monographs*, No. 4, 1944.

Tryon, R. C., and Bailey, D. E. *Cluster Analysis*. New York: McGraw-Hill. 1970.

Turney, J. R. Activity outcome expectancies and intrinsic activity values as predictors of several motivation indexes for technical-professionals. *Organizational Behavior and Human Performance*. 1974, 11: 65–82.

Tyler, L. E. *The Psychology of Human Differences*, 3rd ed. New York: Appleton-Century-Crofts. 1965.

Underwood, B. J. Individual differences as a crucible in theory construction. Address to American Psychological Association, New Orleans, August, 1974.

Velicer, W. F. Comment on the general inapplicability of Ghiselli's moderator system for two predictors. *Journal of Applied Psychology*. 1972, 56: 262–265.

Velicer, W. F. The moderator variable viewed as heterogeneous regression. *Journal of Applied Psychology*. 1972, 56: 266–269.

Vroom, V. H. *Work and motivation*. New York: Wiley. 1964.

Williams, W. E., and Seiler, D. A. Relationship between measures of effort and job performance. *Journal of Applied Psychology*. 1973, 57: 49–54.

2

INDIVIDUAL DIFFERENCES IN THE WORLD OF WORK

Paul R. Lawrence
Harvard University

INTRODUCTION

This conference gives the opportunity to do a stock-taking on fifty years of change in the relationship between man and work. Fifty years is a suitable review point because it approximates the length of one full life of work. This is borne out by the sad fact that the strongest personal link for many of us to the Hawthorne Studies was broken this spring by the death of Fritz Roethlisberger. Even in his last illness the insights from the Western Electric studies were still working for him. His friends found on hospital visits that he cheered us with his discerning and humorous observations on the hospital's social structure. He wryly remarked one day, "The physicians want to be surgeons, the nurses want to be physicians, the aides want to be nurses, and no one wants to fluff my pillow."

So what has happened to the world of work in the past fifty years with special reference to individual differences? Has work changed? Have people changed? Is there in general a good fit or not between the capabilities of people and the jobs they find available? Do all misfits in these terms experience the job blues? Is this a serious problem? Why does it persist? To attempt to answer such broad questions is worthwhile, even though it forces us to generalize far beyond hard evidence. We will start with the question of whether the nature of work itself has changed in any important ways.

HAS THE NATURE OF WORK CHANGED

Today's world of work is made up of many more different kinds of jobs than in 1924. In fifty years thousands of new types and categories of jobs have appeared. The *Dictionary of Occupational Titles* has added over twelve thousand new job definitions to a base of seventeen thousand job definitions since it was first published in 1939. Most of these have arisen in connection with new technologies, such as the obvious examples of computers and space vehicles. Other less obvious jobs have emerged as society achieves the affluence to compensate more people to work as designers, artists, therapists, etc. But have the basic characteristics of jobs changed? Has the mix changed? It is difficult to prove, but I believe the evidence indicates that they have changed.

One of the helpful unifying concepts that has emerged in the study of work is that of *uncertainty*. One can roughly characterize different jobs on a scale from highly certain to highly uncertain. Uncertainty can be thought of as an amalgam of three features of any job: (1) the number of variables involved in its performance; (2) the state of knowledge about the cause and effect relations between these variables; and (3) the length of time it takes to get feedback on the effects of job efforts. Jobs can be thought of as a one-person package of these uncertainties or problems-to-be-solved. This dimension of uncertainty allows an arrayal of the jobs available in 1924 and 1974. The range would be wide in both times, but I would assert that there has been a significant shift to greater uncertainty. There is simply a smaller proportion of unskilled jobs. This has happened for many complex reasons that need not be explored here, except to make the general point that the long term trend to automation is absorbing unskilled jobs even as the newer jobs are appearing in response to the more complex issues of society. I believe a long term and significant move toward job enrichment had taken place long before the term job enrichment was coined as the label of a deliberate program. This is a healthy sign. This chart shows schematically the shift involved. But before adjourning this conference in self-congratulations, a look at the people side of the equation is in order.

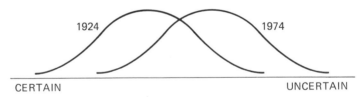

1924   1974

CERTAIN   UNCERTAIN

Figure 1. Estimated distribution of job content in 1924 and 1974.

CHANGES IN THE WORKING POPULATION

How has the working population changed in fifty years? Here the facts and conclusions are somewhat better documented. Postulating a general problem-solving capacity and charting a distribution of that capacity in the working population, I venture that it has shifted significantly upward in the last fifty

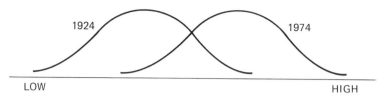

Figure 2. Estimated distribution of human capacity to handle job uncertainty in 1924 and 1974.

years. There are many indications of this. To cite one, in 1920 only some 64% of American young people between the ages of five and 20 were attending school while over 90% were in 1970.

This, too, is a healthy sign. As the job mix moves toward bigger problems to be solved, the people available have at least an equally increased problem-solving capacity. What could be neater. Should not there be a right job for every person? Yet there are widespread signs of blue collar blues, the white collar blues, the professional blues, and even the managerial blues. These work complaints may be muted by the current problems of the economy, but there is every reason to expect them to resurface. The catch is that when the 1924 distribution of people-capacity is placed over the 1924 job uncertainty distribution, there is an area of misfit of people with capacities for problem solving that will be under-utilized given the mix of jobs available. The same comparisons for 1974 show the same gap, and I believe it has actually increased.

These charts are only schematic. I know of no hard data on such broad questions. The only specific evidence of the existence of this gap that I know of comes from a study (Eckhaus, 1964) which found that the educational requirements for most jobs in the United States economy are generally more than obtained by the holders of these jobs. We do not have comparable data from

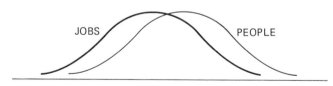

Figure 3. Estimated fit of job content and human capacity in 1924.

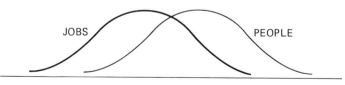

Figure 4. Estimated fit of job content and human capacity in 1974.

1924 to test whether this gap was larger or smaller. There is the danger of over-stating these gaps, but few informed observers doubt they exist.

INDIVIDUAL DIFFERENCES

Do all the people whom these spaces represent acutely feel the job blues? Are they all alienated and frustrated? Behavioral scientists who study such matters have provided two different answers to this question. Herzberg (1959) to cite one well-known source, would answer with an emphatic yes. His research findings indicated to him that the only true motivator of work is work itself. Only when a person is challenged by the problem content of work will he produce the energy and concentration needed for its successful completion. Other factors, such as fair pay and good working conditions, can be necessary for general satisfaction and their absence can serve to demotivate, but they cannot in themselves serve as motivators. Only an opportunity for job achievement and recognition can so serve. On the other hand, the same question asked of Turner and Lawrence (1965) and some others, will elicit a rather reluctant no. This conflict is worth exploring briefly because it goes to the question of individual differences and reflects a widespread confusion.

In the research I did with Arthur Turner, we were testing a hypothesis very similar to Herzberg's, that people would be "turned on" by job autonomy and challenge. Instead of studying professional and white collar employees as did Herzberg, we stuck to a broad sample of blue collar workers. Herzberg found ample evidence to support his hypothesis. To our surprise and chagrin we did not. I used the word reluctantly before to emphasize the mood of our discovery that about half of our sample was not at all motivated by more challenging, responsible work. We did not give up our beliefs easily. We tested to see if their reactions were simply a front or a cover for a more underlying need to achieve. If it was there we could not find it. So we had to conclude that some workers, by no means all, have been nurtured in urban subcultures that have deeply conditioned them to see work as a simple exchange of time and minimal energy for fair pay and decent conditions. They do not expect to live on the job, only off the job. This is in sharp contrast to most of the individuals in Herzberg's study.

If one can believe that Turner and Lawrence's findings (and the fact that they have been supported by subsequent research, has added to my own sense of confidence in them) the working population must be thought of as bimodal as regards the meaning of work in their lives. So if one's experience has made it hard to buy completely Herzberg's argument, he is not alone. But he should not jump to the other extreme. Among the population of people he sampled, the Herzberg hypothesis seems to hold for a high enough proportion to provide a good rule-of-thumb. One should not be tempted to treat it as a universal rule since individuals are different.

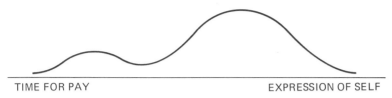

TIME FOR PAY   EXPRESSION OF SELF

Figure 5. Estimated distribution of basic attitudes about work.

THE MISFIT VICTIMS

So my analysis suggests that many of the "misfit victims" will feel frustrated and somewhat alienated, but, due to individual differences, not all of them. Perhaps the meaning of these general conclusions can be brought closer to this conference theme by drawing examples from the original Hawthorne Studies. In the Relay Assembly Test Room experiments, of the five original women in the group, three responded positively to the opportunity for more participation, more latitude about work rules, etc., but by Period VII it was obvious that two did not. While the evidence is not entirely clear, these two women seemed not to behave according to Herzberg's hypothesis. In the face of the prospect of increased job scope they demonstrated "a hostile and uncooperative" attitude and were therefore replaced in the group by two women who "welcomed the opportunity." So even in the Hawthorne experiments there is a clue to this bimodal definition of the meaning of work. Incidentally, this episode has been cited by some critics as evidence that the studies are suspect, on the grounds that the test women were selected to be "management patsies." I suppose this is true, if being productive and involved emotionally in one's work is equated with selling out to management.

Beyond these personal frustrations, does this considerable lack of personal fit with one's job make any significant difference in our society? I believe the overwhelming evidence indicates it does. First of all the logic of the situation argues that underutilized human resources represent a direct loss in productive capacity to society, regardless of whether the lost output is in the form of fewer cars, less food, or less artistic achievement. There are too many worthwhile things that need doing to be complacent about this loss of resources. But behind this logical argument are some quite specific research studies that demonstrate the losses that flow from a poor fit between particular human resources and the particular way work has been structured.

Jay Lorsch and John Morse of U.C.L.A. (1974) have just published findings which bear directly on this question. They found that when a three-way fit existed between the certainty of the task itself, the personal characteristics of a set of employees and the way the organization had structured the work, that there was activated in these employees a strong competence motivation that was associated with relatively high performance. On the other hand, they found that

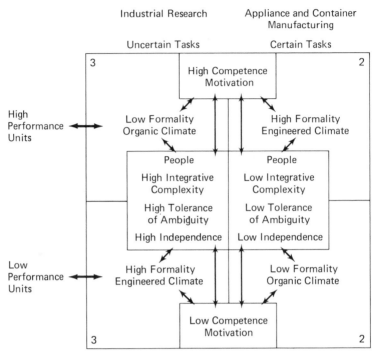

Figure 6.

when there existed a misfit between the certainty of the task, individual characteristics and the way the work was structured, that competence motives were not activated and poor performance was experienced (see the two lower boxes in Figure 6). They, moreover, found these results in settings picked to cover a wide spectrum of industrial conditions from industrial research laboratories to appliance and container factories. Their sample included managers down to the foreman level and therefore probably included mostly people who would confirm the Herzberg hypothesis. It is important to note that in the settings studied, predispositions of the individuals in the research laboratories were statistically similar on three relevant characteristics but were distinctly different from those in the manufacturing setting. Thus, in this study the misfit problem was generated by inappropriate work structure and climate rather than by the selection of people. These new studies provide empirical support for the argument that society as well as the individuals involved pay a high price for the underutilization of human resources. Further, they strongly suggest some ways that management can do something about it. But more on that point later.

It may be difficult to visualize just what is taking place in human terms in the four conditions studied. This may be clarified by examining the character of the chief complaint made by people working in these two lower "misfit" boxes. The complaint in the research laboratory on the lower left is that "too much red tape and mickey mouse rules are frustrating getting a job done." In the "misfit" factories, on the other hand, a more typical complaint is, "the place is too sloppy. We ought to get organized, so we could get something done." It is probably easier to visualize how the research professional could find the loose job structuring and organic climate of the upper left box stimulating to their competence motivation. It may not be so obvious what is going on in the upper right-hand box. Herzberg's theory, as it is generally interpreted, would not have predicted this association of high motivation with highly structured jobs. But anybody who has witnessed an expert military drill team at work cannot deny that some people can find a great opportunity for expressing their competence in a highly structured task. It is difficult to imagine anyone deriving pleasure from marching under the direction of a sloppy incompetent drill sergeant. The Lorsch and Morse findings support the logical argument about the costs of underutilization, but more importantly they indicate an additional potential loss of the extra productive energy that can be derived from the striving for competence.

A final piece of evidence bearing on the question of the consequences of underutilized human resources is the group of Bank Wiring Room men at Hawthorne. Here we see the pattern of a work group frozen into a defensive stance vis-à-vis management, boring themselves with the underutilization of their productive potential, immobilized by their inarticulate fears of the consequences of expressing their competencies on the job. Some of these men would respond in line with the Herzberg hypothesis and some probably would not, but the behavior of all was constrained by defensive group norms. Even today, when executives study descriptions of such groups they acknowledge that such conditions are still very prevalent in industry. The Bank Wiring Room story presents an intimate first-hand picture of the costs of an underutilized group, as current today as when it first happened.

SOLUTIONS TO UNDERUTILIZATION

So misfits still abound, and the gap represented by underutilization of people has, if anything, increased in the last fifty years. The costs go beyond frustration to impact on our ability as a society to meet important needs. The original Hawthorne Studies continue to throw light on this problem both in general impact and in how impacts differ because of individual differences. Subsequent research adds clarity and stronger evidence, but no major reversals. Why does the gap persist in spite of the knowledge and the earnest efforts of many people to close it? I will cite only three important reasons that all too often are ignored.

First of all, this gap persists because one of the basic reasons man has developed organizations has been to reduce uncertainties. This, of course, is by no means all a bad thing. If organizations have helped decrease uncertainties about where the next meal is coming from, and they have, who can knock it? But in some areas, organizations have clearly overshot the mark in reducing uncertainty. The distribution of uncertainty in organizations is very uneven and lumpy. Few company presidents complain of too much job uncertainty, but many hourly people do. Society has trained and turned loose in industry whole armies of industrial engineers who usually see their role as reducing all uncertainties about how blue and even white collar jobs are to be done. This process of job simplification can be a useful contribution to increased productivity if it can be pursued to its logical conclusion of moving human work over the watershed into machine work. But many jobs, such as the classical example of automobile assembly, have defied extensive automation for decades. Yet industrial engineers, like lemmings, continue to press toward simplification of such jobs instead of backing off and enriching them. If jobs are to continue to be performed by humans they should be designed with this fact in clear focus. Management must plan for the performance of work, but the prevalent philosophy is that if a little planning is a good thing, then a lot is that much better. If some uncertainties are not left in each and every job to be handled by each and every employee, then human resources are being wasted. Organizations will need to continue to act to reduce uncertainties, but they must be designed so that everyone involved can make his or her contribution to this process and reduce underutilization of people.

Secondly, I believe that applied behavioral scientists and personnel people must shoulder a goodly share of the blame for the continuing gap. There has been a long-term neglect in developing a major part of the practical technology needed to achieve better individual-to-the-job fits. It is an obvious logical point that it takes two sides to make a good fit. One has to be able to measure nuts as well as bolts to be able to predict a good fit in advance. This point seems to have been ignored for many, many years by industrial psychologists and personnel people. They have focused a great deal of time and energy on measuring the attributes of people and the study of individual differences. A great deal has been learned about how to do this with reasonable accuracy. Any comparable effort to measure job characteristics is simply nonexistent. At best, job descriptions are general statements about what is expected to be accomplished. As far as the human traits go, there are only vague statements about the level and type of formal education expected or the years of experience needed. Rarely is anything said about the kind and complexity of mental work required in a form that relates to measures of human attributes. Little beyond platitudes is said about interpersonal skills, specialized and technical language requirements, emotional stress capacity, time horizon, etc.

Compare, for example, the methods used in selection, placement, and job design, with those involved in making, selling and fitting men's suits. When an order for a new type of suit goes into production, it is geared into considerable data about how men are constructed and how many of each size category are potential customers. Suits are then produced in quantities that reflect the normal size distribution of men. The number 42 on a suit ticket refers to a human feature, the chest measurement, selected as a key variable that can reasonably predict arm length, etc. This is what is missing in our personnel practices. Potential labor market characteristics are not investigated before a batch of jobs is designed into a new plant. In fact on most assembly lines people are assumed to come in only one very, very small size in their problem-solving capacity. When jobs are categorized, it is not in human terms, such as chest size. It is usually in reference to some machine or technology.

To carry the analogy a bit further, a suit store has a salesman who is trained to find out about chest sizes and then to show an array of suits that will come reasonably close to fitting. The customer helps him do this because he is interested in a good fit too. Such straightforward procedures are the exception in industrial personnel practice. Even if a measure is made of the applicant's chest, the right job is hard to find. At the store, once the client has expressed interest in a suit, he is expected to put it on and see how it feels before he buys it. This is virtually unheard of in job fitting circles. Beyond that, if the applicant decides to buy a suit (invest in a long-term job) a technician steps forward to assist in minor alterations to better insure a good fit. Could industrial engineers ever work on this? Sometimes customers even are known to come back after a few weeks with complaints about the fit and something is actually done about it. This is very unlikely in industrial circles. Simply not enough time and energy has been spent in the right places to develop the needed technology and standard practice to achieve a half-decent performance of fitting people and jobs. There are a few encouraging exceptions to this statement such as the more imaginatively designed assessment centers. But the overall picture is bleak. A focus on both sides of the "fit" equation is necessary to bring it into balance.

The final reason for the continuing gap has to do with the preferred direction of error in our personnel practices. This obscure phrase, "preferred direction of error" can be clarified by drawing a final example from the persistent analogy with buying men's suits. When there is any doubt about getting the right size suit, people prefer to err by getting one a little too big, and this is a common practice for growing boys. This is called a growing fit or a planned "error" to allow for predicted growth. Growing boys are not fitted into straitjackets, but this is the customary method of job fitting. The process is unnecessarily inaccurate and compounds this problem by selecting people who can do the job because they are picked to have plenty of capacity to spare. Yet the normal pattern for adults is to increase their complex problem-solving capacity for many, many years after their physical growth stops. In this regard they are growing boys and girls throughout most of their work life. At least their normal tendency is to grow if it isn't stunted by job strait-jackets. When normal growth is blocked, some quite unpleasant things are apt to happen. The normal needs of all people, not just professionals, dictate taking a career rather than a job perspective toward their working life. Everyone needs a "growing fit" with their job to avoid waste and frustration.

The fact that in practice the underutilization error is preferred probably arises from an understandable even if deplorable desire to play it safe. One never knows when the organization might need that extra reserve of talent. So it is stockpiled in spite of the high spoilage rate of human talent. These self-defeating practices may be a result of other questionable assumptions such as that work weeks are fixed in length. Are there not other ways to provide the human talent safety factor without subjecting millions of people to a lifetime of underutilization?

SUMMARY

What can be done to turn these observations on the reasons for underutilization into practical remedial actions? People such as myself, who have become identified with the growing perspective known as the contingency theory of organization, have pushed two rules-of-thumb: (1) that it takes different kinds of organizations and different kinds of people to do different kinds of tasks and (2) that therefore a key management problem is achieving and maintaining the right kind of dynamic compound *fit*. There are few, if any, universally right ways to organize, essentially because of individual differences and task differences. One way to recapitulate the implication of the argument so far is to say that if we are to close the gap of underutilization of human resources, management must improve the "fitting" process at at least three levels. First, managers must review their overall set of jobs or roles that they offer employees and compare them with the modal characteristics of young people coming onto the job market. Is there a gross misalignment or a reasonable match? As Robert Ford, of AT&T "work itself" fame, likes to remark, "Given that some 90% of our young people are graduating from high school, unless industry dramatically changes its job design practices, there will be a terrible rush for that 10%."

At the second level of fitting a specific job to a specific individual, a number of standard practices will have to change. There is a need to carefully categorize the features of jobs in human terms to catch up with our capacity for psychometrics. The applicant must be engaged as a partner in the fitting process and real trial periods for jobs must be provided. All of this is needed to take account of individual differences.

Finally, at a third level, career development must be planned by providing for a growing, stretching job fit and for a semi-planned career sequence. Finding the right career for oneself is and must remain to a large extent a personal concern and responsibility. Few people want their careers chosen for them. But before that personal choice can be made there must be some career paths available. Management must assume responsibility for setting up these paths. All too often jobs are structured into dead ends such as face any fully experienced and trained nurse who must start her medical education at ground zero if she expects to become a doctor. Not all nurses want to become doctors, but the lack of any practical choice might contribute to their disenchantment with fluffing pillows. These, then, are in summary form, the three principal implications for management action to gain and close the gap of underutilizing human resources.

It takes at least 15 to 20 years even today for a significant new finding in the physical sciences to find its way into everyday application. I am confident that it takes two or three times as long in the social sciences. We are still assimilating the social significance of Darwin's findings of 100 years ago. Looking at the fifty years that have elapsed since the start of the Hawthorne Studies, it is, therefore, no cause for despair that many of the insights developed are still not widely applied. Spotty progress has been made. The studies are still a fruitful source of ideas for both research and practice. They are not misleading. There simply is still a great deal of work remaining to be done.

REFERENCES

Eckhaus, R. "Economic Criteria for Education and Training," R. E. Stat, May, 1964.
Herzberg, F., Mausner, B. and Snyderman, B. *The Motivation to Work*, New York: Wiley, 1959.
Lorsch, J. and Morse, J. *Organizations and Their Members: A Contingency Approach.* New York, Harper & Row, 1974.
Turner, A. and Lawrence, P. *Industrial Jobs and the Worker*, Harvard Business School, 1965.

PART II

Management by Involvement and Participation

Few work groups, before or since, have experienced the degree of involvement and participation in the productive process as did those in some of the Hawthorne experiments. Although concepts such as "participative management" or "industrial democracy" are not new, their application to date has been limited. The points of focus for these presentations include the extent of employee needs and desires for involvement and participation, a review of the forces that seem to be raising interest in such management techniques and reasons why further application has not been undertaken.

3
MANAGEMENT BY PARTICIPATION

Alfred J. Marrow
The Harwood Co., Inc.

INTRODUCTION

A cartoon in a recent issue of *The New Yorker* magazine neatly illustrates the problems I shall be discussing. The drawing shows a company president seated commandingly behind his desk. One of his managers is standing obediently in front. The president says, "We do live in a democracy, Perkins, but here we operate under an authoritarian regime."

This cartoon, in my judgment, is funny in its truthfulness, but not at all amusing in its implications. It represents all too realistically the present situation in the vast majority of organizations where the approved way of managing is by command. Such institutions ignore the results of the nine-year Hawthorne research program. They also reject the impressive studies that have been done elsewhere and that demonstrate the beneficial effects of participation for both company and employees.

Though the leaders of organizations recognize that the present work force is better educated, more affluent and brings to the job greater expectations for self-management and self-actualization, they have effected only minor changes in their managerial practices. Most have continued the traditional procedures which reinforce decision-making at the top and deny the employees' potential for responsibility, creativity and productivity. This is still acceptable to many older workers who have become accustomed to thinking in terms of economic rewards. But the young people do not share these material values. Money is important but not at the expense of the life style they want. One result of the outdated managerial practices is substantially to increase the cost of doing business while contributing to the growing unhappiness, unrest and alienation of employees. Another is the slowing down or sabotaging of production.

A large part of the cost of almost everything in our society is labor. We might expect, then, that more leaders would address themselves to the failure of the public and private institutions they head to meet the psychological needs of those they employ and of those they serve, especially since many of their organizations are under sharp attack. Let us take some names from the financial press: Penn Central, Pan American, Lockheed, Wall Street brokerage houses, Consolidated Edison, and Franklin National Bank. They are typical of many institutions afflicted with dry rot, poor morale and ineffectiveness. As of now, they are moving toward collapse.

THE DEVELOPING CRISIS

In most institutions and organizations, the structure, job design and managerial procedures are deficient and outdated. A reordering of their systems is long overdue. The employees are disgruntled and frustrated by the low quality of their work life. They are unwilling to subordinate their personal wants and desires to meet the needs of the organization. They are prepared to risk economic penalties for taking days off, shifting jobs or engaging in sabotage. Inferior products, services and low productivity are tangible evidence of workers' dissatisfaction and anger.

In most organizations, the application of scientifically-derived human relations knowledge and skills has hardly begun. The quantity and quality or relevant knowledge has been growing rapidly but is scarcely utilized. The lag is so great that though fifty years have passed since the Hawthorne Studies, little of our scientific knowledge is being applied. As the so-called "work ethic" disappears, our business, governmental and educational organizations are more and more afflicted with poor quality, low output, costly overruns, inefficiencies, indifferent services, minimal manpower utilization and the exorbitantly high cost of almost everything. In 1945, Elton Mayo wrote that, "We cannot live and prosper with one foot in the 20th century and the other in the 18th. We must seek collaboration, and that collaboration cannot be left to chance."

In the thirty years that have passed since Mayo wrote that, behavioral scientists have greatly expanded their understanding of how greater collaboration can be achieved but, unhappily, little that is known is being used. Some say, perhaps facetiously, that this has happened because the people with power have no knowledge and those with knowledge have no power. But, however it is stated, it points to the fact that people with influence and power are skeptical about the value of behavioral science. That skepticism is a prime, social factor that I should like to emphasize and deplore. It is pronounced and widespread. It is as true of the heads of educational organizations as it is of government and industry.

In Studs Terkel's recent book, *Working*, the author says in the introduction,

"This book being about work is by its very nature about violence—to the spirit as well as to the body—It is about ulcers as well as about accidents—It is above all, about daily humiliations—To survive the day, is triumph enough for the walking wounded—for a Monday through Friday sort of dying." What Terkel is saying in very clear language is that while firms give lip service to there being a meaning to work well over and beyond the reward of the paycheck, little is done to honor it. The present system of management creates frustration at all levels.

AUTHORITARIAN MANAGEMENT AND THE FIRES OF DISCONTENT

A similar gloomy outlook about people who work was also expressed in a comprehensive study entitled, "Work in America", released by the Department of Health Education and Welfare in December, 1972. It was widely reviewed in the national press. In sum, the study reported that "job discontent is hurting the nation and that there is extensive and serious dissatisfaction and even despair at all occupational levels up to and including the managerial."

A salient point in this report is that most managers and supervisors are chosen because they possess authoritarian traits. But this very trait brings managers into daily conflict with their subordinates, particularly those workers, younger and better educated who have grown up in homes and schools where democratic and participative methods are practiced. One major consequence of this is that the employees who are potentially the most productive are the most dissatisfied. All-in-all, the study presents a gloomy picture of the nation's industrial future and with excellent reason. Among the many recommendations made in the H.E.W. report toward revising the unhappiness and the discontent is one that is the central theme of this paper, namely, that industry should give workers more direct participation in decision-making.

Today, industry is overmanaged and overcontrolled. Employees in the future are even less likely to accept rigid control than they do now. They are going to resort more and more to overt acts of retaliation, amounting in many cases to outright sabotage of both product and productivity. In increasing numbers, they will invent subtle but very costly ways of smothering production and twisting the system as their way of saying, "The power-holders will not enjoy their arrogant use of power." Signs of this increased militancy have been pointedly visible. General Motors discovered the sober facts in the much-publicized turbulence in its plant at Lordstown. The leaders of that revolt were the young and the better educated. It is this group who speak openly about their resentment at the humiliation of having no voice in how they are to carry out their jobs. They have experienced the freedom to participate in problem-solving and decision-making in their homes, their schools, and the governing of their country, but not at work where they spend most of their waking hours. Shorter hours and higher pay will not provide a satisfactory answer to the young employee's yearning for self-fulfillment or for the loss of self-esteem from having to perform mind-killing work. Young employees no longer believe that hard work pays off. They have a different notion of what success is. They are not willing to make personal sacrifices for economic security if it doesn't bring self-fulfillment as well.

The feelings of restlessness, anger and hatred that creep out of the factories and shops and office buildings, and into the streets and homes of Americans, come from jobs that provide no challenge or variety, and from bosses who are inconsiderate and autocratic. The on-coming generation have new doubts about the ideals of efficiency. They are unwilling to pay the crushing price of loss of pride, mind-killing monotony, dehumanization and stress diseases in return for the highest wages in history. Their idea of success revolves around forms of self-fulfillment, toward more humanistic ways of living. Material rewards alone turn them off.

A worker who feel he is being turned into a robot, that he stands powerless before the clangorous automatic system, with no hope of changing his drudgery and loss of self-esteem, finds psychic withdrawal the only temporary escape against his growing fury. His morale is low and his productivity minimal. Most economists agree that climbing wages and stable prices are possible only through increased productivity. An annual improvement of 4% is essential if our nation is to move out of the present serious recession without creating a new wage-price spiral with its built-in inflationary forces. During 1973, and the first half of 1974, the productivity rate showed no increase at all despite modernization of equipment and increased automation. Only a small part of the answer to the needed 4% can come from more efficient equipment. The major increase must come from human productivity. This means creating a work climate that satisfies those needs of the worker which wages and hours do not and cannot, and without which he will not work at his best.

Despite the present critical economic situation, neither government "productivity" commissions, nor private business has shown any genuine interest in these extremely significant instances of building teamwork, raising morale and satisfying those needs of employees that motivate them to work at their best and increase their productivity. Productivity growth is what is desperately needed and it is futile for organizations to fall back on traditional methods to achieve it.

PARTICIPATION, NOT CONFRONTATION

It may be that Volvo in its new Virginia plant will be the demonstration needed at this time to convince industrial leaders that participative procedures, self-management and small work groups with decision-making powers are more efficient than the traditional assembly line. Possibly the success of the Volvo program, based largely on the findings of behavioral scientists which most American industry has ignored, will revolutionize the way organizations operate and point the way for the productivity increases that must be achieved if our economy is to recover. The elimination of the assembly line and its dull, simplified jobs at Volvo and the substitution of a program of active participation by work groups in planning their work, setting their own pace and solving their own problems may provide the breakthrough that will show the nation how to gain the productivity increases it needs to overcome the worst recession since the 1930's. Research has found that people on a job, if they have nothing to say about the way things are done, are apt to show very little interest or concern. They drift along, just to "get by" while doing as little as they can. However, if they are involved in face-to-face problem-solving connected with their jobs, they join wholeheartedly in finding practical solutions. They are "participants," not just "hired hands." They no longer feel like robots. They have a piece of the action and can earn genuine feelings of achievement because they really contribute to shaping a company's policy.

Just what is meant by "participation?" There are, of course, many different amounts and kinds of participation. Here we refer to the ability of people to influence to some degree the decisions that affect them and their jobs. Such participation applies to subordinates at every level. Impressive evidence has been amassed by psychologist Rensis Likert and others showing that managers and supervisors as well as office workers and machine operators favor a system of participatory management above any other kind. It is ego enhancing, puts limits on arbitrary control, and often brings material rewards. In the all-too-rare instances where they have been used with commitment and seriousness, participatory practices have provided workable and profitable answers. The methods used have been based on hard-gotten, hard-tested facts collected by trained psychologists and applied by concerned businessmen who had a great deal at stake.

Some guidelines developed from our studies are essential. Genuine "participation" must be consistent with what is truly feasible. Employees should not be invited to "decide" anything unless the decision is really to be up to them. Or else they should be asked for their counsel, not their consent. The distinction between, "I'd like your opinion," and "It's up to you," should be clearly made, to the precise degree of participation sought.

Will the employees' opinions be of much value? That depends, of course, on how well-informed they are about the subject discussed. About matters which they know best, their own jobs, they are likely to have far more informed opinions than top managers or the men in the board room who lack firsthand experience with the details of a particular task. Employees can make practical and helpful suggestions because they know more about the departments in which they work and of the capabilities of themselves and their fellow workers than do remote senior executives. What if the employees offer suggestions that are turned down? In our experience, participants will show readiness to work out whatever policy is finally adopted. The upshot is likely to resemble that of a political election. Every year elections are held in this country. Not everyone's choice can win, but having had the chance to vote, most of the losers will go along with the winner. Having invited a frank expression of opinion, management might be embarrassed to hear criticism. That is one of the great virtues of "participation." Obviously, if top management is surprised by such frank comment, there has been a barrier to good communication which is always a dangerous condition. An additional point to be stressed, is that when an employee is invited to participate in decision-making, the subject must be one that matters to him. His role in it must not exceed what is relevant or of consequence to him.

Some enthusiasts assume that the higher the degree of participation, the better. But its effectiveness actually depends on how much that participant knows. Many problems are beyond the scope of the average employee. If he is not included, he will understand. The employee is apt to know his limitations as well as, and perhaps better than, everyone else. Participative practices have been criticized because group decision takes more time than does a unilateral decision by management. That criticism is valid. Participation does indeed take more time. But the ultimate cost is considerably less.

It is appropriate to declare here that there is nothing inherently "bad" about an employee sometimes being a nonparticipant. His attitude largely depends on the context. Often, of course, he is relieved to be omitted from a decision that does not directly concern him. Sometimes there are people who react negatively to participation. They are the dependent sort who would rather lean on someone else than take personal responsibility.

Participation provides many added satisfactions to the employees involved. It gives them feelings of self-esteem when their views are considered important. It helps provide a cooperative social atmosphere during important organizational meetings and it offers everyone the personal gratification of problem-solving. It also provides each employee with increased opportunities to raise issues of self-interest in a climate that is both protective and receptive.

SOME MANAGEMENT CONTRADICTIONS

A small number of organizations have been redesigned to provide for the exchange of valid information, encourage open communication, raise the level of trust, and involve all employees in decisions that affect their lives. But most companies have not ventured beyond the stage of more sloganeering. Even though today's executives have acquired more knowledge about human behavior, that has had no effect on their personal behavior in dealing with human problems. Their knowledge has not centered on their growth and development as persons.

One noticeable change is that managers today rarely admit to being authoritarian. The present posture is verbally to espouse views supportive of democratic procedures and greater self-management. But despite the verbal commitment, the way they relate to others has not changed. This is not to imply that such executives are feigning a democratic point of view. They are seemingly unaware of the contradictions between their professed concepts and their actual behavior. Many executives fail to see how their behavior exploits others. They identify their personal success with the general good. They view the world in terms of their own private needs. The incongruence between espoused theory and actual behavior can be seen with examples drawn from two prominent leaders in public life. These instances are not intended to represent conclusions drawn from scientific research. On the contrary, they are merely observations that provide illustrative material that can help us understand the inconsistency that so often occurs between professed views and actual behavior.

Robert Moses of New York received national recognition for his services as the one public official who could get things done. His achievements were perceived as being in the public's interest. At one time, he held 12 separate city and state positions simultaneously. But to the people who worked for him, his reputation was very different from his public image. To them, he was an absolute and ruthless dictator who spent his life amassing power and using it against anyone who stood in his way. While he publicly advocated social planning and depended on the public for his support, he never encouraged sharing of decision-making. Everyone in his organization knew there was just one decision-maker and that was Moses.

In assessing the 30 years of leadership by Moses, Robert Caro, the author of Moses' biography, *The Power Broker*, writes, "In evaluating his leadership, we must consider the homes he destroyed, the lives he ruined, the neighborhoods he bulldozed, the humiliations he piled on subordinates, the careers he crushed, the hundreds of millions of dollars he wasted—how he brutalized the poor and appeased the powerful." Apparently, Moses was able to blind himself to all this. He could ignore his own self-centered motivations and publicly speak of his devotions to the democratic process and the power of the people to be the ultimate decision-makers. But he never recognized the gap between creed and deed.

The second example is another public official, the widely known reform mayor of New York, Fiorello LaGuardia. As mayor, LaGuardia proclaimed his devotion to the democratic way of life and publicly denounced the political bosses who made decisions in back rooms without consulting the people. Yet, to everyone who worked with him, he was considered a bullying, petty tyrant.

When a city council member said to Mayor LaGuardia, "It is the business of the majority to advance a constructive program," LaGuardia replied with a grim smile, *"In this administration, I am the majority."* Typical of his interpersonal behavior with subordinates was this incident. At a meeting of all city commissioners, LaGuardia sharply rebuked his secretary and, as she left the room deeply embarrassed, he shouted, "If you were any dumber, I'd appoint you a commissioner."

Both of these men by their highhanded and autocratic leadership and craving for power contributed to the deterioration of New York City and its current reputation as being "unmanageable" and beyond recovery. Though widely scattered, there are now enough documented successful case studies to provide ample evidence that a participative managerial system can heighten performance, increase employee and managerial satisfaction and improve the health of both the organization and its employees.

SUCCESSFUL CASES USING PARTICIPATIVE METHODS

Convincing data have been available, and tested under the most exacting conditions in a number of organizations for more than twenty-five years. In the next few pages are summarized the findings of three significant projects often referred to as the Marrow-Harwood studies (1957, 1967, 1972), that demonstrated the superiority of participative methods. These are just a few of many similar projects that were completed over a twenty-five year period at a manufacturing plant in Marion, Virginia. A number of distinguished psychologists, among them Kurt Lewin, Alex Bavelas, John R. P. French, Jr., Gilbert David, Ian Ross, Stanley Seashore, and David Bowers, collaborated with me at various times on this long range program of on-the-job studies.

The first project concerned the obstinate resistance of production workers to changes in their methods and job tasks. Such changes were required, however, by competitive conditions, new technology, and shifts in consumer demands. An experiment was planned to test whether or not employee participation in problem-solving and in decision-making would help overcome the workers entrenched resistance. Three groups were formed, but for the purposes of this brief summary only two will be mentioned. The first, a nonparticipative group, was transferred to new work in the usual manner. Group members were told that changes were being made, the production manager explained the new job assignments and new piecework rates.

The second group, the participative group, was given a complete explanation of why the change was mandatory and the problems the management faced. Group members were asked to discuss cost reduction and a shift in job methods as a joint problem of the management and the workers. It was stated this way, "We don't want to sacrifice quality, we don't want you to lose income, but we must reduce our prices to get new business. What suggestions can you offer?"

After the two groups were transferred to the new units, their performance was compared. The nonparticipative group dropped 35% in productivity after the changeover and showed no improvement for a month afterwards. Nine percent of the operators in that group quit. Others filed grievances about the pay rates. Morale was exceptionally low. At the end of six weeks, the performance was so poor that management decided to dissolve the group and assign its members to other work stations.

The participative group reacted differently. By the second day they were back to their former level of production, and after three weeks, they had raised their production level 14% higher than before the transfer. No one quit and no grievances were filed with the union.

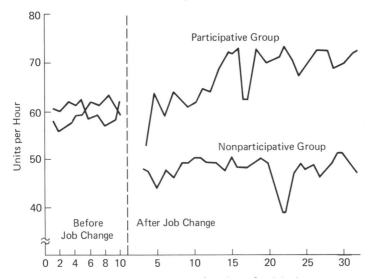

Figure 1. Output by two groups of workers after job change.

The evidence was unmistakably clear that the participative group had handled the problem created by the transfer in a far superior way. It was possible to confirm this even more dramatically about two and one-half months later. The earlier nonparticipative group, which had been broken up, was reassembled and its members transferred to new jobs. Now, however, management followed the participative procedures that had been used with the first experimental group. This time productivity recovered rapidly. Within a week, the group attained a new and much higher level of output. There was no manifestation of hostility and no one left. The participative approach was successful in this instance at the blue-collar level.

The second study I will describe involves middle management. The company had long discussed, but never started, a profit-sharing plan for supervisors. The management felt strongly that a plan which the staff itself helped to develop would have a better chance of succeeding than one merely designed for it. First of all, the plan would result from their own decisions, based on their own deliberations. Moreover, the staff would have a clearer understanding of how important its role was in keeping down costs. Their discussions would drive home the influence of their own leadership skills on the gains and losses effected by daily performance.

Management felt certain that economies would result, but nobody expected anything like the dramatic gains that followed the introduction of the new plan. After four months, there was a 58% decrease in make-up to standard pay (for workers who were not producing enough to earn the minimum wage). There was a 53% drop in employee turnover, a 12% drop in absenteeism and a 9% rise in production throughout the whole plant. (See Table 1.)

TABLE 1.   Effect of supervisory profit-sharing plan.

Item	Average Rate Four Months Preceding Plan	Average Rate Four Months After Plan	Percent of Improvement
Turnover	8.2	4.4	53
Absenteeism	6.1	5.4	12
Make-up pay	31.0	13.0	58
Average hourly production	56.5	61.7	9

The third study was made possible by the unusual occurrence of the purchase by the Harwood Companies of its largest competitor, the Weldon Manufacturing Company. From the standpoint of a behavioral science experiment, this was a lucky acquisition. It had never been possible in the past to compare two contrasting ways of managing two seemingly similar organizations. Now the opportunity arose though the occurrence was unintended. Each firm employed about 1,000 people. Their main plants were each about thirty years old; they put the same raw materials through similar manufacturing processes, on much the same kind of machinery, and sold them at competitive prices in similar and even overlapping markets.

It had been agreed that Weldon's entire staff was to be retained. The Weldon Companies' two owner-managers would become salaried managers, but otherwise the management would go on as before. The firms were to continue to operate separately and maintain separate identities. However, not long after the merger, it became clear to Harwood's top executives that, despite all the similarities, there was an irreconcilable conflict between the managerial systems of the two companies. In contrast to Harwood's emphasis on participative methods in dealing with managerial problems, Weldon operated under the traditional authoritarian system. A survey of Weldon's management and employees showed that the authoritarian attitude depicted in *The New Yorker* cartoon was prevalent and breeding poor production and big problems at Weldon. Good business dictated that the Weldon system be quickly changed.

In condensed form, Figure 2 compares the conditions in the Weldon and Har-

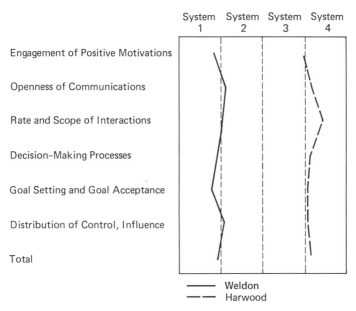

Figure 2. Operating characteristics 1962.

wood plants according to ratings made on the Likert scale (Likert, 1961). The profile for the Weldon organization runs along the border-line System 1, the exploitative-authoritative system. Harwood's profile ran well into System 4, the participative.

The results of an employee attitude survey were fed back to the Weldon staff. There was no indication in the summary as to what the solutions might be. These were to be worked out jointly between Weldon supervisors and their subordinates. The problems were profound and potentially dangerous. From a business standpoint, the differences between Weldon and Harwood plants could hardly have been more complete. For the year 1962, before efforts to change Weldon began to have a significant impact, Harwood was superior to Weldon in every area studied. Some examples are shown in Table 2. The evaluation presented such a dismal financial picture of Weldon that the survival of Weldon was very much in question.

TABLE 2. Comparison of organizational performance, Weldon and Harwood, 12 months, 1962 (percent).

Area of Performance	Weldon	Harwood
Return on investment	−15	17
Production efficiency	−11	6
Average earnings above minimum	None	17
Make-up pay to reach minimum	12	2
Average monthly absenteeism	6	3
Average monthly turnover	10	2

Harwood felt it had no choice. To protect its investment in Weldon, it had to find ways to encourage the Weldon people to work at their best and to increase their productivity. There were large questions to be answered. Could the habits and attitudes of Weldon people be unfrozen enough for useful change to come about? Could change occur without disrupting the entire organization and causing wholesale quitting and sabotage of the new program? Could the supervisory staff, which was as suspicious and anxious as the rest of the work force, be persuaded to take on the risks and responsibilities that lay ahead? Most important, would participation and trust be acceptable to people who had spent their working lives in a very different environment?

The answers to these questions were all yes. By 1964, the main economic goals of the program had essentially been achieved, as Table 3 shows. Productivity had increased by 25%, turnover had dropped by 60%, absenteeism had been lowered by 50% and return on capital had improved by 32%. The effect

TABLE 3. Indicators of organization efficiency in production, Harwood and Weldon, 1962 and 1964 (percent)

Area of Performance	Weldon		Harwood	
	1962	1964	1962	1964
Return on capital invested	−15	+17	+17	+21
Make-up pay	12	4	2	2
Production efficiency	−11	+14	6	16
Earnings above minimum (piece-rate and other incentive employees only)	None	16	17	22
Operator turnover rates (monthly basis)	10	4	$\frac{3}{4}$	$\frac{3}{4}$
Absences from work (daily rate, production employees only)	6	3	3	3

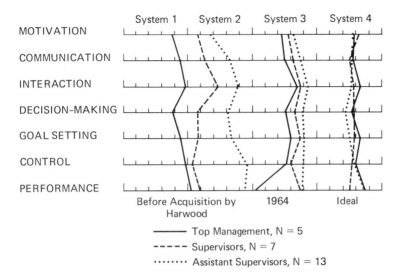

MOTIVATION

COMMUNICATION

INTERACTION

DECISION-MAKING

GOAL SETTING

CONTROL

PERFORMANCE

System 1   System 2   System 3   System 4

Before Acquisition by   1964   Ideal
Harwood

——— Top Management, N = 5
– – – – Supervisors, N = 7
········ Assistant Supervisors, N = 13

Figure 3. Weldon's progress toward participative management.

of the changes in Weldon to a participative system is illustrated in the following diagram, using the Likert rating procedure. Weldon had now shifted to System 3, the "consultative" model, from System 1 in 1962. Harwood's program to implant participation in the Weldon organization succeeded. Production, performance and profits increased while simultaneously personal relations, morale, and trust had radically and rapidly improved.

BARRIER TO ACCEPTANCE

Participative methods are being used successfully in many countries around the world. Arnold Tannenbaum has studied such methods in factories in Yugoslavia, Italy, Austria and Israel. The name by which the participative system is described varies. Some call it co-determination, others term it worker councils and joint consultation. But the principles and the results are essentially the same as we have experienced in the United States. Why in the light of so much hard data are so many organizations still ripe with conflict, their workers ambivalent and their leaders authoritarian? Why have so many firms resisted a program of active participation? Why, in the past 50 years, has there been so little implementation of the findings from the Hawthorne Studies and the others that have followed? What are the barriers to wider application? Why has progress been so slow?

There are many answers. One of the most important in my judgment is the resistance of the power holders who head our institutions. In my experience, they are most responsible for blocking the changes in their managerial system that would give their employees an opportunity to exercise greater control over their own activities. A number of hypotheses drawn from clinical experience and from such research studies as *The Authoritarian Personality* offer explanations of why the needs of top executives gain fulfillment through adding power and not sharing. Men and women who have climbed the rough journey to the top characteristically object to any change that will restrict their control. They have attained their elite positions because they possess a vigorous drive for achievement that is intrinsic in the American Dream. Power to them means the ability to prevent changes as well as to affect and influence other people's behavior. Status, authority, prestige are central considerations in their need for domination. To them, winning and being in command are what count. If it evokes animosity, they do not really care.

To feel successful, they must constantly assert or demonstrate power. Once in charge, their typical behavior is to avoid compromise, negotiation, persuasion, or sharing for they feel that it implies weakening their grip. Sometimes this drive for power is neurotic and often it is exploitive and manipulative. At other times, the drive results from the influence of the work ethic that overvalues material success. But, invariably, the men and women in positions of power believe that holding on to the job is more important than the well-being of the organization. We have experienced this phenomena in our consultant services to universities, government agencies, business institutions. In every situation we studied, the top leader fiercely resisted giving up any of his important prerogatives. Autocratic leaders seem to develop protective shells like turtles against any change brought about by outside pressure. New ideas bounce off their psychic shells like soft rain.

It is probably true that all human beings are born with a drive for power. How it is shaped during childhood often determines whether it is turned to constructive or destructive ends. But once power has been fought for and acquired, the holder will strongly oppose any diminution of his established control. Most of those who have gained power also possess a high level of anxiety, and the behavior of people with high anxiety is to be low risk-takers. Once at the peak, they constantly feel threatened. If their right to dictate were reduced, their anxiety would have to be faced. For power, though precariously based, does allay hidden anxiety.

Such executives fear becoming obsolete and are uncertain about the future, so they struggle against any attempts to limit their control over others. A sudden loss of power is recognized as being one of the most traumatic and painful experiences a leader, especially one with a good deal of hidden anxiety, can undergo. People in positions of high prestige and influence recognize this and are aware of the emptiness, hopelessness and desolation they will feel if stripped of the status and ceremonial trappings brought by their high office. They ward off any encroachment which could arouse inner tension. The causal factors that produce a leader with a neurotic power drive are beyond the scope of this presentation. We know that such a person can be outwardly charming, speak with authority on arcane subjects, be rich and cultured and own superb art collections. We also know that any effort to alter behavior by appeals to logic or persuasion will fail.

What can be done? Our own experience and the published research suggests that scientific tools are available to improve the process of selecting executives for key positions. Further research is needed but even with our incomplete knowledge, it is now possible to develop diagnostic series of instruments that would embrace measurements of leadership skills, readiness to share power, emotional maturity, sensitivity to the needs of others, ability to give and take feedback. Once a man has been appointed to a position of power, strong emphasis should be placed on training him for top management, along with personal counselling and experiential learning. These would help him function more effectively by providing him with a clearer understanding of his motives, his sense of values, his emotional maturity and his impact on the people with whom he works. The Watergate disaster points out the benefits of such a diagnostic and training program. A leader's sharing of power is what is at stake. Redistributing it has its costs and these must be paid for in coins of time, authority and prerogative.

SUMMARY

American industry, personal industriousness, as well as the corporate venture, has reached a turning point. We must learn how to operate with a maximum of collaboration and a minimum of hierarchy in a climate where cooperation replaces conflict. Fortunately, there are men in nearly every organization who already possess the desirable leadership temperament. They are sensitive to the needs of others and are supportive of the employees' desires for intrinsically satisfying jobs. There are some such executives, but far from enough of them. We need to concentrate now on exploring the executive mind and the promptings of those who assume leadership. We must shift the weight of our research and learn as much about the men in the executive suite as we already know about the men with the blue collar.

It may seem a long way from management-by-participation to backache, tension headache and coronary disease, but the human system is interrelated. Franz Alexander said, "The fact that the mind rules the body. . .is the most fundamental fact that we know about life." It is in the mind that we confront many of our problems, not in the stomach or joints. The daily nervous and mental frustrations that our workers experience also take a serious toll of their health, and that means in the aggregate, the national health. Such psychosomatic illnesses also add to the general inefficiency and the excessive cost of our industrial production.   Rising absenteeism from the job, malingering and vandalism are alarming symptoms of the psychological malaise that is spreading everywhere in our country. Work must provide a more attractive lure. It must offer mental stimulation, challenge and a lift to personal morale which it is inherently quite able to do.

If our basic problems are human ones, then executives must build more bridges between the behavioral sciences and business management. If they succeed, then the critically needed changes can be made by skillful and conscious choice. If they don't, the changes are likely to be made for them by militant employees who will upset the power balance of the past, sabotage and topple the traditional pyramidal organization structure and possibly create a serious economic catastrophe.

One might have expected many more significant changes towards participative management in the fifty years that have passed since the Hawthorne Studies. But that expectation was too optimistic. Today we hear with increased frequency the dismaying term "unmanageable" in explaining the low productivity of our nation's organizations. Our society is out of gear. What happens next will be determined by how enlightened the managers are of the country's vast technical and intellectual resources. Such managers have the power to convert the aspirations of their employees into a tangible and dynamic reality, a constructive force toward building a better and happier future society. Now, as never before, the most promising option is a scientific yet humanistic approach with a passionate concern by leaders to release to the full the latent talents and energies of the people they direct so that employees will work at their best and productivity will increase.

REFERENCES

Adorno, Brunswick, Levinson, Sanford *et al. The Authoritarian Personality.* New York, Harper Bros., 1950.
Likert, R. *New Patterns of Management.* New York, McGraw-Hill, 1961.
Marrow, A. J. *Making Management Human.* New York, McGraw-Hill, 1957.
Marrow, A. J. *The Failure of Success.* New York, American Management Association, 1972.
Marrow, A. J., Bowers, D. J. and Seahorse, S. E. *Management By Participation.* New York, Harper & Row, 1967.

4

IN SEARCH OF THE HAWTHORNE EFFECT

Robert L. Kahn
University of Michigan

INTRODUCTION

In 1798 the great English physician, Edward Jenner, published his *Inquiry into the Cause and Effect of Variolae Vaccinae*. This paper proposed an explanation for the acute infectious nature of smallpox, a disease which had been pandemic in Europe and epidemic in Britain. More important for its immediate contribution to life and health, Dr. Jenner's monograph described his discovery that smallpox could be prevented by means of inoculation with infectious matter from the blisters of a lesser but related disease, cowpox.

Jenner was approaching the age of fifty when he published these research findings, but he had been a medical apprentice of less than twenty years when he first remarked the apparent immunity of Gloucestershire milkmaids to smallpox and noted that cowpox and smallpox were somehow antagonistic to each other. His insistence on explaining an unexpected observation led to one of the most important discoveries in the history of medicine.

It is debatable, I suppose, whether Jenner's discovery was a proper instance of scientific serendipity, and in any case the word had scarcely entered the English language. Horace Walpole coined it from the title of a fairy tale, *The Three Princes of Serendip*, whom he describes as "always making discoveries, by accidents and sagacity, of things they were not in quest of." Jenner's initial discovery of the apparent antagonism between cowpox and smallpox was serendipitous. Thereafter his discoveries could scarcely have been more purposeful.

A clearer and a more recent example of serendipity is provided by the well-known circumstances through which Alexander Fleming came to discover penicillin. Fleming was engaged in research on influenza when he noticed that mold had developed accidentally on one of the culture plates which he was using for his work with staphylococcus bacteria. Around the mold Fleming observed an area that was free of the staphylococcus. This accident and observation oc- cured in 1928. Within a year Fleming had done experiments proving that a liquid culture of this mold, even when diluted 800 times, prevented the growth of staphylococcus. He published the results in the *Journal of Experimental Pathology*, calling his discovery penicillin, after the botanical name for the class of molds from which it was derived.

There is implicit in these examples a great instruction to scientists on dealing with the significant unexpected. Having identified an unexpected finding, we must explain it, descern its causes, and describe the conditions under which it occurs. In the case of Edward Jenner, between his youthful observations in Gloucestershire and his epochal invention of smallpox vaccination lay some thirty years of recurring effort to explain why milkmaids did not show the then common susceptibility to smallpox. He found that cowpox took two different forms, only one of which protected against smallpox, and then only when it was communicated at a particular stage of the disease. Only after the unexpected had been thus explained and specified did the immunization of mass populations become safe and practicable.

THE HAWTHORNE EFFECT

To discuss unexpected research results on the 50th anniversary of the Haw- thorne Studies is by no means unexpected. The best known finding from those famous researches is perhaps the "Hawthorne effect," a phrase that has become synonymous in social science for almost any unintended experimenter effect. I believe, however, that the main significance of the so-called Hawthorne effect has been buried beneath that phrase. The significance of the finding has to do with participation, not the minor amusement of taking part in a brief experi- ment or the implausible response to mere managerial attention, but participation in more important terms like taking part in the decisions that affect one's life. The remainder of this chapter will review the evidence for this point of view and consider its implications for social research and social policy.

The Object of Attention

Two things impress the reader who attempts to follow the comments of scholars on the Hawthorne Studies; their number and their agreement. Theorists and appliers of theories, psychologists and sociologists, students of organizations and researchers on groups all mention Hawthorne, and almost invariably mention as well the mysterious "effect." I offer a sampler, chosen for variety and credibil- ity of source rather than absolute representativeness.

In the *Handbook of Social Psychology* (1969), Herbert Simon and Andrew Stedry offer a list of "the hypotheses that have been pretty well validated" in the shared territory of psychology and economics. The Hawthorne effect is number one. "When special attention is given to a group of workers by management (say, by enlisting them in an experimental situation), production is likely to rise independently of changes in actual working conditions." That states the myth in its purest form: increased productivity in exchange for a little attention. It is the embodiment of a managerial dream.

Donald T. Campbell (1957) in a classic article on "factors relevant to the validity of experiments in social settings," wrote that "the Hawthorne studies (Mayo 1933) illustrate . . . sympathetic changes due to awareness of experimentation rather than to the specific nature of X" (that is, the experimental variable itself).

Anne Anastasi (1968), summarizing the field of applied psychology for the *International Encyclopedia of the Social Sciences*, stated that "the term Hawthorne Effect is now commonly used to designate the influence that participating in an experiment may have upon the subject's behavior."

Frederick Mosteller (1967), in an essay on nonsampling errors, speaks of the Hawthorne effect as an example of the contrariness of experimental subjects, animal and human, in responding in ways unpredicted by the experimenter:

"Psychologists sadly say that even under the most carefully controlled conditions, laboratory animals do as they please. Humans do even worse. When Roethlisberger and Dickson (1939) carried out their experiments to find conditions that would maximize productivity of factory teams at the Hawthorne Works of Western Electric, they found that every change—increasing the lighting or reducing it, increasing the wage scale or reducing it—seemed to increase the group productivity. *Paying attention to people, which occurs in placing them in an experiment, changes their behavior. This rather unpredictable change is called the Hawthorne effect.*"

Such quotations could be continued to the point of reader and writer exhaustion. Except for an earlier comment by Daniel Katz and me (1966), I have found few deviant interpretations.*

THE HAWTHORNE EFFECT REINTERPRETED

One is tempted to respond to Mosteller's cavil against experimental subjects, good-natured as it is, with the Skinnerian dictum: The rat is always right. When an experimental subject behaves in an unexpected way, the research worker is presented with a new task, the discovery of the unintended stimulus to which he has observed an unpredicted response. Such a search may take the form of

---

*Most thorough of these is H. M. Parsons' (1974) reinterpretation of the Hawthorne effect in terms of operant reinforcement. See also Carey (1967).

meticulous re-examination of experimenter behavior, differentiation of the original stimulus situation into smaller testable components, or attempts at replication by other experimenters under conditions of different and additional controls.

Simon's reference to "special attention" would thus raise the question of what kinds of experimenter attention evoke additional productive behavior and what kinds do not. Campbell's reference to "awareness of experimentation" would raise similar questions about what aspects of the experiment the subjects were aware of and *why* their awareness motivated them to expend greater effort at their task.

It is surprising that such questions have not been prominently raised, in light of the conspicuous difficulty of creating organizational change and especially of increasing productivity. Research on the effect of conventional training methods, too seldom done, is generally discouraging. (See Fleishman 1953, 1961; Mann 1957, for example.) Research on the organizational effects of sensitivity training ("laboratory" training, T-groups) compels the conclusion that such experiences do not in themselves produce increments in performance (Bowers 1973). Yet such programs certainly give their subjects "special attention by management." Why no Hawthorne effect? Is the Hawthorne effect perhaps characterized by an elusive Zen quality, so that it is achieved only when we are not aiming for it?

An interesting clue, although a negative one, is provided by a research project of Frederick Herzberg (1968) on job enrichment. This project is described in a well-known article in the *Harvard Business Review* and carries the slightly provocative title, "One More Time: How Do You Motivate Employees?" Herzberg's answer to this question involves enriching jobs in "vertical" terms, adding to quality rather than merely to numbers of specific functions or "hygienic" rewards. That is the main point of the article; the clue for us searchers after the Hawthorne effect comes in a parenthetical statement. Herzberg is explaining that one of his experiments with job enrichment involved an experimental group (enriched) and a control group which "continued to do its job in the traditional way. There were also two uncommitted groups of correspondents formed to measure the so-called Hawthorne effect—that is, to gauge whether productivity and attitudes toward the job changed artificially merely because employees sensed that the company was paying more attention to them in doing something different or novel. The results for these groups were substantially the same as for the control group, and for the sake of simplicity I do not deal with them."

This is a plausible and encouraging set of findings. Two groups of employees were given the allegedly potent Hawthorne treatment, and their behavior was not different from that of the control group. More replications of this design are needed, but assume, for purposes of the present argument, that the results are correct and replicable. Where do they lead?

At the very least, they tell us that awareness of participating in an experiment, even an experiment of considerable scope conducted in an industrial setting, does not in itself lead to an increase in productivity. The Hawthorne effect is not unvarying or even dependable, and the problem is then to find under what circumstances it is evoked. Or more modestly, what are the important differences between the Hawthorne experiments in which the effect was generated and Herzberg's experiment in which it was not?

Many answers can be given to that question including type of work, duration of the experiment itself, and even the cultural or normative differences between 1974 and 1924. My own answer, however, involves the hypothesized effect of participation itself; not participation in an experiment but participation in shaping the conditions and expectations of a major life role. I have become convinced that the young women in the Relay Assembly Test Room were offered and increasingly took the opportunity to alter their work roles in content, duration, pace, rewards, and relationship to conventional authority. There was, in short, a genuine transfer of power, in significant degree and for no trivial period of time.

The Latin sources of the word participate, after all, mean literally to take a part or share, not merely to play a role. I think the experimental subjects were closer to the root meaning of the term than many of their academic interpreters. As evidence for the modification of the then conventional supervision and the development of participation among the workers in the test room, consider the following descriptive statements from Roethlisberger and Dickson (1939):

1. There was from the beginning a reduction in the closeness of supervision. "In planning the studies, no definite arrangements for supervision had been made. The girls had been previously under the direct supervision of a group chief, who in turn reported to a section chief, whose superiors were the assistant foreman and foreman of the department. Inasmuch as the test room observer could assume responsibility of most of the day-to-day supervision, it was unnecessary to transfer the group chief to the test room." (Pages 36 and 37)
2. The test room observer, however, "was chiefly concerned with creating a friendly relation with the operators which would ensure their cooperation." (Page 36)
3. (Period II) "When it was time for the second physical examinations, the girls, with Operator 1 as spokesman, expressed a dread of the examinations and objected to submitting to them so frequently. In order to dispel some of their qualms, the investigators again explained the purpose of the examinations and made arrangements for the operators to go to the hospital together instead of separately as before. After the examinations, the physicians and other members of the hospital staff met with the girls for a

friendly talk, the purpose of which was to break down the formality of the occasion. During this meeting, it was suggested that ice cream be served on these occasions. This suggestion met with the immediate approval of the operators, who offered to furnish a cake. Plans were made for a 'party' at the next meeting. This method of treating the occasion seemed to satisfy the girls, for when the next examinations came around, they made no complaints." (Page 34)   This would be an interesting example of reciprocal influence under any circumstances. As a negotiation between medical staff and 20-year-old factory workers of an earlier generation, it is remarkable.

4. (Period III)   At the beginning of this period, the six young women in the test room became a separate wage incentive payment group. In the regular department they had been part of a large group, and they had been paid as members of that group of about 100 employees. "They were told, then, that a method of payment would be introduced after the test was well under way which would *assure* them of earnings equal to what they had been getting in the past, with the possibility that these earnings would actually be increased should their output in the test room increase over what it had been in the regular department." (Page 35)   In short, the test room operatives moved to a pay system that was more visibly related to the performance of the primary group and offered opportunity for greater earnings.

5. (Period IV)   This period involved the introduction of rest periods. Consider, however, the participative process by which rest periods were introduced: "Finally, in accordance with the general test room policy, it was decided to consult the girls themselves before the times for the rests were definitely fixed.

   A meeting was called for August 5, 1927, at the superintendent's office. The girls were shown their output curves, and the low and high points in the day were pointed out. When asked at what times they would like to have their rests, they unanimously voted in favor of 10 o'clock in the morning and 2 o'clock in the afternoon. Accordingly, the investigators agreed to institute rest pauses at these times. The working hours were thus reduced to 47.05 hours per week, a decrease of 1.9 per cent from the standard 48-hour week." (Page 40)

6. Meantime, the interpersonal relationships between "supervisors" and employees had been changing, as Roethlisberger and Dickson gently put it, toward "a rather free and easy relation with the test room authority." (Page 46)   The evidence for this consists mostly of conversational exchanges between the test room employees and the observer, who was the only "supervisor" on the immediate premises.

7. (Period V)   "In this period an . . . incident occurred which threw much

light on the girls' attitudes toward . . . authority." (Page 47) The investigators planned to institute a method of deferring a part of the money earned above the usual rate, expecting that payment of this bonus might be more effective on a monthly basis. The women objected to the deferment. ". . . as soon as they (the investigators) became aware of the operators' reaction they quickly decided to drop the proposed alteration in method of payment." (Page 48)

8. (Period VII) This period was notable for the abandonment of five-minute rest periods, to which the women had objected, and the institution of longer, less frequent rest periods, which they had requested. In addition, a "lunch" was to be provided in the morning at company expense. "In determining what should be served for these lunches, the company doctors were consulted and also the girls themselves. Arrangements were made with the organization in charge of the company restaurant to prepare and serve the food. When the final plans were made, the girls were called again into a meeting in the superintendent's office, and this next feature was discussed with them." (Page 51)

The reactions were positive, not without some skepticism, and full of increasing confidence. Thus, Operator 3: "How long are they going to feed us?" Operator 4: "They'll have to keep it up now or we won't work here." (Page 52)

9. The limits to autonomy and participation were also illustrated during Period VII, when two operators were dismissed from the experimental group for "hostile and uncooperative attitudes," which seem to have been inferred from "excess talking" and reduced productivity. The operators' defense, "We thought you wanted us to work as we feel." was judged insufficient, and two new subjects, chosen for their cooperative attitudes, were introduced as replacements. (Pages 53-55)

10. (Periods VIII-X) The experimentation with hours of work was clearly an initiative of the investigators rather than a participative expression by the operators. It is worth noting, however, that significant areas of choice were given—the opportunity of choosing between either starting work one-half hour later in the morning or stopping work one-half hour earlier in the afternoon. They unanimously chose the latter alternative." Further, "during Period IX the girls again chose to stop early—one hour earlier than usual." (Pages 60-63)

11. The questionnaire responses during these periods indicated that the operators themselves were much aware of their increased power and autonomy: "greater freedom," "absence of bosses," "opportunity to set one's own pace and to earn what one makes without being held back by a big group," "more freedom," "less supervision," and the like. (Page 66)

12. The extent to which the operators had acquired a participative role in the

design of the experiment itself was illustrated as Period XI began. "Quite obviously, the next step in the experiment would have been to return to the full 48-hour week without rest periods, as originally planned. But the investigators had promised the operators an experiment with a five-day week at some time during the summer months. As it was already the end of June, it seemed desirable to again postpone the return to the original conditions of work in favor of the five-day week experiment." Moreover, ". . . the operators were paid their basic hourly rate for Saturday mornings, the time not worked. Just why this arrangement was made was never explicitly stated by the investigators." (Page 68)

13. Finally, we have during Periods XII and XIII frequent examples of the extent to which a kind of power-equalization between "supervisor" and "supervised" had occurred in the test room. The observer had at one point stated that conditions in the larger department were similar to those in the test room. The operators, who knew better, responded:

Operator 2: Yes, but you can't scream and have the good times out there that we do in the test room and the *fun* in the test room is what makes it worthwhile.
Operator 3: Yes, there are too many bosses in the department.
Operator 1: Yes, Mr. _____ (observer) is the only boss we have.
Operator 2: Say, he's no boss. We don't have any boss.
Observer: (starting to speak) But you know . . .
Operator 3: Shut up.
Operator 2: Look at that. Look at the way she tells her boss to shut up.
(Page 71)

I believe that any conscientious reader of the original materials will be led to the conclusion that operators in the test room were during those five years participating increasingly in decisions that affected their lives on the job, the quality of the working experience, the amount of time available to them for leisure activities, and the money they received for their work. These, I believe, were the stimuli to which they were responding, and their responses are consistent with the findings of subsequent research in which major participative changes have been introduced.

Participation, Performance, and Satisfaction

A great deal of research has been done on the correlates and effects of participation, primarily in terms of productivity and satisfaction. The books and articles describing this work constitute a large and various literature, some of it restrained and conservative in interpretation, some of it throbbing with the enthusiasm of advocacy and a priori conviction. This large body of material is further complicated by unresolved differences in the definition of participation itself and by unspecified differences in organizational setting, extent of participation, and choice of criterion measures. Moreover, subjective reports and objective or independent data on the participative process are often confounded. It is, in short, a difficult literature to summarize.

Several good summaries are available, nonetheless. Likert (1961, 1967), whose "System 4" theory of overlapping groups is essentially a theory of participative decision-making, offers a scholarly, convincing (and admittedly partisan) summary of much of the relevant organizational research on the subject. Vroom (1964, 1969) has reviewed much of the same material, somewhat more critically, and addresses himself to a good many laboratory findings, as well. None of these reviews deals with the various formal systems of participation that have developed outside the United States, but a recent chapter by Tannenbaum (1974) describes these programs in some detail. The conclusions of these several review articles and chapters are stated below.

(1) Participation is consistently and significantly associated with satisfaction. The satisfaction of subordinates with their jobs is positively related to the extent to which they participate in and exert influence on decisions affecting them in the work situation. This relationship holds for auto workers (Jacobson 1951), research scientists (Baumgartel 1956), telephone operators and service representatives (Wickert 1951), utility employees (Ross and Zander 1957), clerical workers (Morse 1953), Norwegian factory workers (French, Israel, and As 1960), insurance clerks (Morse and Reimer 1956), aircraft workers (Meyer, Kay and French 1965), and many other kinds of groups.

(2) The relationship between participation and satisfaction differs for people of different personality characteristics, being most strongly positive among persons high in need of independence and low on authoritarianism. (Tannenbaum and Allport, 1956; Vroom, 1960)

(3) Participation is generally associated with group or unit effectiveness, although there are findings to the contrary and the magnitude of the relationship appears to depend to some extent on the particular criterion of effectiveness that is used. Vroom (1969) considers three such criteria, decision quality, likelihood of implementation, and decision time.

(4) Research on the quality of group versus individual decisions has been done in the laboratory for the most part, and leaves uncertain the extrapolation of findings to the organizational context. The laboratory findings show persistent differences in content between group and individual decisions, and the group decisions tend to be superior in quality. Tasks have involved management problems, mathematical puzzles, military riddles, question games, and the like. Vroom (1969) presents a summary of this material, and Lorge, et al. (1958) did an earlier extensive review. Conditioning or moderating factors yet to be thoroughly understood include the nature of the task, the relative experience

and knowledge of group members (including the formal leader), and the stage of problem-solving at which group process is introduced. There is some evidence that interaction inhibits the "creative" phase of problem-solving and contributes most to the evaluation of alternative courses of action.

(5) Participation is consistently and positively related to the implementation of decisions. More research has been done on this hypothesized effect of participation than on any other, and the findings that support it are very numerous. The early researches of Lewin and his colleagues in bringing about changes in the pattern of food consumption concentrated on the implementation of decisions rather than on the initial determination of decision content or choice (Lewin 1947; Radke and Klisurich 1947; Simmons 1954). The subsequent industrial experiment of Coch and French (1948) also dealt primarily with the implementation of a decision to reduce costs and change methods of work, although the participants were perhaps free to oppose or revise that decision. Bennett (1955), in an ingenious experiment designed to dissect out the crucial factors in the participative experience, found that an individual's behavior in implementing a decision depended upon his being asked actually to make a decision or commitment and upon the visible consensus of the group with respect to carrying out the decision. In short, as Vroom (1969) concludes, ". . . the participation of individuals or of groups in decisions which affect them appears to be positively related to their acceptance of decisions and to the efficiency with which the decisions are executed, *other things being equal . . .*" (Page 237)

(6) Participation takes time; its benefits are not cost-free. The research on this aspect of participative decision-making is perhaps less definitive; certainly the issue of decision-time by groups as compared to individuals has been less researched. The research that has been done (Taylor and Faust 1952; Davis and Restle 1963, for example) shows that decision-time increases with the size of the group participating in making the decision. Guetzkow and Simon (1955) did an excellent experiment addressed to a somewhat different issue, which suggests the same conclusion. They demonstrated that a "participative" communications network required more time than a "hierarchical" network to reach a decision about how to solve a problem, but did not require more time thereafter.

The fact that costs and time are attached to participation should surprise no one. The question is whether these costs are outweighed by the improvement in quality, the additional commitment to implementation, the presumptive reduction in needed surveillance, and (if satisfaction be allowed some weight in the equation) the increase in satisfaction of human needs. One need not be a zealot to conclude that the evidence favors participative decision-making.

Almost all the research on participation in the United States has been conducted at the level of groups or organizational units like departments or local offices. Much of such research has been done in the laboratory, as we have seen. The research on participation done in live organizational settings has, for the

most part, described variations in supervisory or managerial behavior that occurred within the formal constraints of conventional hierarchical structures. A
few experimental studies have been based on programs of training or organizational change, but such programs were also nested in larger organizational
structures of conventional design. There are, however, systems of formal participation that are comprised of entire organizations or societies, and that involve
structural changes in employee representation, allocation of rewards, and the
like.

Such participative systems have been well summarized in a recent chapter by
Tannenbaum (1974). The story involves many systems and many countries,
kibbutz industries in Israel, self-management (workers' councils) in Yugoslavia,
codetermination in any number of western European countries, and experiments
in industrial democracy in Norway and Sweden. The conclusions thus far
available from these experiences (which cannot readily be compared with each
other because of cultural and contextual differences) argue that participation
does work, but not always. Sometimes the formal stipulations are not introduced without the hoped-for effects. But, as Tannenbaum says, ". . . the predicted effects *do* occur, in at least some cases: the system is legitimated and
accepted in the eyes of many workers and managers, control is effective, morale
is as high as can be expected in industrial work, and many participative organizations are efficient and profitable. . . . The demand for participation is not likely
to be less in the future than in the past, and the question for many, therefore,
is not whether participation works but rather *how* to make it work."

CONCLUSION

A single sentence summarizing the results of this excursion into the realm of the
Hawthorne effect and the research on participation would go as follows: Real
participation has real effects. When people take a significant and influential part
in decisions that they value, the quality of decisions is likely to be improved and
their implementation is almost certain to be improved.

Having said this, we must recognize that there are many ways in which managerial practices touted as participative fall short of this modest definition. Two
of the most common involve (1) the restriction of employee participation to
peripheral issues (picnics rather than pay) and (2) the presentation of grand
participative schemes or blueprints that managers do not, in fact, carry out. The
first of these failures can be thought of as real participation around fake issues;
the second as fake participation around real issues. Neither of them is participation as we have defined it and neither can be expected to produce the results
that real participation can generate.

It goes without saying, or it should, that participation in organizations must be
limited for the sake of sanity as well as efficiency. Many principles have been

proposed to determine who should be involved in what decision. An additional principle, which distinguishes among three major areas in the work role may be that which involves the area of autonomy, the area of participation, and the area of relevant nonparticipation.

One can think of these areas as arising from a series of dichotomies. First, in any job, there is an area of autonomy, in which the worker may do as he likes without affecting others particularly. This can be distinguished from the area of "nonautonomy," in which by definition the worker is controlled. The area of "nonautonomy" or controlled activities can in turn be dichotomized, into an area of participative control, in which the worker is controlled by decisions in which he has had a part; and the area of nonparticipative control, in which the worker is controlled by decisions in which he has not had a part. Finally, even the area of participative control can be dichotomized to distinguish between decisions in which the worker participates directly, and decisions in which he participates by representation or some other indirect means. The results of this dichotomizing can be more easily drawn than described:

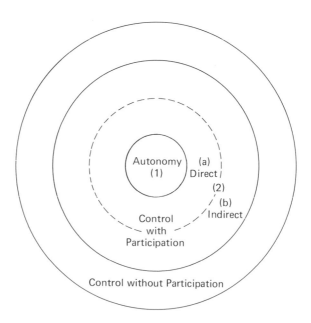

To design a new organization along participative lines, we might begin by asking how to maximize area one: To what extent can the person be autonomous without handicapping individual or organizational performance? The next question would take similar form with respect to the area of participation: In how many of the decisions that will affect him can the person participate without handicapping individual or organizational performance? The distinction between direct and indirect participation could be made in similar fashion. That is, one would attempt to maximize direct as compared to indirect participation. The area of decision-making by which the person was affected but in which he did not participate would thus be treated as a residual, to be minimized.

There are many schemes for attaining something along these lines. There are many obstacles, including the resistance of management to the sharing of prerogatives, and the resistance of unions to proposals that modify worker-management relationships or affect conventional styles of collective bargaining. Also important are the obstacles of ignorance and uncertainty, the research not yet done, and the questions not yet answered.

The stakes, however, are tremendous. To begin with, they involve the gross national product and all that it represents of material aspiration and hope. But the principle of participation affects the quality of people's lives in more ways than that. If the experience of working is unalterably dull and negative, then to improve the quality of a person's life one must reduce the amount of time he spends working, which means fewer hours per day, days per week or year, years per lifetime. If work is exciting and fulfilling and growth-inducing, then work itself enhances the meaning and quality of life. Participation, real participation, is one of the few things than endow work with such qualities.

In the fifty years since the first experiments were begun at the Hawthorne plant, far less has been done with the participative implications of the data than with the implications for group norms, informal organization, supervisory etiquette, and off-the-job influences. These facts say more about the times and the society than about the original data. I hope that social science and social practice may now be more ready for the full message of those early experiments.

REFERENCES

Anastasi, A. Applied psychology. In D. L. Sills (ed.) *International Encyclopedia of the Social Sciences.* New York: The Macmillan Company and The Free Press. 1968, **13:** 84–95 (quote p. 88).

Baumgartel, H. Leadership, Motivations and Attitudes in Research Laboratories. *J. soc. Issues.* 1956, **12:** 24–31.

Bennett, Edith Becker. Discussion, decision, commitment and consensus in 'group decision.' *Hum. Relat.* 1955, **8:** 251–273.

Bowers, D. OD techniques and their results in 23 organizations: the Michigan ICL study. *J. Appl. Beh. Sci.* 1973, 9 (1). 21–43.

Campbell, D. T. Factors relevant to the validity of experiments in social settings. *Psychol. Bull.* 1957, **54:** 297–312.

Carey, A. The Hawthorne studies: a radical criticism. *American Sociological Review.* 1967, **32** (3): 403–416.

Coch, L., and J. R. P. French, Jr. Overcoming resistance to change. *Hum. Relat.* 1948, **1:** 512–532.

Davis, J. H., and F. Restle. The analysis and prediction of group problem solving. *J. abnorm. soc. Psychol.* 1963, 66: 103–116.

Fleishman, E. A. Leadership climate, human relations training, and supervisory behavior. *Personnel Psychology.* 1953, 6: 205–222.

Fleishman, E. A. *Studies in Personnel and Industrial Psychology.* Homewood, Illinois: Dorsey, 1961.

French, J. R. P., Jr., J. Israel, and D. As. An experiment on participation in a Norwegian factory. *Hum. Relat.* 1960, 13: 3–19.

Guetzkow, H. and H. A. Simon. The impact of certain communication nets upon organization and performance in task-oriented groups. *Managemt. Sci.* 1955, 1: 233–250.

Herzberg, F. One more time: how do you motivate employees? *Harvard Business Review.* 1968, 46: 53–62.

Homans, G. C. In G. E. Swanson, T. M. Newcomb, E. L. Hartley (eds.), *Readings in social psychology.* New York: Holt, pp. 637–649, (Rev. ed. 1952).

Jacobson, E. Foreman-steward participation practices and worker attitudes in a unionized factory. Unpublished doctoral dissertation, University of Michigan, 1951.

Katz, D., and R. L. Kahn. *The social psychology of organizations.* New York: Wiley, 1966.

Lewin, K. Group decision and social change. In T. M. Newcomb and E. L. Hartley (eds.), *Readings in social psychology.* New York: Holt, 1947, pp. 330–344.

Likert, Rensis. *New Patterns of Management.* New York: McGraw-Hill, 1961.

Likert, Rensis. *The Human Organization.* New York: McGraw-Hill, 1967.

Lorge, I., D. Fox, J. Davits, and M. Brenner. A survey of studies contrasting the quality of group performance and individual performance: 1930-1957. *Psychol. Bull.* 1958, 55: 337–372.

Mann, F. C. Studying and creating change: a means to understanding social organization. In C. M. Arensberg et al. (eds.), *Research in industrial human relations.* New York: Harper, 1957, pp. 146–167.

Mayo, E. *The human problems of an industrial civilization.* Boston: Harvard University Graduate School of Business, 1933.

Meyer, H. H., E. Kay, and J. R. P. French, Jr. Split roles in performance appraisal. *Harvard Business Review.* 1965, 43: 123–129.

Morse, Nancy C. *Satisfactions in the white-collar job.* Ann Arbor: University of Michigan, Institute for Social Research, Survey Research Center, 1953.

Morse, Nancy C. and E. Reimer. The experimental change of a major organizational variable. *J. abnorm. soc. Psychol.* 1956, 52: 120–129.

Mosteller, Frederick. Nonsampling errors. In D. L. Sills (ed.), *International Encyclopedia of the Social Sciences.* New York: The Macmillan Company and The Free Press, 1967, 5: pp. 113–132 (quote p. 115).

Parson, H. M. What happened at Hawthorne? *Science,* 183 (8 March 1974): 922–932.

Radke, Marian, and Dana Klisurich. Experiments in changing food habits. *J. Amer. Diet Assoc.* 1947, 23: 403–409.

Roethlisberger, F. J., and W. J. Dickson. *Management and the worker.* Cambridge: Harvard Univ. Press, 1939.

Ross, I. C., and A. Zander. Need satisfactions and employee turnover. *Personnel Psychol.* 1957, 10: 327–338.

Simon, Herbert A. and Andrew C. Stedry. Psychology and economics. In Gardner Lindzey and Elliot Aronson (eds.), *Handbook of Social Psychology.* Reading, Massachusetts: Addison-Wesley, 1969, 5, pp. 269–314 (quote p. 294).

Simmons, W. The group approach to weight reduction: I. A review of the project. *J. Amer. Dietet. Assoc.* 1954, 30: 437–441.

Tannenbaum, A. S. Systems of fromal participation. In G. Strauss, R. Miles, C. C. Snow and A. S. Tannenbaum (eds.), *Organizational behavior: research and issues*. Madison, Wisconsin: Industrial Relations Research Association, 1974.

Tannenbaum, A. S., and F. H. Allport. Personality structure and group structure: an interpretive study of their relationship through an event-structure hypothesis. *J. abnorm. soc. Psychol.* 1956, **53**: 272–280.

Taylor, D. W., and W. L. Faust. Twenty questions: efficiency in problem solving as a function of size of group. *J. exp. Psychol.* 1952, **44**: 360–388.

Vroom, V. H. *Some personality determinants of the effects of participation.* Englewood Cliffs, N. J.: Prentice-Hall, 1960.

Vroom, V. H. *Work and Motivation.* New York: Wiley, 1964.

Vroom, V. H. Industrial social psychology. In Gardner Lindzey and Elliot Aronson (eds.), *Handbook of Social Psychology.* Reading, Massachusetts: Addison-Wesley, 1969, **5**, pp. 196–268.

Whitehead, T. N. *The Industrial Worker.* Cambridge, Mass: Harvard University Press, **1**, 1938.

Wickert, F. R. Turnover and employees' feelings of ego-involvement in the day-to-day operations of a company. *Personnel Psychol.* 1951, **4**: 185–197.

PART III

Organizations—Formal and Informal—Groups, Cliques, Constraints and Control

The Hawthorne Studies provided rich, descriptive information about not only the formal organization of the factory, but also the elaborate informal structure of the work place. The effect of this second structure was well-documented as to its effect on work performance.

The importance of these groups, though acknowledged, has not been used to any appreciable degree in considering alternative ways of organizing the factory. In fact, at times it appears that management may totally ignore this phenomenon. Once again, the issues pertaining to social organization of people by others and by themselves should be examined.

5
SUPPOSE WE TOOK
GROUPS SERIOUSLY . . .

Harold J. Leavitt
Stanford University

INTRODUCTION

This chapter is mostly a fantasy, but not a utopian fantasy. As the title suggests, it tries to spin out some of the things that might happen if we really took small groups seriously; if, that is, we really used groups, rather than individuals, as the basic building blocks for an organization.

This seems an appropriate forum for such a fantasy. It was fifty years ago, at Hawthorne, that the informal face-to-face work group was discovered. Since then groups have been studied inside and out; they have been experimented with, observed, built, and taken apart. Small groups have become the major tool of the applied behavioral scientist. Organizational Development methods are group methods. Almost all of what is called participative management is essentially based on group techniques.

So the idea of using groups as organizational mechanisms is by no means new or fantastic. The fantasy comes in proposing to start with groups, not add them in; to design organizations from scratch around small groups, rather than around individuals.

But right from the start, talk like that appears to violate a deep and important value, individualism. But this fantasy will not really turn out to be anti-individualistic in the end.

The rest of this chapter will briefly address the following questions: (1) Is it fair to say that groups have not been taken very seriously in organizational design? (2) Why are groups even worth thinking about as organizational building materials? What are the characteristics of groups that might make them interesting enough to be worth serious attention? (3) What would it mean "to take groups seriously?" Just what kinds of things would have to be done differently?

(4) What compensatory changes would probably be needed in other aspects of the organization, to have groups as the basic unit? And finally, (5), is the idea of designing the organization around small face-to-face groups a very radical idea, or is it just an extension of a direction in which we are already going?

Haven't groups been taken seriously enough already? The argument that groups have not been taken "seriously" doesn't seem a hard one to make. The contemporary ideas about groups didn't really come along until the 30's and 40's. By that time a logical, rationalistic tradition for the construction of organizations already existed. That tradition was very heavily based on the notion that the individual was the construction unit. The logic moved from the projected task backward. Determine the task, the goal, then find an appropriate structure and technology, and last of all fit individual human beings into predefined man-sized pieces of the action. That was, for instance, what industrial psychology was all about during its development between the two world wars. It was concerned almost entirely with individual differences and worked in the service of structuralists, fitting square human pegs to predesigned square holes. The role of the psychologist was thus ancillary to the role of the designers of the whole organization. It was a back up, supportive role that followed more than it led design.

It was not just the logic of classical organizational theory that concentrated on the individual. The whole entrepreneurial tradition of American society supported it. Individuals, at least male individuals, were taught achievement motivation. They were taught to seek individual evaluation, to compete, to see the world, organizational or otherwise, as a place in which to strive for individual accomplishment and satisfaction.

In those respects the classical design of organizations was consonant with the then existent cultural landscape. Individualized organizational structures blended with the environment of individualism. All the accessories fell into place: individual incentive schemes for hourly workers, individual merit rating and assessment schemes, tests for selection of individuals.

The unique characteristic of the organization was that it was not simply a race track within which individuals could compete, but a system in which somehow the competitive behavior of individuals could be coordinated, harnessed and controlled in the interest of the common tasks. Of course one residual of all that was a continuing tension between individual and organization, with the organization seeking to control and coordinate the individual's activities at the same time that it tried to motivate him; while the competitive individual insisted on reaching well beyond the constraints imposed upon him by the organization. One product of this tension became the informal organization discovered here at Western; typically an informal coalition designed to fight the system.

Then it was discovered that groups could be exploited for what management saw as positive purposes, *toward* productivity instead of away from it. There followed the era of experimentation with small face-to-face groups. We learned to patch them on to existing organizations as bandaids to relieve tensions between individual and organization. We promoted coordination through group methods. We learned that groups were useful to discipline and control recalcitrant individuals.

Groups were fitted onto organizations. The group skills of individual members improved so that they could coordinate their efforts more effectively, control deviants more effectively and gain more commitment from subordinate individuals. But groups were seen primarily as tools to be tacked on and utilized in the pre-existing individualized organizational system. With a few notable exceptions, like Rensis Likert (1961), most did not design organizations around groups. On the contrary, as some of the ideas about small groups began to be tacked onto existing organizational models, they generated new tensions and conflicts of their own. Managers complained not only that groups were slow, but that they diffused responsibility, vitiated the power of the hierarchy because they were too "democratic and created small in-group empires which were very hard for others to penetrate." There was the period, for example, of the great gap between T-group training (which had to be conducted on "cultural islands") and the organization back home. The T-groupers therefore talked a lot about the "reentry problem," which meant in part the problem of movement from a new culture (the T-group culture) designed around groups back into the organizational culture designed around individuals.

But of course groups didn't die despite their difficulties. How could they die? They had always been there, though not always in the service of the organization. They turned out to be useful, indeed necessary, though often unrecognized tools. For organizations were growing, and professionalizing, and the need for better coordination grew even as the humanistic expectations of individuals also grew. So "acknowledged" groups (as distinct from "natural," informal groups) became fairly firmly attached even to conservative organizations, but largely as compensating addenda very often reluctantly backed into by organizational managers.

Groups have never been given a chance. It is as though someone had insisted that automobiles be designed to fit the existing terrain rather than build roads to adapt to automobiles.

Are groups worth considering as fundamental building blocks? Why would groups be more interesting than individuals as basic design units around which to build organizations? What are the prominent characteristics of small groups? Why are they interesting? Here are several answers:

First, small groups seem to be good for people. They can satisfy important membership needs. They can provide a moderately wide range of activities for individual members. They can provide support in times of stress and crisis. They are settings in which people can learn not only cognitively but empirically to be reasonably trusting and helpful to one another. Second, groups seem to be good problem finding tools. They seem to be useful in promoting innovation and creativity. Third, in a wide variety of decision situations, they make better decisions than individuals do. Fourth, they are great tools for implementation. They gain commitment from their members so that group decisions are likely to be willingly carried out. Fifth, they can control and discipline individual members in ways that are often extremely difficult through more impersonal quasi-legal disciplinary systems. Sixth, as organizations grow large, small groups appear to be useful mechanisms for fending off many of the negative effects of large size. They help to prevent communication lines from growing too long, the hierarchy from growing too steep, and the individual from getting lost in the crowd.

There is a seventh, but altogether different kind of argument for taking groups seriously. Thus far the designer of organizations seemed to have a choice. He could build an individualized *or* a groupy organization. A groupy organization will, de facto, have to deal with individuals; but what was learned here so long ago is that individualized organizations, must de facto, deal with groups. Groups are natural phenomena, and facts of organizational life. They can be created but their spontaneous development cannot be prevented. The problem is not shall groups exist or not, but shall groups be planned or not? If not, the individualized organizational garden will sprout groupy weeds all over the place. By defining them as weeds instead of flowers, they shall continue, as in earlier days, to be treated as pests, forever fouling up the beauty of rationally designed individualized organizations, forever forming informally (and irrationally) to harass and outgame the planners.

It is likely that the reverse could also be true, that if groups are defined as the flowers and individuals as the weeds, new problems will crop up. Surely they will, but that discussion can be delayed for at least a little while.

Who uses groups best? So groups look like interesting organizational building blocks. But before going on to consider the implications of designing organizations around groups, one useful heuristic might be to look around the existing world at those places in which groups seem to have been treated somewhat more seriously.

One place groups have become big is in Japanese organizations (Johnson & Ouchi, 1974). The Japanese seem to be very groupy, and much less concerned than Americans about issues like individual accountability. Japanese organizations, of course, are thus consonant with Japanese culture, where notions of individual aggressiveness and competitiveness are de-emphasized in favor of self-effacement and group loyalty. But Japanese organizations seem to get a lot done, despite the relative suppression of the individual in favor of the group. It also appears that the advantages of the groupy Japanese style have really come to the fore in large technologically complex organizations.

Another place to look is at American conglomerates. They go to the opposite extreme, dealing with very large units. They buy large organizational units and sell units. They evaluate units. In effect they promote units by offering them extra resources as rewards for good performance. In that sense conglomerates, one might argue, are designed around groups, but the groups in question are often themselves large organizational chunks.

Groups in an individualistic culture. An architect can design a beautiful building which either blends smoothly with its environment or contrasts starkly with it. But organization designers may not have the same choice. If we design an organization which is structurally dissonant with its environment, it is conceivable that the environment will change to adjust to the organization. It seems much more likely, however, that the environment will reject the organization. If designing organizations around groups represents a sharp counterpoint to environmental trends maybe we should abort the idea.

Our environment, one can argue, is certainly highly individualized. But one can also make a less solid argument in the other direction; an argument that American society is going groupy rather than individual this year. Or at least that it is going groupy as well as individual. The evidence is sloppy at best. One can reinterpret the student revolution and the growth of anti-establishment feelings at least in part as a reaction to the decline of those institutions that most satisfied social membership needs. One can argue that the decline of the Church, of the village and of the extended family is leaving behind a vacuum of unsatisfied membership and belongingness motives. Certainly popular critics of American society have laid a great deal of emphasis on the loneliness and anomie that seem to have resulted not only from materialism but from the emphasis on individualism. It seems possible to argue that, insofar as there has been any significant change in the work ethic in America, the change has been toward a desire for work which is socially as well as egoistically fulfilling, and which satisfies human needs for belongingness and affiliation as well as needs for achievement.

In effect, the usual interpretation of Abraham Maslow's need hierarchy may be wrong. Usually the esteem and self-actualization levels of motivation are emphasized. Perhaps the level that is becoming operant most rapidly is neither of those, but the social-love-membership level.

The rising role of women in American society also has implications for the groupiness of organizations. There is a moderate amount of evidence that American women have been socialized more strongly into affiliative and relational sorts of attitudes than men. They probably can, in general, more comfortably work in direct achievement roles in group settings, where there are strong relational bonds among members, than in competitive, individualistic settings. Moreover it is reasonable to assume that as women take a more important place in American society, some of their values and attitudes will spill over to the male side.

Although the notion of designing organizations around groups in America in 1974 may be a little premature, it is consonant with cultural trends that may make the idea much more appropriate ten years from now.

But groups are becoming more relevant for organizational as well as cultural reasons. Groups seem to be particularly useful as coordinating and integrating mechansims for dealing with complex tasks that require the inputs of many kinds of specialized knowledge. In fact the development of matrix-type organizations in high technology industry is perhaps one effort to modify individually designed organizations toward a more groupy direction; not for humanistic reasons but as a consequence of tremendous increases in the informational complexity of the jobs that need to be done.

What might a seriously groupy organization look like? Just what does it mean to design organizations around groups? Operationally how is that different from designing organizations around individuals? One approach to an answer is simply to take the things organizations do with individuals and try them out with groups. The idea is to raise the level from the atom to the molecule, and *select* groups rather than individuals, *train* groups rather than individuals, *pay* groups rather than individuals, *promote* groups rather than individuals, *design jobs* for groups rather than for individuals, *fire* groups rather than individuals, and so on down the list of activities which organizations have traditionally carried on in order to use human beings in their organizations.

Some of the items on that list seem easy to handle at the group level. For example, it doesn't seem terribly hard to design jobs for groups. In effect that is what top management already does for itself to a great extent. It gives specific jobs to committees, and often runs itself as a group. The problem seems to be a manageable one: designing job sets which are both big enough to require a small number of persons and also small enough to require only a small number of persons. Big enough in this context means not only jobs that would occupy the hands of group members but that would provide opportunities for learning and expansion.

Ideas like evaluating, promoting, and paying groups raise many more difficult but interesting problems. Maybe the best that can be said for such ideas is that they provide opportunities for thinking creatively about pay and evaluation. Suppose, for example, that as a reward for good work the group gets a larger salary budget than it got last year. Suppose the allocation for increases within the group is left to the group members. Certainly one can think up all sorts of difficulties that might arise. But are the potential problems necessarily any more difficult than those now generated by individual merit raises? Is there any company in America that is satisfied with its existing individual performance appraisal and salary allocation schemes? At least the issues of distributive justice within small groups would presumably be open to internal discussion and debate. One might even permit the group to allocate payments to individuals differentially at different times, in accordance with some criteria of current contribution that they might establish.

As far as performance evaluation is concerned, it is probably easier for people up the hierarchy to assess the performance of total groups than it is to assess the performance of individual members well down the hierarchy. Top managers of decentralized organizations do it all the time, except that they usually reward the formal leader of the decentralized unit rather than the whole unit.

The notion of promoting groups raises another variety of difficulties. One thinks of physically transferring a whole group, for example, and of the costs associated with training a whole group to do a new job, especially if there are no bridging individuals. But there may be large advantages too. If a group moves, its members already know how to work with one another. Families may be less disrupted by movement if several move at the same time.

There is the problem of selection. Does it make sense to select groups? Initially, why not? Can't means be found for selecting not only for appropriate knowledge and skill but also for potential ability to work together? There is plenty of groundwork in the literature already.

After the initial phase, there will of course be problems of adding or subtracting individuals from existing groups. We already know a good deal about how to help new members get integrated into old groups. Incidentally, I was told recently by a plant manager in the midwest about an oddity he had encountered; the phenomenon of groups applying for work. Groups of three or four people have been coming to his plant seeking employment together. They wanted to work together and stay together.

Costs and danger points. To play this game of designing organizations around groups, what might be some important danger points? In general, a group-type organization is somewhat more like a free market than present organizations. More decisions would have to be worked out ad hoc, in a continually changing way. So one would need to schedule more negotiation time both within and between groups.

One would encounter more issues of justice, for the individual vis-a-vis the group and for groups vis-a-vis one another. More and better arbitration mechanisms would probably be needed along with highly flexible and rapidly adaptive record keeping. But modern record keeping technology is, potentially, both highly flexible and rapidly adaptive.

Another specific issue is the provision of escape hatches for individuals. Groups have been known to be cruel and unjust to their deviant members. One existing escape route for the individual would of course continue to exist: departure from the organization. Another might be easy means of transfer to another group.

Another related danger of a strong group emphasis might be a tendency to drive away highly individualistic, nongroup people. But the tight organizational constraints now imposed do the same thing. Indeed might not groups protect their individualists better than the impersonal rules of present day large organizations?

Another obvious problem: If groups are emphasized by rewarding them, paying them, promoting them, and so on, groups may begin to perceive themselves as power centers, in competitive conflict with other groups. Intergroup hostilities are likely to be exacerbated unless we can design some new coping mechanisms into the organization. Likert's proposal for solving that sort of problem (and others) is the linking pin concept. The notion is that individuals serve as members of more than one group, both up and down the hierarchy and horizontally. But Likert's scheme seems to me to assume fundamentally individualized organizations in the sense that it is still individuals who get paid, promoted and so on. In a more groupy organization, the linking pin concept has to be modified so that an individual might be a part-time member of more than one group, but still a real member. That is, for example, a portion of an individual's pay might come from each group in accordance with that group's perception of his contribution.

Certainly much more talk, both within and between groups, would be a necessary accompaniment of group emphasis; though we might argue about whether more talk should be classified as a cost or a benefit. In any case careful design of escape hatches for individuals and connections among groups would be as important in this kind of organization as would stairways between floors in the design of a private home.

There is also a danger of over-designing groups. All groups in the organization need not look alike. Quite to the contrary. Task and technology should have significant effects on the shapes and sizes of different subgroups within the large organization. Just as individuals end up adjusting the edges of their jobs to themselves and themselves to their jobs, we should expect flexibility within groups, allowing them to adapt and modify themselves to whatever the task and technology demand.

Another initially scary problem associated with groups is the potential loss of clear formal individual leadership. Without formal leaders how will we motivate people? Without leaders how will we control and discipline people? Without leaders how will we pinpoint responsibility? Even as I write those questions I cannot help but feel that they are archaic. They are questions which are themselves a product of the basic individual building block design of old organizations. The problem is not leaders so much as the performance of leadership functions. Surely groups will find leaders, but they will emerge from the bottom up. Given a fairly clear job description, some groups, in some settings, will set up more or less permanent leadership roles. Others may let leadership vary as the situation demands, or as a function of the power that individuals within any group may possess relative to the group's needs at that time. A reasonable amount of process time can be built in to enable groups to work on the leadership problem, but the problem will have to be resolved within each group. On the advantage side of the ledger, this may even get rid of a few hierarchical levels. There should be far less need for individuals who are chiefly supervisors of other individuals' work. Groups can serve as hierarchical leaders of other groups.

Two other potential costs: With an organization of groups, there may be a great deal of infighting, and power and conflict issues will come even more to the fore than they do now. Organizations of groups may become highly political, with coalitions lining up against one another on various issues. If so, the rest of the organizational system will have to take those political problems into account, both by setting up sensible systems of intercommunications among groups, and by allocating larger amounts of time and expertise to problems of conflict resolution.

But this is not a new problem unique to groupy organizations. Conflict among groups is prevelant in large organizations which are political systems now. But because these issues have not often been foreseen and planned for, the mechanisms for dealing with them are largely ad hoc. As a result, conflict is often dealt with in extremely irrational ways.

But there is another kind of intergroup power problem that may become extremely important and difficult in groupy organizations. There is a real danger that relatively autonomous and cohesive groups may be closed, not only to other groups but more importantly to staff advice or to new technological inputs. These problems exist at present, of course, but they may be exacerbated by group structure. I cannot see any perfect way to handle those problems. One possibility may be to make individual members of staff groups part time members of line groups. Another is to work harder to educate line groups to potential staff contributions. Of course the reward system, the old market system, will probably be the strongest force for keeping groups from staying old-fashioned in a world of new technologies and ideas.

But the nature and degree of many of the second order spinoff effects are not fully knowable at the design stage. We need to build more complete working models and pilot plants. In any case it does not seem obvious that slowdowns, either at the work face or in decision-making processes, would necessarily accompany group based organizational designs.

Some possible advantages to the organization. Finally, from an organizational perspective, what are the potential advantages to be gained from a group based organization? The first might be a sharp reduction in the number of units that need to be controlled. Control would not have to be carried all the way down to the individual level. If the average group size is five, the number of blocks that management has to worry about is cut to 20% of what it was. Such a design would also probably cut the number of operational levels in the organization. In effect, levels which are now primarily supervisory would be incorporated into the groups that they supervise.

By this means many of the advantages of the small individualized organization could be brought back. These advantages would occur within groups simply because there would be a small number of blocks, albeit larger blocks, with which to build and rebuild the organization.

But most of all, and this is still uncertain, despite the extent to which we behavioral scientists have been enamoured of groups, there would be increased human advantages of cohesiveness, motivation, and commitment, and via that route, both increased productivity, stronger social glue within the organization, and a wider interaction between organization and environment.

SUMMARY

Far and away the most powerful and beloved tool of applied behavioral scientists is the small face-to-face group. Since the Western Electric researches, behavioral scientists have been learning to understand, exploit and love groups. Groups attracted interest initially as devices for improving the implementaiton of decisions and to increase human commitment and motivation. They are now loved because they are also creative and innovative, they often make better quality decisions than individuals, and because they make organizational life more livable for people. One can't hire an applied behavioral scientist into an organization who within ten minutes will not want to call a group meeting and talk things over. The group meeting is his primary technology, his primary tool.

But groups in organizations are not an invention of behavioral types. They are a natural phenomenon of organizations. Organizations develop informal groups, like it or not. It is both possible and sensible to describe most large organizations as collections of groups in interaction with one another; bargaining with one another, forming coalitions with one another, cooperating and competing with one another. It is possible and sensible too to treat the decisions that emerge from large organizations as a resultant of the interplay of forces among groups within the organization, and not just the resultant of rational analysis.

On the down side, small face-to-face groups are great tools for disciplining and controlling their members. Contemporary China, for example, has just a fraction of the number of lawyers in the United States. Partially this is a result of the lesser complexity of Chinese society and lower levels of education. But a large part of it, surprisingly enough, seems to derive from the fact that modern China is designed around small groups. Since small groups take responsibility for the discipline and control of their members many deviant acts which would be considered illegal in the United States never enter the formal legal system in China. The law controls individual deviation less, the group controls it more (Li, 1971).

Control of individual behavior is also a major problem of large complex western organizations. This problem has driven many organizations into elaborate bureaucratic quasi-legal sets of rules, ranging from job evaluation schemes to performance evaluations to incentive systems; all individually based, all terribly complex, all creating problems of distributive justice. Any organizational design that might eliminate much of that legalistic superstructure therefore begins to look highly desirable.

Management should consider building organizations using a material now understood very well and with properties that look very promising, the small group. Until recently, at least, the human group has primarily been used for patching and mending organizations that were originally built of other materials.

The major unanswered questions in my mind are not in the understanding of groups, nor in the potential utility of the group as a building block. The more difficult answered question is whether or not the approaching era is one in which Americans would willingly work in such apparently contra-individualistic units. I think we are.

REFERENCES

Johnson, Richard T. and William G. Ouchi. Made in America (under Japanese management). *Harvard Business Review*, September–October 1974.

Li, Victor. The Development of the Chinese Legal System, in John Lindbeck (ed.), *China: The Management of a Revolutionary Society*. Seattle: University of Washington Press, 1971.

Likert, Rensis. *New Patterns of Management*. New York: McGraw-Hill, 1961.

6

THE HAWTHORNE GROUP STUDIES REVISITED: A DEFENSE OF THEORY Y

Edgar H. Schein
Massachusetts Institute of Technology

INTRODUCTION

This chapter is motivated by two basic concerns: 1) one on the part of the Western Electric Company that some of the findings of the Hawthorne Studies, particularly those dealing with worker group behavior, have not had a major impact on industrial relations or organizational psychology, and the other 2) on my part that the group behavior of workers has often been misinterpreted to be evidence against McGregor's Theory Y.

To be specific, a number of authors have attempted to argue that because workers are often alienated from work and/or are often fundamentally in conflict with the organization that employs them it is not possible to apply participative theories in many kinds of situations, and by implication therefore, they argue that Theory Y is inadequate or wrong. It is alleged that union or other group membership limits the degree of participation possible and makes workers unresponsive to certain kinds of management incentives. The smart manager is advised to learn something about intergroup conflict resolution, collective bargaining, and other power/political strategies if he is to solve his productivity problems.

In this chapter I will attempt to re-examine these various arguments, and will attempt to show that not only is Theory Y valid and sufficient for what it tries to do, but that most of the evidence from worker group behavior is, in fact, in support of Theory Y. The key to this argument will be to show that 1) Theory Y is a theory of human motivation, not a theory of how to manage or run an organization; 2) Theory Y does not argue that human needs and organizational goals are always congruent and integratable, but that such integration is possible

if management chooses to make it possible; 3) Theory Y does not imply participative management or any other kind of management—it is only a statement
about what people are fundamentally like, and what kind of organizational behavior they are capable of, if the conditions within the organization are appropriate—and; 4) Most of the research on group behavior, including the research on
reference groups, union-management conflict, and conflict resolution supports
the Theory Y assumptions about human behavior.

Further, I will argue that where management practices have failed to elicit a
high degree of motivation and involvement from workers, it was because of
inconsistencies and conflicts within the managerial practices themselves, not because of the resistance of workers or the interests of unions. If management
wants to reduce union-management conflict, increase productivity and worker
involvement, and elicit high levels of commitment from workers, it is often
within its power to do so, but not without major cultural changes within the
philosophies which govern most organizations and which put a higher premium
on values other than productivity and worker involvement.

To reiterate what McGregor said many years ago, when workers fail to exhibit
behavior consistent with Theory Y assumptions at their place of work, it is likely
that they have been trained by past management practices, organizational traditions, and control systems to seek their involvement elsewhere, possibly in their
peer groups and/or unions, possibly in their family and/or leisure time activities.
But this does not constitute evidence for anything other than the fact that management has not been willing to pay the price to unlock worker motivation, or
possibly has not found it necessary to do so because adequate levels of productivity and quality could be obtained without high levels of worker commitment.

Why is it so important to justify Theory Y? My basic belief, based on now 15
or more years of working with all kinds of organizations, is that we need more
Theory Y managers at all levels of organizations, but especially at the higher levels. As organizations and technology become more complex in response to more
turbulent environments, it becomes more and more important for managers to
hold the set of assumptions about human behavior which McGregor attempted
to capture in his Theory Y notion. This is not to say that we need more of any
given type of managerial style or system be it participative management, delegation or power equalization. It is only to emphasize the needed capacity on the
part of the manager to view human behavior objectively and realistically, and to
adapt the right managerial tactics according to the dictates of the task he is facing. As I will try to show, Theory Y gives him this flexibility because it gives
him an accurate appraisal of human behavior. Theory X is a distortion which
limits the freedom of choice of the manager because of the limiting assumptions
it makes. I see no inconsistency between contingency theories of organization
and Theory Y because Theory Y as originally conceived *is* a contingency theory.

WHAT DID THE HAWTHORNE GROUP STUDIES SHOW?

The now classic Bank Wiring Room studies led, in a sense, to the "discovery" that worker peer groups and cliques influenced in a substantial manner the productivity level, the quality level, the relationship to supervision, and the implementation (or lack thereof) of company policies (Roethlisberger and Dickson, 1939, Homans, 1950). Here are some of what I consider to be the major findings from the Bank Wiring Room study:

(1) The workers in the room developed a group structure around the nature of their work, the geography of the work place, and their personalities. This group structure operated not only on the informal level but began to influence in various ways the formal routine of the group. For example, workers traded jobs, a specific violation of company policy based on industrial engineering studies which argued that given job requirements were matched with worker skill levels such that job trading should have reduced quality. The workers undermined or sabotaged these standards by putting pressure on the supervisors by building hidden flaws into the equipment and making the supervisors look bad so that they would cooperate with the job trading practices.

(2) The workers undermined or sabotaged the management control system by developing their own norms of "a fair day's work for a fair day's pay," and by creating a system of sending work out of the room. This made it appear as if the group had the desired "straight line output" when, in fact, the workers stored up extra product from days when they felt energetic and fed that into the system on days when they had underproduced. This artificial creation of a straight line output was condoned by supervision, and the obvious restriction of output which was involved in the concept of a fair day's work was also tolerated. Indeed, it is alleged in the study that management was, on the whole, satisfied with the productivity of the work group even though it was clearly below its physiological or mental fatigue limit.

(3) Workers did not respond logically to management's incentive system. Indeed, the productivity of individual workers had more to do with group membership and the internal conflicts which developed between two cliques within the room, than it had to do with individual motivation, talent, or managerial incentives. Workers spend a lot of time pressuring each other to live within the production norms of the group, and the high producers were socially ostracized. Workers spent a great deal of energy and creativity on essentially nonproductive activities, and in fact, spent energy on defeating some of the goals and policies of management.

These findings were the first of their kind, but they have been reproduced and documented frequently in other studies of employee behavior. Particularly, the studies of William F. Whyte (1955) and Chris Argyris (1957) have documented the degree to which energy is channeled by workers into antimanagement, non-productive kinds of activities, and Dalton's classic study of management worker interrelations (1959) shows how the informal relations among members of the organization are actually necessary for tasks to be accomplished. Data such as these as well as studies of union–management conflict (Stagner, 1956), have been cited as evidence that Theory Y is an erroneous concept of worker motivation, and that there is little hope of integrating worker needs with organizational goals. But before leaping to that conclusion, a re-examination of Theory Y is in order.

WHAT DOES THEORY Y STATE?

Theory Y states, in essence, that man is capable of integrating his own needs and goals with those of the organization; that he is not inherently lazy and indolent; that he is by nature capable of exercising self-control and self-direction, and that he is capable of directing his efforts towards organizational goals. It is what McGregor called a "cosmology," a world view, a set of assumptions about what human nature is really like which is carried by a person inside his head. Every-one has his or her theory of what motivates people, what makes them tick, what is their human nature. The behavior exhibited toward people tends to be a re-flection of those deep-down inner assumptions which one makes. McGregor was seeking an articulation of a set of assumptions which most nearly fitted what is known about adult human behavior, in the same sense in which Argyris articu-lated in his early writings the characteristics of a mature adult (Argyris, 1957).

To reiterate, Theory Y is a set of assumptions about human nature which a given person holds, consciously or unconsciously inside his own head. It is not a managerial philosophy. It is not a management style. It is not a property of an organization or a management system. It is not a set of external managerial behaviors, strategies or tactics. It is the inner set of assumptions from which people derive some of their overt behavior.

To put it in McGregor's own words:

"Theory X and Theory Y are *not* managerial strategies: They are underlying beliefs about the nature of man that influence managers to adopt one strategy rather than another. In fact, depending upon other characteristics of the manager's view of reality and upon the particular situation in which he finds himself, a manager who holds the beliefs that I called Theory X could adopt a considerable array of strategies, some of which would be typically called "hard," and some which would be called "soft." The same is true with respect to Theory Y." (1967, p. 79).

McGregor goes on to say that he would not change the major assumptions stated above, but that insofar as Theory X and Theory Y are cosmologies which are properties of an individual person, it is possible to discover among managers other sets of assumptions about human behavior. McGregor argued, however, that Theory Y was the set of assumptions most consistent with what we know about human behavior. This position is still correct. If one wants to identify that set of assumptions which best fits what we know about human behavior, Theory Y is the most nearly correct. Furthermore, McGregor did not feel that he had created Theory X and Theory Y but that he was describing the cosmology of effective and ineffective managers whom he encountered in his consulting. He pointed out over and over again in his teaching that Theory Y was a description of how effective managers viewed human behavior.

When I attempt to get this point across in a classroom I find myself relying on a simple tactic. I give the students two questionnaires to fill out. One questionnaire is a set of assumptions about human nature derived from McGregor's writing. The respondent is asked to indicate how much he agrees with statements such as:

1. It is only human nature for people to do as little work as they can get away with.
2. When people avoid work, it is usually because work has been deprived of its meaning.
3. People tend to raise their standards if they are accountable for their own behavior and for correcting their own mistakes.

Next I give the students a second questionnaire which deals with the students' own managerial behavior, how participative they are, how much they delegate, how much they attempt to elicit from subordinates a degree of self-control, etc. We then score each questionnaire separately so that each student now has two different scores to look at for himself. One score is his Theory X-Theory Y score, his statements about his agreement or disagreement with certain assumptions about human behavior; the second score is his tendency to use participative types of managerial strategies and tactics. It immediately becomes apparent to the students that the correspondence between the two sets of scores is far from perfect. In fact, they tend to correlate at about the .6 level, suggesting that if one believes in Theory Y assumptions, one tends also to believe in participation, but that there is no necessary or automatic connection between the two sets of concepts.

We then explore managerial situations where Theory Y managers may want to use autocratic methods or tight control systems because 1) the task demands it, or 2) there are time pressures, or 3) the subordinates have lived for so long in an organization climate where they expect autocratic methods that they would not know how to respond constructively to participative methods, etc. We also explore the idea that the Theory Y manager diagnoses carefully the organizational situation he finds himself in, including the culture and climate of the organization, its past history of management practice, the nature of this work force, the kind of technology it has, the degree of unionization and its labor relations history. The Theory Y manager may be predisposed toward involving people, but there is nothing in the theory that dictates that he must do so, nor is there any implication in the theory that participative methods will work under all circumstances.

Why has there been so much confusion about this point? I believe that McGregor himself muddied the conceptual waters when he linked to his analysis of managerial cosmologies a value position that it was management's obligation to create opportunities for self-actualization. This is pointed out most clearly by McGregor (1957, p. 15) in his original statement from his paper, "The Human Side of Enterprise."

1. Management is responsible for organizing the elements of productive enterprise—money, materials, equipment, people—in the interest of economic ends.
2. People are *not* by nature passive or resistant to organizational needs. They have become so as a result of experience in organizations.
3. The motivation, the potential for development, the capacity for assuming responsibility, the readiness to direct behavior toward organizational goals are all present in people. Management does not put them there. It is a responsibility of management to make it possible for people to recognize and develop these human characteristics for themselves.
4. The essential task of management is to arrange organizational conditions and methods of operation so that people can achieve their own goals *best* by directing *their own* efforts toward organizational objectives.

In point 1, McGregor clearly links management to the economic goals of organizations. Point 2 is the essential statement of human nature that is claimed here as being a correct statement in terms of whatever data are available. Point 3 mixes an assumption about human nature with which I agree, with a value position which is articulated in the last sentence of point 3, with which I do not agree. Point 4 is clearly a value position which should be argued as a separate issue and should be clearly differentiated from the assumptions about human nature.

The evidence from industrial relations research is clearly in contradiction to a simple adoption of point 4 as a viable philosophy of management. As Landsberger (1958), Strauss (1970), Mills (1970) and others argue very effectively, it is often neither possible nor desirable for management to attempt to create conditions for the integration of individual and organizational objectives. Given McGregor's own philosophy and utopian vision of what organizations could be, it is easy to see why he added the value position to the theoretical position. But the fact that he confused the issue should not blind one to the fact that he was probably much more right about his scientific position (that it is possible for people to achieve their own goals best through directing their efforts toward organizational objectives) than he was about his value position (that it is management's task to make this integration possible across a wide variety of technologies and organizational situations).   Other variables such as those argued by organizational sociologists, industrial relationists, and economists must be seriously considered before one develops any particular managerial philosophy, strategy, and tactics, whether participative or not.

My own value position which I have tried to articulate in *Organizational Psychology* (1970) is that the manager must be a good situational diagnostician and be flexible in his behavior. He must be logical and think rationally. If he is to perceive clearly what his behavioral options are, he must also see clearly the relationship between his assumptions about human nature and those behavioral options.   If he holds Theory X assumptions, he is not being logical or responsive to data, and will, therefore, be limited in his choices of managerial style. If he holds Theory Y assumptions, he is more likely to examine the full range of alternatives available to him and choose wisely among them, taking into account the technological, economic, and group realities which face him. Clearly one of his options, the one favored by Argyris (1964), Likert (1967), Herzberg (1966), Marrow et al. (1967), and others associated with participative methods and job enrichment, is to try to arrange conditions to make it possible for his employees to meet their needs best by linking themselves to organizational goals.   If he chooses that option, having made a thorough diagnosis of the factors which will aid and hinder such integration, he must also face the problem of setting into motion a major change effort which will build the support systems necessary to make that option work.*   All too often the manager expects instant success and, if he does not get it, assumes that his basic theory of people was wrong, rather than questioning his own strategy and tactics of implementation.

For example, many companies have launched programs of management by objectives or performance appraisal systems based on mutual target setting between boss and subordinate only to find after a few years that the paper work was dutifully being carried out but organizational effectiveness had not increased.   The problem in most such cases is that a management system which requires Theory Y managers is put into an organization which has too many Theory X managers and too many autocratic or paternalistic traditions. Such systems can only work if one starts with Theory Y managers and changes the organization's traditions.

Given these considerations, I think one can favor the selection and/or training

---

*Such change efforts have come to be labeled "organization development" and have been described in a number of recent publications (Beckhard, 1969; Bennis, 1969; French & Bell, 1973; Schein, 1969, etc.)

of Theory Y managers, without in any way committing oneself to a participative, power equalization, or human relations philosophy of management. I believe that organizations need Theory Y managers, especially as the environmental pressures on organizations become more complex. It is then up to those managers to decide what kind of management strategy will work best in their situation. The social scientist should support their efforts by continuing to give them data about what happens under varying conditions, but I would certainly argue against any prescriptions (in the name of Theory Y or any other theory) of the participative or job enrichment or self-actualization-through-work kind of philosophy. Here I would align myself squarely with the industrial relationists in arguing for contingency theories and caution in generalizing across tasks, industries, etc.

DO THE BANK WIRING ROOM STUDIES AND SUBSEQUENT RESEARCH REFUTE THEORY Y?

Now to a crucial logical point. If workers behave in a demonstrably anti-organizational, anti-managerial manner as they did in the Bank Wiring Room, or as they do in a highly unionized conflict-ridden industry like the automobile industry, does this mean that Theory Y assumptions are incorrect? If workers feel more linked to external reference groups in the community, or if they are alienated from their work, of if they put family concerns ahead of work concerns, does this constitute negative evidence for Theory Y? Clearly, the answer is no. Such data do constitute negative evidence for participative management, but they do not constitute negative evidence for Theory Y. In all of the situations described above, workers are energetic and involved, but usually in anti-management activities. It is not inconsistent with Theory Y when workers expend effort to resist, sabotage, undermine, or take advantage of management efforts, if those workers feel linked to anti-organizational peer groups, external reference groups, or are alienated from the work itself because of technological or economic factors.

To put it positively, workers who are expending great quantities of energy defeating management's control systems, or workers who are sluffing off on their job while expending great energy on their hobbies at home, or workers who are busy becoming leaders in their militant union, are all behaving consistently with Theory Y.* But the organization or group which has captured their involvement happens to be different from the employing organization.

---

*There are, of course, immature, neurotic or psychotic individuals in the work force who are genuinely unmotivated and indifferent across all areas of their life to self-direction and self-actualization. Such people do exist, but they are by most psychological theories considered to be immature or neurotic and hardly models on which to build any theory of healthy human behavior.

CONCLUSIONS: WHAT SHOULD MANAGEMENT BE AND DO?

A summary model. The arguments laid out above can best be summarized with the aid of Figure 1. My basic argument is that we must learn to separate conceptually the manager's assumptions about human nature, whether he is basically Theory X or Theory Y, from his action tendencies or style and his actual managerial behavior.

I believe that a Theory X manager will have action tendencies to control and limit employee behavior in terms of control systems, industrial engineering standards, and his own sterotypes of what is good and bad management. I believe he will be conceptually limited, inflexible, and therefore, have a predisposition to develop autocratic or paternalistic solutions to management problems.

In contrast, I believe that a Theory Y manager, by virtue of his more realistic appraisal of human nature, will have action tendencies toward involving employ-

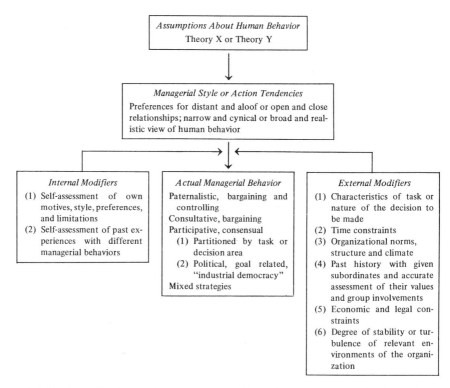

Basic Conclusion: The Theory Y manager is more likely to make an accurate internal and external diagnosis and consequently choose a behavior pattern that is appropriate to the realities of the situation.

Figure 1. How theory Y relates to managerial style and behavior.

ees as much as the task and total situation warrants. He will be more diagnostic in his orientation, more realistic in his appraisal of task, time pressures, organization climate, type of subordinates he is dealing with, the reference groups and membership groups which are operating, the legal and economic constraints in the situation, and his own personal limitations. He will, of necessity, consider a broader range of leadership or managerial behaviors, and will behave in a consultative and/or participative manner only when the situation and task warrants such behavior. He will also diagnose the various decision or task areas he is responsible for and will probably vary his behavior according to the diagnosis along some dimension of participation (Tannenbaum & Schmidt, 1958).

Having elaborated the difference between the Theory X manager and the Theory Y manager, I would like to restate my major conclusion:

As organizational task and environments become more complex and require more diagnosis and flexible action, organizations will need more Theory Y managers, especially at the higher levels.

In effect, I am saying that the Contingency Theory of organizations (e.g., Morse & Lorsch, 1970, Galbraith, 1973) is correct but it takes a Theory Y manager to implement it. The Theory X manager is too limited in his diagnostic skill and too inflexible to vary his style according to the needs of the task, etc. Applying this conclusion to the Hawthorne group studies, I would argue that to manage groups in such a way as to insure maximum productivity for the organization and maximum security or safety from exploitation for the workers, it is necessary to have Theory Y managers. Employees would indeed be exploited by the Theory X manager because of his beliefs that the employees are out to exploit the organization. It takes a Theory Y manager who realizes that employee behavior is a product of past organizational history, outside groups such as unions, occupational traditions, etc., to develop bargaining strategies which will be integrative rather than exploitative.

Will a Theory Y person automatically be a good manager? One might assume from much of the above argument that holding Theory Y assumptions about people will make one a good manager, while Theory X assumptions about people will make one a bad manager. I am not asserting that conclusion. I am asserting that the Theory Y person will have greater potential for being a good manager, especially at higher and more complex managerial jobs. He must have the relevant training and experience for this potential to become actual. The other side of the coin is that the Theory X person who receives excellent management training can probably be effective in many kinds of managerial situations but his potential will be limited by the inflexibility of his style. To be very clear, both types of people need training and experience in being a manager before they can become effective at any level. But certain kinds of developmental training such as training in group dynamics and the management of complex, matrix situations will be more successful with the Theory Y person because the concepts are more congruent with his initial assumptions.

A related question is whether it is possible for a Theory X person to become a Theory Y person. My answer is Yes, but only through fairly significant growth or development experiences over a period of time. Initial assumptions about human behavior are probably learned fairly early in life and are taken for granted by the individual. Only when he encounters some strong disconfirming experiences will he begin to question his initial assumptions and begin to reassess the nature of the reality around him. Such initial disconfirmation happens often in sensitivity training where a person learns that his fellow participants can be trusted more than he had assumed. Once such a person begins to re-examine his work relationship and cautiously experiments with higher levels of trust, he finds confirmation for a new point of view and moves gradually toward more of a Theory Y orientation. Such growth experiences are neither easy nor automatic, but I am willing to assert on the basis of my own experience that such growth is possible.

Some concrete applications. In order to illustrate the above conclusions, let us examine how a Theory Y manager would deal with certain situations especially those which are alleged to show that Theory Y is not valid. For example, Mills (1970) points out that when several units of a company or several companies are dealing with a single national union that is attempting to apply a coordinated strategy, the employees of a given plant or company may be asked to continue a strike even though the local labor–management relations at the plant might not warrant it. There is little that the management of that plant can then do to improve relations, since the employees are constrained by their dual loyalties to the company as well as the union. In this situation, I believe that a Theory X manager would probably become angry, feel that the continued strike was proof of his cynical view of human nature, and set about to increase management controls in order to weaken the union. The Theory Y manager, facing the same situation, would understand the delemma of double loyalty and his employees' decision to strike. He would understand that they had, in effect, no choice, would not become angry or cynical, but would set about to work out a realistic plan with his own employees which would minimize the long-range negative impact of the strike on his own plant. He would reassure his employees that he understood their position and would put his energies into dealing with the national union (the outside group) rather than trying to undermine or weaken his own employees' union commitments.

Mills also argues:

"The view that true employee participation can occur only in the union context stems from the belief that only where a labor organization exists is an employee able to participate without fear of reprisal from management . . . Only freedom from arbitrary dismissal or other denial of privileges can make the employee at all independent . . . An employee, protected by a set of rules and due process, is believed to be a free man in the industrial framework." (Mills, 1970, p. 5).

The employee is indeed unsafe from a Theory X manager because of the manager's cynical view of the employee's motivation.* A Theory Y manager would recognize that employees need due process and would strengthen those parts of the contract which provided the necessary safeguards and protection. He would set about to build up trust levels which would make it possible for employees to participate in those decision areas where they have a genuine input and stake in the decision.

Plant managers who are strongly Theory Y in their personal beliefs and who want to stimulate a climate of greater trust have been able to do so over a period of time even with strong and initially cynical unions. The result is not that the union goes away or is weakened, but that the time needed to reach an agreement through collective bargaining is dramatically shortened. Once there is a degree of mutual trust, the union is still there but the dealings with the union take on more of a problem-solving character instead of hostile bargaining between enemies. Once the problem-solving climate has been established, it is possible for the union and management to look for integrative solutions. In this context, the Theory Y manager seeks to strengthen the union since he recognizes the need for it, and welcomes the problem-solving process which collective bargaining makes possible. Once the employee learns that both management and his union are attempting to do what is best for everyone concerned, there is less need for the kind of self-protection which the workers in the Bank Wiring Room exhibited. Is this utopian? Possibly, but I know of enough examples from my own consulting experience to prove that one can improve the industrial relations climate markedly if one finds Theory Y managers to run plants and to negotiate with workers.

Mills' assumption that the worker ". . . is likely to limit his 'participation' to what he thinks his supervisor would like to hear," (Mills 1970, p. 6) is probably correct in the kind of climate which is typically established by Theory X managers, but it is not inherent in the labor–management context. I would agree with Mills that "In general, the process of participative management is more difficult and complex than has been recognized." (Mills, 1970, p. 6). This is

---

*The data from the Bank Wiring Room are a perfect example of what happens when mutual mistrust arises between workers and managers. Management creates a set of rules and controls to minimize the negative impact of what is presumed to be the worker's tendency to be lazy (Theory X). The worker responds by defeating the rules and controls of management as a self-protective device because he mistrusts management. The workers believed that if they produced more, the piece work rate would be cut, even though none of them had any firsthand experience of such cuts in the past.

partly because of the danger that management, in its efforts to reward participation will give in too much on issues of efficiency. But there is nothing in Theory Y that says one has to give in. Rather, the Theory Y manager would assert that a worker is capable of understanding and accepting the economic constraints which operate in a business and which force management to seek a high degree of efficiency and effectiveness. But the manager must not only have the faith that the worker can understand and accept such constraints, he must also make the effort to think it through clearly and communicate his logic clearly to the worker. All too often, the manager is not clear in his own mind why he will not go along with a particular union demand, or will not make the effort to explain to the union why the company cannot afford a particular benefits package or pay raises. Part of the reason may be that management has not seen fit to educate the workers in the economic realities of their particular company, partly because management operates too much on Theory X assumptions. The Theory Y manager would lay the groundwork by educating workers in the economics of the industry, and would find it easier to argue against unrealistic demands from unions, because the criteria of what is realistic would be jointly shared between labor and management.

Participative management can be a fraud and fraught with dangers for the workers, as Mills points out, but only when participation is practiced by Theory X managers who are looking for a way to defraud their workers. The Theory Y manager would not undertake a participative program in the first place unless he could see overall gains for both the company and the workers. So it does little good to argue about the merits or demerits of participation per se. What I am arguing is that whether or not it works and whether or not it is safe for the worker to participate has much more to do with the nature of the industry and the task, and has much more to do with the manager's assumptions about human nature, whether he is a Theory X or Theory Y kind of manager.

What if a company is operating in an industrial relations climate where strong trade unions consistently undermine productivity by limiting what the employee can work on? If such a company has Theory Y managers at its top levels, it can set out to change the total climate by working with the trade unions at a national level. One large industrial conglomerate which decided that its total survival depended upon changing its basic relationship with its unions nation-wide, launched a 20 year change program which involved simultaneous programs at the national level aimed at changing relations with the national offices of the union, massive efforts to find more Theory Y managers for the major plants, large-scale change programs to examine the pro's and con's of more participation at the shop floor level on a plant by plant basis, education programs for all levels of plant management, a new incentive scheme more consistent with the changing goals of the company, trial sites and research evaluations of pilot aspects of the program and many other separate activities. Clearly if a company decides it is important enough, there is much that it can do to overcome an unfavorable industrial relations climate.

If such programs fail, it is often because the task that workers are asked to perform is technologically meaningless and/or frustrating, leading to alienation and the organization of defensive counter-organizational groups. Giving workers a "sense" of participation in inherently meaningless work would only be thought of by a Theory X manager.

The Theory Y manager, in that type of situation, would not use participative methods because he would recognize that in the long run workers would become angry over phony participation and would then group together against him. Instead, he would acknowledge that the situation was inherently noninvolving and would undertake to assess the costs and benefits of a change in the technology. If the economic realities preclude changing the technology (as may be the case in the auto industry), the Theory Y manager would "level" with his employees and would accept their demands for higher pay or fringe benefits to compensate them for the inherently meaningless work. He would consult them on how to make the plant more human, but he would acknowledge frankly the economic facts which would make a change in the task technology impossible. The Theory X manager sometimes falls into the trap of wanting his cake and eating it too. He wants worker motivation without creating a task which permits involvement. Asking workers to participate in tasks which do not permit involvement is simply self-defeating, and the Theory X manager is more likely to fall into this trap because of his lack of diagnostic skill and action flexibility.

Theory Y and group dynamics. Many critics of the human relations movement, participative management, and by implication Theory Y, argue that intergroup conflict within the organization (e.g. union–management conflict, interdepartmental conflict, etc.) are not only inevitable but can be a productive force both for employees and management. Out of the inherently different interests of different groups can come new ideas and new solutions to problems.

Strauss put it this way:

"There is general agreement that, on occasion, conflict can be very useful to organizations both as a means of bringing issues to top management's attention which might otherwise be ignored and as a form of competition within the firm which serves as a substitute for that of the market place. The trick is how to handle such conflict so that it remains productive." (1970, p. 179)

Strauss goes on to review the work of Landsberger, Whyte, Sayles, Walton, Lawrence and Lorsch, all of whom deal with lateral conflicts as an inevitable aspect of organization, and as something which can be made productive for the organization.

The main problem with the analysis is that it fails to distinguish task or work related conflict (which implies highly involved employees competing to implement their view of what is best for the total organization) from intergroup or interindividual conflict based on personal power needs, representing the interest of outside groups or needs for self-protection from higher levels of management.

A Theory Y manager is ready to deal with task related conflict and to set integrative solutions provided the organization is prepared to adjust work flows, organization structure, etc. to permit the solution to be implemented. The Theory X manager assumes that conflict is always motivated politically and selfishly, and therefore seeks to bargain his way out of it rather than even considering integrative solutions. In other words, the tactics of conflict resolution used by the manager will be related to his assumptions about people, as Blake has shown in analysing the conflict resolution styles of his different "grid" types (Blake and Mounton, 1964). The production oriented, 9,1, manager tends to suppress conflict or simply decide one way or the other. The abdicating 1,1 or compromising 5,5 manager tends to try to compromise by mutual bargaining or to avoid recognizing conflict in the first place. The 1,9 manager gives in to worker pressure. Only the 9,9 manager, the one who would, in McGregor's terminology, be a Theory Y person, attempts to find integrative solutions because he believes that each party to the conflict is acting in good faith. Blake's ability to adapt Sherif's intergroup conflict resolution model into successful strategies around labor–management issues, interfunctional issues, interdivisional issues, and merger/acquisition issues testified to the correctness of those assumptions (Blake and Mouton, 1964, Sherif 1956). But it takes a skilled Theory Y manager to implement the Blake conflict resolution model.

All of the above points imply a degree of diagnostic skill in handling groups and handling conflict situation. The Theory Y manager is more likely to be able to learn these skills than the Theory X manager. It has been my observation that most managers, whether X or Y, lack group dynamics skill to a significant degree.* This lack of skill shows up in mismanaged staff meetings, underproductive committees, conflict ridden task forces and project teams, and mis-managed intergroup relations. Clearly, having Theory Y assumptions does not make one an expert in handling group situations, but one needs Theory Y assumptions in order to believe in groups in the first place (Schein, 1970). The Theory Y manager is more likely to recognize that groups are a fact of life to be dealt with and managed. As the examples above have tried to show, he will accept the reality of dual loyalties in his employees and will accept the realities of interfunctional or interdivisional conflict within his organization. He will analyze the

---

*An increasing amount of my consultation work with managers and management teams is focusing on the management of meetings, groups, teams, task forces, etc., teaching line managers how to be better "process consultants." (Schein, 1969)

costs and benefits of such conflict and then will need group skills to either manage the conflict productively or to create a reward system which reduces the conflict in the first place. He will recognize that conflict is not inevitable, but is the result of how groups and individuals are managed. He will know when conflict is productive (in task areas) and when it is destructive (in interpersonal areas).*

Examples such as the Scanlon Plan, wartime economies, Alfred Marrow's two companies, some of the plants in Proctor and Gamble and General Foods, recent experiments within Western Electric, the team production experiences in the aircraft industry and, more recently in Volvo, show that it is possible for groups to work with and for the organization that employs them. But it takes Theory Y managers to use them productively, and it takes tasks and organizational conditions that make such group involvement possible and productive. Once and for all, the Contingency Theories and Industrial Relations theories *are* consistent with and complementary to Theory Y. The conceptual confusion which has muddied this field for so long is unnecessary.

REFERENCES

Argyris, C. *Personality and Organization*, New York: Harper, 1957.

Argyris, C. *Integrating the Individual and the Organization*, New York: Wiley, 1964.

Beckhard, R. *Organization Development: Strategies and Models*, Reading, Mass: Addison-Wesley, 1969.

Bennis, W. G. *Organization Development: Its Nature, Origin and Prospects*, Reading, Mass: Addison-Wesley, 1969.

Blake, R. R. and Mouton, J. S. *The Managerial Grid*, Houston: Gulf Publications, 1964.

Dalton, M. *Men Who Manage*, New York: Wiley, 1959.

French, W. L. and Bell, C. H. *Organization Development*, Englewood Cliffs, N.J.: Prentice-Hall, 1973.

Galbraith, J. *Designing Complex Organizations*, Reading, Mass: Addison-Wesley, 1973.

Galbraith, F. *Work and the Nature of Man*, New York: World, 1966.

Homans, G. C. *The Human Group*, New York: Harcourt, Brace & World, 1950.

Kelly, J. *Organizational Behaviour: An Existential-Systems Approach*, Rev. Ed., Homewood, Illinois: Richard D. Irwin, Inc., 1974.

Landsberger, H. A. *Hawthorne Revisited*, Ithaca, New York: New York State School of Industrial and Labor Relations, Cornell University, 1958.

Likert, R. *The Human Organization*, New York: McGraw-Hill, 1967.

Marrow, A. J., Bowers, D. C. and Seashore, S. S. *Management by Participation*, New York: Harper, 1967.

McGregor, D. The Human Side of Enterprise, *Leadership and Motivation*, Cambridge, Mass: The MIT Press, 1966.

McGregor, D. *The Professional Manager*, New York: McGraw-Hill, 1967.

---

*Theory X managers who learn group dynamics skills often come across as stilted, phony, and manipulative and eventually lose the support of their group.

Mills, D. Q. Industrial Relations and the Theory of Human Resources Management, *Sloan Management Review*, 1970, **12**: pp. 1–14.

Morse, J. and Lorsch, J. W. Beyond Theory Y, *Harvard Business Review*, May–June, 1970, pp. 61–68.

Roethlisberger, F. J. & Dickson, W. J. *Management and the Worker*, Cambridge, Mass: Harvard University Press, 1939.

Schein, E. H. *Process Consultation: Its Role in Organizational Development*, Reading, Mass: Addison-Wesley Co., 1969.

Schein, E. H. *Organizational Psychology*, 2d ed., Englewood Cliffs, New Jersey: Prentice-Hall, 1970.

Sherif, M. Experiments on Group Conflict and Cooperation, *Scientific American*, **195**: 1956, pp. 54–58.

Stagner, R. *The Psychology of Industrial Conflict*, New York: Wiley, 1956.

Strauss, G. Organizational Behavior and Personnel Relations, *A Review of Industrial Relations Research*, 1970, **1**: pp. 145–206.

Tannenbaum, R., and Schmidt, H. W. How to Choose a Leadership Pattern, *Harvard Business Review*, March–April, 1958.

Whyte, W. F. *Money and Motivation*, New York: Harper, 1955.

PART IV

The Design of Work—Should It Be For a Human or a Machine?

There is probably no topic in recent times that has generated as much commentary as the issue of job design or, as it is sometimes called, job restructuring or job enrichment. The positions on this topic cover the range from that represented in *Work in America* to the many writings on "how to do it" to those which are skeptical and even scathing in their criticism.

The following presentations consider the many aspects of job design— including the range of possible changes, their impact and their potential consequences. Also pertinent is a review of those factors which encourage or hinder the initiating and sustaining of design changes.

7

ON THE COMING DEMISE OF JOB ENRICHMENT*

J. Richard Hackman

Yale University

INTRODUCTION

In the years since the groundbreaking Hawthorne Studies, increasing numbers of behavioral science "solutions" to organizational problems have been proposed. Typically a newly-conceived solution is first tried out with great success in one or two organizations. It then is picked up by the management journals and the popular press, and spreads wildfire-like across the country. And then, after a few years, it fades away as disillusioned managers and employees conclude, sometimes reluctantly, sometimes angrily, that the "solution" was not all it had been cracked-up to be.

It looks as if work redesign or job enrichment or job enlargement, call it what you will, is to be the darling of the early 1970s. It began in this country with the pioneering research of Charles Walker and Robert Guest (1952), Frederick Herzberg and his associates (Herzberg, Mausner & Snyderman, 1959; Herzberg, 1966; Paul, Robertson & Herzberg, 1969), Louis Davis (1957; 1966), and a few others. Successful tests were conducted in a few forward-looking organizations, prominently including the studies at AT&T shepherded by Robert Ford and his associates (Ford, 1969). Now change programs focussing on work redesign are

---

*This paper originally was presented in November, 1974 at a symposium sponsored by the Western Electric Company to commemorate the 50th anniversary of the beginning of the Hawthorne Studies. The research on which the paper is based was supported by the Office of Naval Research (Organizational Effectiveness Research Program, Contract No. N00014-67A-0097-0026, NR 170-744) and by the U.S. Department of Labor (Manpower Administration, Grant No. 21-09-74-14). Grateful acknowledgement is made to the numerous organizations that allowed us to examine their work redesign activities, warts and all, and to the following individuals who collaborated in the research: Kenneth Brousseau, Daniel Feldman, Linda Frank, Robert Janson, Andrea Miller, Greg Oldham, and Kenneth Purdy.

flooding the country, stories on "how we profited from job enrichment" are appearing in management journals, and the labor community is struggling to determine how it should respond to the tidal wave that seems to be forming.

The question of the moment is whether the redesign of work will evolve into a robust and powerful strategy for organizational change or whether it, like so many of its behavioral science predecessors, will fade into disuse as practitioners experience failure and disillusionment in its application. The answer is by no means clear.

In this chapter, I report some observations and impressions about work redesign as a strategy for individual and organizational change with particular emphasis on factors which determine whether it will succeed or fail in a given instance. These observations are based on experiences my associates and I have had in fifteen to twenty organizations over the last two years. We have been developing and refining an instrument for the diagnosis of jobs and the evaluation of job redesign projects (Hackman & Oldham, in press). In the process, we have visited numerous organizations where job redesign activities were being planned, implemented, or gotten over. We have talked with workers, managers, and internal and outside consultants. In several cases, we have used our instrument to make quantitative evaluations of organizational change projects involving the redesign of work.

In interpreting our observations and conclusions, it is important to understand that we have not researched the "superstar" projects. Not a single one of our tests has been conducted at a brand new plant, designed, staffed, and managed in accord with the freshest precepts of behavioral science. Instead, we have focussed our attention on "regular" organizations, organizations struggling to figure out, sometimes with professional help and sometimes not, just how one goes about reaping the purported benefits of job enrichment.

What we have seen out there in the "organizational heartland" is not very encouraging. If our observations are representative (and, holding aside the superstar projects, there are reasons to believe that we have seen some of the more thoughtfully-done work redesign projects) job enrichment is failing at least as often as it is succeeding. And people, not all of them of sympathetic mind, are finding out.

For illustration, consider how job enrichments are initiated and how word is spread about their effects. The impetus may come when a manager hears of the idea from a colleague, or reads a glowing case report, and decides to try out job enrichment in his own unit. Or, perhaps, a consultant will convince a manager that it is "just what he needs." Or a vice-president will be converted during a seminar for top management, and will decree that all units responsible to him must have at least one job enrichment project underway by a certain date.

For whatever reason, a target job is selected and is "enriched." But something goes wrong, and it doesn't work. Because there are few decent measures of the outcomes of organizational change projects, the vice-president does not find out (he gets the same slide and flip-chart show in any case). But the manager responsible for the project knows it didn't work, because most of the old problems are still there and maybe even a few new ones have been added. But he is not talking. He will not talk because he believes that somehow he personally screwed it up. Reading additional case studies of job enrichment successes (the only ones published) confirms his feeling of personal failure and his resolve to stay quiet.

Then he goes to a convention or to a management seminar. He has a few drinks, and starts sharing war stories with a (safe) colleague from another organization in another industry. He finds, to his surprise and relief, that exactly the same thing has happened to the other fellow, and that he, too, thought for sure that he personally had fouled it up. Attribution of responsibility for the failure of job enrichment gradually begins to move from internal to external targets, and soon the network reverberates with a new and reassuring message: *Job enrichment doesn't work*. That is what is starting to happen now. The message soon will be scrawled upon the pages of the *Harvard Business Review*, the success of the superstar projects will be carefully explained away (as, indeed, William Gomberg (1973) already has attempted to do for the broad-gauged experiment at General Foods in Topeka), and work redesign as an organizational change strategy will find itself at death's door.

That will be sad. Because the redesign of work differs in some important ways from other behavioral science approaches to changing life in organizations. Five ways in which work redesign is unique are suggested below. Together, I believe, they make a rather compelling "case" for the preservation and further development of work redesign as a change strategy.

WHY WORK REDESIGN SHOULD SURVIVE

Changing jobs changes the basic relationship between a person and his/her work. When all the outer layers are stripped away, this is where most of the problems and most of the opportunities in contemporary organizations reside. The interface between people and the tasks they do therefore represents an especially powerful point of leverage for making changes in organizations.

Frederick Taylor realized this when he set out to design and manage organizations "scientifically" at the beginning of the century (Taylor, 1911). But while we may credit Taylor for addressing the heart of the matter, we must fault him for altering the relationship between workers and their work in a way that placed the needs of the organization in opposition to many of the needs of the workers themselves. Taylor and his associates apparently realized this, and dealt with the problem by instituting financial incentive plans to make the workers "want" to work hard toward organizational goals—and by placing such an elaborate set of supervisory controls on the workers that they scarcely could behave otherwise.   Automated machines later led to increased incongruence between individual and organizational goals, even in companies not managed in accord with the precepts of scientific management.

The response of industrial psychologists to this trend was, in general, to try to help solve the problems created by scientific management and by automation, e.g., by finding ways to select individuals who were appropriate to perform the tasks organizations designed, and to "prop up" the often waning motivation of workers to carry out those tasks. The human relations movement, the design of piece rate and other incentive systems and experimentation with various supervisory styles were all more or less aimed at compensating for or overcoming the "natural" pulling apart between the worker and his work. It can be argued that the failure of behavioral scientists to have more impact on organizations has largely to do with their acceptance of the assumption (shared with management, to be sure) that the work itself was inviolate, that the role of behavioral scientists was simply to help organizations select and motivate people within that terribly significant premise.

Work redesign raises the possibility that by changing the way the work itself is arranged it may be possible to bring individual and organizational goals back together again. By providing workers with additional challenge, responsibility, and feedback in their duties, it appears it may be possible to move from extrinsic props to worker motivation to genuinely internal work motivation—the worker doing the work because it interests and challenges him, and rewarding himself for "work well done" when he performs effectively.

Work redesign changes behavior, and does so directly. People do the tasks they are given. How well they do them depends on many factors, including how the tasks are designed. But people do them.

On the other hand, people do not always behave consistently with their attitudes, their level of satisfaction, or what they cognitively "know" they should do. Indeed, it now is well-established that one's attitudes often are determined by the behaviors one engages in—rather than vice-versa, as traditionally has been thought (Bem, 1970; Kiesler, Collins & Miller, 1969). This is especially the case when the individual perceives that he has substantial personal freedom or autonomy in choosing how he will behave (Steiner, 1970).

Enriching jobs, then, may have a twin virtue. First, behavior itself is changed. Second, an increase usually is realized in the degree to which the individual experiences high levels of autonomy and personal discretion at work—increasing the likelihood that the individual will develop attitudes that are supportive of his new on-the-job behaviors.

The approach of work redesign, then, does not rely on getting attitudes changed first (e.g., inducing the worker to "care more" about the work outcomes as in zero defects programs) and hoping that the attitude change will generalize to work behavior. Instead, the strategy is to change the behavior itself, and to change it in a way that gradually leads to a more positive set of attitudes about the work, the organization, and the self.

When behavior is changed through the redesign of work, it tends to stay changed. After jobs are changed, it usually is rather difficult for workers to "slip back" into old ways of proceeding. The old ways simply are inappropriate for the new tasks, and the structure of those tasks reinforces the changes that have taken place. One need not worry much about the kind of backsliding that occurs so often after training or attitude modification activities, especially those that occur off-site. The stimuli that influence the worker's behavior are very much on-site, every hour of every day. And once those stimuli are changed, they are likely to stay that way—at least until the job is once again redesigned.

Work redesign offers—indeed, often forces into one's hands—numerous opportunities for initiating other organizational changes. When jobs are redesigned in an organization such that many people are doing things differently than they used to, new problems inevitably surface and demand attention. These can be construed solely as problems or they can be treated as opportunities for further organizational development activities. For example, technical problems are likely to develop when jobs are changed, offering the opportunity to smooth and refine the work system as a system. Interpersonal issues are likely to arise, almost inevitably between supervisors and subordinates, but also between peers who now have to relate to one another in new ways. These offer the chance for developmental work aimed at improving the social and supervisory aspects of the work system.

Because such problems are literally forced to the surface by the job changes, all parties may feel a need to "do something" about them. The "something" can range from using the existence of the problems as an occasion for declaring that "job enrichment doesn't work," to simply trying to solve the problems quickly so the project can proceed, to using the problems as a point of entry for work on other organizational issues. If the latter stance is taken, the behavioral science professional may find himself pleasantly removed from the old difficulty of selling his wares to skeptical managers and employees who are not really sure there is anything wrong.

Moreover, if such "spin-off" problems are addressed effectively, the overall management style of the organization may begin to change. Managers sometimes view personnel problems as simply a matter of finding the right pegs (people) to fit existing holes (jobs) in the organizational pegboard—shaving and hammering those pegs (training and motivation) as necessary to get them to fit. Work redesign, when followed up competently, can help managers move toward the view that *both* the pegs and the holes are fair game for change in trying to achieve the best possible fit between the organization and the people who carry out its work.

If work redesign succeeds in generating increased employee motivation toward achieving organizational goals, the nature of the managerial job itself ultimately may change. Rather than having the problem of "how to keep people from loafing on the job," for example, the manager may have to deal with quite a different issue: namely, what to do next to keep his people challenged. That is, what does one do after jobs have been enriched, the people have conquered the newly-enlarged jobs, and they now are hungry for yet more challenge in their work? A tough managerial problem, to be sure, but rather a more pleasant one than that of trying to find ways to keep recalcitrant and perhaps hostile workers plugging away on a deadening, routine job.

Work redesign, in the long term, can result in organizations that rehumanize rather than dehumanize the people who work in them. Despite the popular overblowing of the "work ethic issue" in recent years, the evidence is convincing that organizations can and do sometimes "stamp out" part of the humanness of their members—and especially that natural motivation toward growth and personal development that is so clearly and brawlingly present in infants (cf., Kornhauser, 1965). By the time children have finished school, or at least by the time they have done ten years in a work organization, their motivation toward personal growth and development may have been rendered near latent.

Work redesign can help individuals regain the chance to experience the "kick" that comes from doing a job well, and can encourage them to once again care about their work and about developing the competence to do it even better. These payoffs from work redesign go well beyond simple "job satisfaction." Cows grazing in the field may be satisfied, and employees in organizations can be made just as "satisfied" by paying them well, by keeping bosses off their backs, by putting them in pleasant work rooms with pleasant people, and by arranging things so that the days pass without undue stress or strain.

The kind of satisfaction at issue here is different. It is a satisfaction that develops only when an individual is stretching and growing as a human being, increasing his sense of his own competence and self-worth. Whether creation of opportunities for personal growth is legitimate as a goal for work redesign activities is a value question good for hours of discussion; the case for the value of work redesign strictly in terms of organizational health easily can rest on the first four points discussed above. But the potential impact of work redesign programs on the people who do the work, as human beings, should be neither overlooked nor underemphasized.

As described above, the potential of work redesign as a strategy for change may sound absolutely glowing. It should. The evidence—although it presently is scattered and sadly nonsystematic—is convincing that job redesign really can "work" in the sense of leading to the kinds of positive outcomes suggested above.* Yet the emphasis, for now, must carefully be placed on the word "potential" because that potential infrequently is realized in work redesign projects being undertaken in contemporary organizations. Here are some of the major reasons for this state of affairs.

WHAT GOES WRONG

There is an almost endless list of things that can go wrong when a work redesign project is carried out in an organization. Listed below are seven especially serious pitfalls which often were encountered by the organizations we observed.**

Sometimes the work itself does not actually change. While it is true (as suggested earlier) that when jobs are changed they tend to stay changed, it also is the case that it is relatively difficult to actually alter the way work is structured. It is, for example, typically much harder to change jobs than it is to introduce attitude improvement programs, objective-setting activities, training courses, and numerous other organizational development activities. The reasons for the difficulty are manifold: (a) at the purely bureaucratic level, the entire personnel-and-job-description apparatus often must be involved to get the changes approved, documented, and implemented; (b) if the organization is unionized, the planned changes often must be negotiated a priori—sometimes a formidable task; (c) simple inertia sometimes keeps people from "really" changing what is done—providing instead mere window dressing to make things appear different; and (d) when even one job in an organization is changed, all the interfaces between that job and related jobs must often be dealt with as well, and in even moderately complex work systems that is no small matter.

Because of these and other forces against change, work redesign projects frequently are carried out that have, in actuality, very little to do with the work people do at all. In one organization, for example, the informal word among managers at the end of a work redesign trial was that "we tried job enrichment and it failed." But our research data (which measured the objective characteristics of the jobs people did once before and twice after the change) showed that, while all manner of things did change as part of the job enrichment program, the work itself was not among them.

Correlational analyses of data collected in that organization showed that there were very positive relationships between the amount of skill variety, autonomy,

---

*For numerous examples of successful job enrichment projects, see Davis & Taylor (1972), Glaser (1974), Maher (1971), Rush (1971), and Walters & Associates (in press).
**For other treatments of problems often encountered in the conduct of job enrichment projects, see Beer (1975), Glaser (1974), and Sirota & Wolfson (1972a; 1972b).

and feedback in various jobs and the satisfaction, motivation, performance, and attendance of the job incumbents. These across-job relationships were present prior to the change project, and they were there afterwards. But it also was the case that those people who held the "good" jobs before also held them afterwards, and those people whose jobs originally were routine, repetitive, and virtually without feedback had essentially identical jobs after the work was "redesigned." Chairs were moved about, supervision was changed, names of jobs and work units were altered, and in general a great stirring about took place. But the jobs themselves were not changed. And the effect (after about six months) was a slight deterioration in worker satisfaction and motivation (Frank & Hackman, 1975).

It is easy, apparently, for those responsible for work redesign activities to delude themselves about what is actually being altered in such projects—and to avoid thereby the rather difficult task of actually changing the structure of the jobs people do.

Even when jobs actually are changed, their positive effects sometimes are diminished or even reversed by insufficient attention to the impact of the changes on the surrounding work system. It was suggested earlier that one of the positive features of work redesign is its use as a lever for opening up other aspects of the work system for change and development. The other side of the same coin is that if insufficient attention is given to the "spin-off" effects of job changes, they may backfire and ultimately result in an organizational situation that is worse off than it was prior to the change program.

We have observed this phenomenon in more than one organization, and the nature of the "backfire" has varied from case to case. In one situation, the computer system (which was crucial to orderly workflow) was affected by the change and was unable to handle the now different schedule of data input. The result was excessive delays, creating both attitudinal difficulties on the part of individuals whose jobs had been enriched, and a decrease in the promptness of client service. In another case, work was redesigned so as to push down to workers a number of responsibilities that previously had been handled by supervisors. Initially the workers seemed to be prospering in their new responsibilities (even though objectively the changes were not all that radical). But a post-test revealed a deterioration in morale, especially in the area of superior-subordinate relationships. Apparently the supervisors had found themselves with little work to do after the change (the employees were handling much of what the supervisors used to do), and when they turned to higher management for instructions, they were told to "develop your people—that's what a manager's job is." The supervisors had little idea of what "developing your people" involved, and in many cases operationalized that instruction by standing over the employees' shoulders and correcting each error they could find. Resentment between the supervisor and the employee groups quickly developed, and more than overcame any positive benefits that had accrued from the changes in the job (Lawler, Hackman & Kaufman, 1973).

The implication is clear: those implementing job redesign in the organizations we observed are giving insufficient attention both prior to the change in planning activities and afterwards to the ways the change may affect other aspects of the social and technical systems in the workplace. And the result is often a "failure" of work redesign, one which might have been avoided by more careful attention to the systemic nature of the organizational unit.

Rarely is a systematic diagnosis of the target jobs undertaken prior to planning and executing the actual changes.   At worst (and we have observed it happen—with unfortunate consequences) job enrichment is undertaken because someone in high management orders it done (for reasons never stated), or because a consultant with goods to sell finds a line manager who can be sold. The characteristics of the focal job, of the people doing the job, or of the unit in the organization where the job was located carry essentially no weight in deciding where work is to be redesigned or how it is to be done.

Slightly (only slightly) better was one organization where a line manager and an internal consultant (both of whom were inexperienced in work redesign) decided that a particular job "seemed appropriate" for job enrichment. After consulting a few case reports of successful projects, they decided what specific changes "seemed right" and proceeded immediately to implement them. Neither data nor theory entered into the planning or the implementation in any meaningful way.

More adventurous (or more thoughtful) managers and consultants sometimes decide that since employees probably know their work better than anyone else, they should be involved in deciding how (rarely whether) their jobs should be changed. A diagnosis of sorts is carried out in such cases, because employees usually do know what is right and what is wrong with their work. However, employees typically do not know much about theory that could be helpful in designing jobs so that the joint outcomes for individuals and organizations are maximized. Therefore their advice often tends to be oriented simply toward the removal of "roadblocks" in the work. While managers and consultants could teach the employees the principles of job enrichment theory, we have not observed this done.*

---

*When questioned on this point, managers in one organization reported that they did not believe that the employees (to whom they were about to give considerable additional responsibility and initiative for planning and carrying out the work of the organization) were capable of understanding and using theory. Perhaps an equally reasonable explanation is that the managers themselves did not understand the theories—or that they were embarrassed by them.

An adequate diagnosis of a job being considered for enrichment would involve, at minimum, assessment of the degree to which the job as a whole is objectively open to change and improvement, and identification of those specific job characteristics that should be modified to have the greatest impact on the motivating properties of the job. Only rarely did we see explicit and systematic attention given to diagnostic questions such as these. Instead, managers and consultants tended to rely on intuitive or on "shotgun" approaches to planning for work redesign—sometimes with employee involvement, sometimes without it. And the result, in many cases, was a job enrichment effort that failed because it was aimed at an inappropriate target.

Rarely is the work system surrounding the focal job assessed for its "readiness" for change prior to work redesign. There are now reasonably clear data that job enrichment does not work for all individuals in all organizational circumstances. Yet our observations of in-practice installations of job enrichment show (almost universally) little apparent awareness of or sensitivity to the "readiness" for job enrichment of the target employees or of the surrounding social system. For example, line managers typically expressed initial doubts that their employees could handle the contemplated additional responsibilities— or that they would want to try. Sometimes, as planning for work redesign proceeded, managers would become convinced of the contrary. But only rarely did we observe anyone actually acting on the assumption that individuals may differ in psychological readiness for an enriched job.

Even less frequently was an explicit assessment made of the readiness of the management team itself to deal with the kinds of problems that inevitably arise when major organizational changes are made. In one case, the management team nearly collapsed when the first serious change-related problem emerged. Time and energy that was needed for the change project was spent instead working on the intrateam issues that had been flushed out by the problem and another "job enrichment failure" was added to the tally while the managers talked and talked. An adequate diagnosis of the readiness of the management team for change-management would have increased the likelihood that the problematic intrateam issues would have been dealt with before the work redesign activities themselves were initiated.

The commitment of middle and top management to job enrichment also deserved explicit diagnostic attention, but, in the cases we observed, rarely received it. Whether organizational change activities must begin at the top or whether work redesign is a strategy for change that can spread from the bottom up remains an important and unresolved question (Beer & Huse, 1972). It is, however, almost always the case that middle and top management can terminate a project they find unsatisfactory, whether for good reasons or on a whim. But rather than working to assess and cultivate the commitment of higher management to job enrichment, most implementation teams we observed sufficed by finding a high-level "sponsor" for the project and then counting on him to protect the project from high-level meddling. When such an individual has a change of heart, gets transferred, or even (in one case we observed) takes a vacation, the project may find itself out from under its protective umbrella and in serious organizational jeopardy.

Rarely are work redesign projects systematically evaluated. When we asked managers and consultants whether they evaluated their work redesign projects, the answer was nearly always in the affirmative. But when we then asked to see the evaluation, the response, disappointingly frequently, was something like "Well, let me tell you . . . only one week after we did the actual job enrichment, this guy who had been on the lathe for fifteen years came up to me, and he said. . . ." Sometimes, however, "harder" data are pointed to—especially reduction in personnel in the unit where job enrichment took place. Surely such data reflect higher productivity per worker, but they are of little help in understanding the full richness of what happened, and why. Of great importance in unionized organizations, they are hardly the kind of data that will engage the enthusiasm of the bargaining unit for further implementations of work redesign.

It is easy to explain why decent evaluations of work redesign projects are not done. There are lots of good reasons; like not having the capability of translating human gains into dollars and cents; like there being so many influences on measured productivity and unit profitability that it is hard to separate out what was due to the job changes; like having an organization-wide accounting system that cannot handle the costs of absenteeism, turnover, training, and extra supervisory time; like not really "trusting" measures of job satisfaction.

The reasons can be convincing. Until one asks what was done to try to overcome the problems, and gets as a response something like "Well, we really didn't think we could get the accountants to help out, so. . ." One is left with several unhappy hypotheses: (a) the implementors do not know how to do a decent evaluation, nor how to get assistance in doing one; (b) evaluation per se is not considered to be an important part of work redesign by those who implement it; or (c) the orientation to have the program appear successful is so strong that the implementors cannot afford the (very real) risk of conducting a systematic evaluation. (Often, for example, job enrichment is "sold" to higher management and is very much identified as "Joe's program." Joe, understandably, thereafter has a large personal stake in managing the image of the program within the organization—and a systematic evaluation takes out of his hands one important aspect of the image that eventually emerges.)

For whatever the reasons, the frequent result is that *nothing is learned from the work redesign project that would be helpful in doing it better next time* (other, perhaps, than an increase in the intuitive understanding of what to "watch for" on the part of those individuals most intimately involved with installation of the program). Nothing is generated to convince a skeptical middle manager (or even a sympathetic one) that this activity is worthy of continued experimentation, of further trial-and-error iteration, and of additional investment of managerial time and organizational resources. "Let me tell you what this guy said. . ." just doesn't go over very well with a skeptical manager. Nor is it the stuff of which generalizable behavioral science knowledge is made.

Neither consulting staffs nor line managers nor union officers are obtaining appropriate education in the theory, strategy, and tactics of work redesign. In a few of the organizations we observed, no educational preparation for job enrichment projects was undertaken whatever—other than routine reading in management journals. In other organizations, key personnel would visit one or two organizations where work redesign projects had been carried out successfully. Sometimes a group from the organization would attend a one- or two-day workshop offered by an educational institution or consulting firm to learn the basics of job design.

But the orientation toward learning was, unfortunately, very much in the "satisfying" mode. That is, once those responsible for implementation felt comfortable with the basic ideas and principles of job enrichment, their commitment to learning dropped to near zero, and/or was overwhelmed by the day-to-day pressures of getting the project planned and installed. The loss of interest in learning, in many cases, perpetuated throughout the life of the project and beyond. (We observed a manager in one organization, for example, suffer through what was clearly a rather unsuccessful job enrichment project and then, a few months later, begin planning a new one—doing everything exactly the way he had done it before.)

Of special importance in the conduct of any organization development activity— and job enrichment is no exception—is the role of the internal consultant. Often one hears such individuals complain that they are not sufficiently respected as professionals in their organizations, that they constantly have to fight the battle of gaining "field credibility." This is understandable. A line manager, or a union officer, should very much want to see evidence of the competence of the person who would bear primary professional responsibility for the project about to be done in his or her unit. He or she should not be satisfied with war stories that had happy endings, despite any protestations that systematic evaluation is next to impossible given the state of the art.

It is also true, however, that sometimes line managers want altogether unrealistic amounts of reassurance about the competence of the staff consultants they will be dealing with, or that they seek unrealistically high estimates of the probability of success of the project being contemplated. Our observations suggest that consultants too often collude in such hand-holding activities rather than helping managers and union officials face up to the genuine risks and uncertainties in the project, and encouraging them to cultivate the project as a site for personal and organizational learning.

It usually is the responsibility of internal behavioral science professionals to make state-of-the-art information about the strategy and tactics of work redesign available to those who will be planning and executing the project. If internal resources are not at a sufficiently high level, steps should be taken to upgrade the expertise of key organization members and/or to bring into the organization outsiders who do have the knowledge and skill needed for the project. We observed such developmental activities all too rarely in the organizations we visited. When consultants were engaged from the outside, for example, their advice was indeed used, but typically as a guide to "what to do now" rather than in a fashion that would upgrade the competence of those internal personnel who were centrally involved in the project. In such circumstances, the chances are very slim that significant learning and increased professionalization of internal personnel will occur as a by-product of the change project.

Work redesign projects often are themselves managed in accord with the dictates of traditional bureaucratic practice. Job enrichment projects, by their nature, are oriented toward helping individual workers (or groups of workers) become more autonomous and self-directed in carrying out their work activities. In a successful project, the people at the bottom of the organization are considered to be capable of doing the work of the organization with a minimum of interference, and of having the competence and the sense of responsibility to seek appropriate assistance when they need it. They are, in effect, encouraged to manage fairly autonomously their role relationships as well as their actual task work.

This requires, for effectiveness in the long-term, attention not only to the task itself, but also to the work system and how it is managed. As suggested earlier, the job and the organizational surround must be congruent with and supportive of one another. The problem is that too often the process of implementing job enrichment is strikingly incongruent with the end state being worked toward.

It is unrealistic, I believe, to expect that one can achieve a more flexible, bottom-loaded work system by implementation procedures that are relatively rigid and bureaucratic, and that operate strictly from the top down. At the least, such implementation will raise questions in employees' minds about the genuineness of the change activity ("They're dictating to me again, but this time about how I should take more responsibility and initiative for achieving the organization's goals"), often with unfortunate consequences for the level of employee trust in the project and commitment to it.

Yet again and again we observed standard, traditional organizational practices being used to install work redesign. More often that not employees were the last to know what was happening, and only rarely were they given any real opportunity to actively participate in and influence the changes. In many cases employees were never told why the changes were being made. Privately, afterwards, managers would ask themselves, "I don't understand why they did not respond more enthusiastically. Don't they realize how we are going to make their work a lot more pleasant and interesting?" They did not realize the basic incongruence between the goals being aspired to and the phrase "how *we* are going to make . . ."

SOME INGREDIENTS FOR EFFECTIVE IMPLEMENTATION

For all these reasons—and, undoubtedly, more that we have not observed—job enrichment projects are failing and leaving bad tastes in the mouths of both the managers responsible for implementing them and the employees who are supposed to benefit from them. The failures are relatively quiet now; soon they will become loud.

But I do not want to end on such a pessimistic note. We also saw in our travels some rather successful projects and like everyone else read the glowing reports of job enrichment successes in the professional literature. There are, I believe, some ingredients that are common to many of the more successful projects. A few that seem to me especially important are reviewed below.

Key individuals responsible for the work redesign project move TOWARD the especially difficult problems, and do so early. There is apparently a great temptation to get the project "sold" to management and union leadership, and only then to begin negotiations on the difficult problems. This seems entirely reasonable: if such problems were raised while authorization to undertake the project was being sought, the probability of a refusal would be higher. It appears, nevertheless, that in the long run it may be wiser to risk not doing a project for which the tough issues cannot be resolved a priori than to do one under circumstances that require compromise after compromise to keep the project "alive" after it has begun.

Particular issues that, in my view, require explicit attention from the outset (and that too often are reserved for "later" discussion) include—

(1) Explicit specification of the nature and extent of the commitment of management and union leaders, including the circumstances under which a decision may be made to terminate the project. Of special import is making sure that management and union leadership realize that there will be problems created by undertaking the project (especially in the early stages) and gaining commitment of these individuals to protect the project during these "down" phases.

(2) Discussion of criteria against which the project ultimately will be evaluated and the means by which evaluation will be done—including the measures that

will be used. Given that there are serious measurement difficulties in assessing any work redesign project, it is important to make sure that all parties, including management and union sponsors, are aware of these difficulties—and are committed at the outset to the evaluation methodology.

(3) Establishment of organizational learning as a goal that is shared by all involved parties—in addition to the typical goals of personal and organizational benefit. Critical to achieving a goal of learning, of course, is the development of feedback mechanisms to ensure that the learnings gained (whether they be of the "successful tactics we discovered" or the "roadblocks we unexpectedly encountered" variety) are available to appropriate individuals to be assimilated by them.

A theory-based diagnosis of the target job(s) is undertaken prior to implementation. Most work redesign projects, if grounded in theory at all, tend to be based either on the motivator-hygiene theory of Herzberg (1966) or (less frequently) on some version of socio-technical systems theory (e.g., Emery, 1959). The reason is simply that, until recently, these two paradigms have been about the only ones available for guiding work redesign activities. Now, however, a number of alternative conceptual approaches to work redesign have begun to appear—some of which specify explicit "principles" for improving jobs (see Glaser, 1974 for a partial review). As a result, the knowledgeable practitioner currently has considerable choice about the conceptual approach he will take in planning a work redesign project.

Probably some of the theories are better than others. Yet our observations suggest that it may not be that important which particular theory is used. More crucial to the success of a project, it appears, is that those responsible for designing the changes have firmly in mind some set of general principles for guiding their redesign activities and that they conduct a preliminary diagnosis of the work system based rather explicitly on those principles. The theory is important, but primarily because it facilitates the development of specific objectives for the change project, and because it specifies the kinds of data about the job, the people, and the stiuation that are required for planning the changes and, later, for evaluating them.

Among the general issues often addressed in successful diagnoses we observed (which were conducted from a variety of theoretical perspectives) are the following:

(1) Can the jobs under consideration be meaningfully changed, i.e., will job enrichment make enough of a difference in the jobs to have an effect on the people who do them? (Some jobs are "about as good as they can be" at present; real changes in others would involve enormous expenditure of capital or alteration of unalterable technology.)

(2) If the jobs are open to meaningful change, what specific aspects of the work are particularly problematic at present? What other aspects of the job provide opportunities for change that could increase the level of self-motivation of employees in their work?

(3) Are the employees reasonably ready for change and capable of handling their new duties afterwards? Are they reasonably satisfied with bread-and-butter issues of pay, supervision, and job security or would an attempt to improve jobs run into resistance and hostility because of existing dissatisfaction with such items? It is especially important to collect explicit, reliable data on such issues, because these are matters for which a relatively high level of misperception and stereotyping on the part of managers may be expected. In particular, managers often overestimate the present satisfaction of employees with the bread-and-butter issues, and underestimate employees' psychological readiness and technical competence to take on added responsibility and challenge in their work.

(4) Is management itself ready to handle the extra burdens and challenges that will be created by the change? Some management teams are not, and it is better to find out early than to risk a major breakdown during week one of the project.

(5) What other aspects of the work system are likely to be affected by the change (including management, related peer groups, and clients), are they ready and able to handle the change, or is prior developmental work required before beginning on the target jobs themselves?

Such diagnoses are not easy to make. They involve hard, sometimes anxiety-arousing questions, and the answers which emerge are not always optimistic ones. Moreover, the tools and methodologies required for undertaking them are only now beginning to become available (cf., Hackman & Oldham, in press; Jenkins, Nadler, Lawler & Cammann, in press; Sirota & Wolfson, 1972b). But our observations suggest that the diagnostic task itself may be one of the most crucial of all in a work redesign project.

Specific changes are planned explicitly on the basis of the diagnosis, and are done so publicly.   There appear to be at least three major advantages to being public and explicit in the translation from the theory through the diagnosis to the actual action steps that will be taken to modify jobs. First, by basing action plans explicitly on the diagnostic results, the project is protected from boiling over into all manner of irrelevancies—such as the perennial "parking problem" and the occasional "washroom problem." This is not to say that such other problems should not be dealt with; but it does suggest that if one is undertaking the redesign of work, the changes should have to do with the work itself. Action steps that are planned on the basis of a theory-based diagnosis of the work situation appear much less likely to miss the mark than those stemming from a more general probing of "what can we do here to improve things?"

Secondly, when the diagnosis is carried out and discussed publicly, all relevant parties (including those employees whose jobs may be changed) have the chance to become more involved in the redesign activities, more knowledgeable about them (and therefore less threatened by them), and more willing to contribute ideas and energy toward making them successful. Indeed, the quality of the diagnostic data themselves may be enhanced when the planning process is public and discussable since respondents may try especially hard to provide valid data for the diagnosis when they understand that changes in their own work will be planned on the basis of what they say.

Finally, by tying changes explicitly to the diagnostic results, the probabilities are dramatically increased that systematic understanding can emerge from the project that will help in the development of more effective action principles of work redesign. It will be easier to "trace back" to the reasons why such-and-such a change was tried, and discern where things went wrong (and where things went right) when the links between diagnosis and action are made explicitly and in advance (cf., Hackman, Oldham, Janson & Purdy, 1974).

Contingency plans are prepared ahead of time for dealing with the inevitable "spin-off" problems and opportunities that emerge from work redesign activities. By making such plans, and making them both explicitly and a priori, a number of advantages accrue. First, employees, managers, and consultants all know (and share the knowledge) that certain types of problems (e.g., tension in superior-subordinate relationships; technical problems; coordination difficulties at the interfaces of work systems; etc.) are likely to emerge. In more than one organization we observed, this simple understanding appeared to keep surprise and dismay at manageable levels when such problems did appear, and thereby may have decreased the chance for people to conclude prematurely that "it failed." Moreover, preplanning for possible problems leads to an objective increase in the readiness of all parties to deal with them when they do emerge. Problems in organizations seem to crop up at the most frantic, generally worst possible moment. Therefore, having a few contingency plans filed away can lessen the chances that unexpected problems will sap all available energy as people try to cope with them, thereby draining away the energy and morale required to keep the project itself afloat.

In the work redesign projects we observed, needs arose for additional employee and managerial training, for reconsideration of the pay plan, for revision of selection and placement procedures, and so on. All of these issues—which indeed, bear on almost every aspect of organizational functioning—simply cannot (and probably should not) be planned for in detail ahead of time. Until a project is underway one cannot know what the specific nature of the need or the problem will be. But one can be ready to deal with common and general problems that may appear. For example, the training department can be alerted that some training may be required if managers find themselves in difficulty supervising the employees after the work is redesigned; those responsible for the reward system can be asked to engage in some contingency planning on the chance that the new work system may require nontraditional compensation arrangements; and so on. To recapitulate: one does not begin with these matters; but one is well-advised to anticipate that certain of them will arise, and to prepare to deal with them when and if they do.

Those responsible for the work redesign project are ready and able to evaluate, iterate, and evaluate again throughout the life of the project. A striking feature of the successful projects we observed was the orientation of key personnel to *learning* from the change activities—including those activities that could be viewed as interim failures. Given that there is no neat "package" available for undertaking work redesign in all circumstances, it seems essential that implementors will have to learn as they go how most effectively to design, implement, and manage enriched jobs in the local organization.

The costs of pretending expertise when that expertise is not really present are, in my view, too high to bear. Also high are the costs of adopting an open, evaluative stance, a stance that allows learning from failures as well as success, a stance that involves experimentation with evaluation methodologies as well as with the content of work redesign. But, to my view, these latter costs are much preferable because they can lead to longer-term increases in knowledge and expertise, and because they can help increase the base of understanding on which other people in other organizations can plan their own work redesign activities.

The message of this chapter is simply that implementation of job enrichment is about as tough a managerial and consultative challenge as there is. But the potential of work redesign, the gains that can be realized, also are very substantial. Unless the challenge of implementation is approached with the seriousness it deserves, I fear, the opportunity for personal and organizational change through the redesign of work may slip away for many years.

REFERENCES

Beer, M. The technology of organizational development. In M. D. Dunnette (ed.), *Handbook of Industrial and Organizational Psychology*. Chicago: Rand McNally, 1975.
Beer, M. and Huse, E. F. A systems approach to organization development. *Journal of Applied Behavioral Science*, 1972, 8: 79–101.
Bem, D. J. *Beliefs, Attitudes and Human Affairs*. Belmont, Calif.: Brooks/Cole, 1970.
Davis, L. E. Toward a theory of job design. *Journal of Industrial Engineering*, 1957, 8: 19–23.
Davis, L. E. The design of jobs. *Industrial Relations*. 1966, 6: 21–45.
Davis, L. E. and Taylor, R. N. *Design of Jobs*. London: Penguin, 1972.
Emery, F. E. *Characteristics of socio-technical systems*. Document No. 527, Tavistock In-

stitute of Human Relations, 1959. Excerpted in L. E. Davis and J. C. Taylor (eds.) *Design of Jobs*. London: Penguin, 1972.

Ford, R. N. *Motivation through the work itself*. New York: American Management Association, 1969.

Frank, L. L. and Hackman, J. R. *A failure of job enrichment: The case of the change that wasn't*. Technical Report No. 8, Department of Administrative Sciences, Yale University, 1975.

Glaser, E. M. *Improving the quality of worklife . . . And in the process, improving productivity*. Los Angeles: Human Interaction Research Institute, 1974.

Gomberg, W. Job satisfaction: Sorting out the nonsense. *AFL-CIO American Federationist*, June, 1973.

Hackman, J. R. & Oldham, G. R. Development of the Job Diagnostic Survey. *Journal of Applied Psychology*, in press.

Hackman, J. R., Oldham, G., Janson R. and Purdy, K. *A new strategy for job enrichment*. Technical Report No. 3, Department of Administrative Sciences, Yale University, 1974.

Herzberg, F. *Work and the nature of man*. Cleveland: World, 1966.

Herzberg, F., Mausner, B. and Snyderman, B. *The motivation to work*. New York: Wiley, 1959.

Jenkins, G. D. Jr., Nadler, D. A., Lawler, E. E., and Cammann, C. Standardized observations: An approach to measuring the nature of jobs. *Journal of Applied Psychology*, in press.

Kiesler, C. A., Collins, B. E. & Miller, N. *Attitude Change*. New York: Wiley, 1969.

Kornhauser, A. *Mental Health of the Industrial Worker*. New York: Wiley, 1965.

Lawler, E. E., Hackman, J. R. and Kaufman, S. Effects of job redesign: A field experiment. *Journal of Applied Social Psychology*, 1973, 3: 49–62.

Maher, J. R. *New perspectives in Job Enrichment*. New York: Van Nostrand Reinhold, 1971.

Paul, W. J. Jr., Robertson, K. B. and Herzberg, F. Job enrichment pays off. *Harvard Business Review*. 1969, 47: 61–78.

Rush, H. M. F. *Job design for motivation*. New York: The Conference Board. 1971.

Sirota, D. and Wolfson, A. D. Job enrichment: What are the obstacles? *Personnel*, May–June, 1972a, 8–17.

Sirota, D. and Wolfson, A. D. Job enrichment: Surmounting the obstacles. *Personnel*, July–August, 1972b, 8–19.

Steiner, I. D. Perceived Freedom. In L. Berkowitz (ed.) *Advances in Experimental Social Psychology* (Vol. 5). New York: Academic Press, 1970.

Taylor, F. W. *The principles of scientific management*. New York: Harper, 1911.

Walker, C. R. and Guest, R. H. *The man on the assembly line*. Cambridge, Mass.: Harvard University Press, 1962.

Walters, R. W. and Associates. *Job Enrichment for Results*. Reading, Mass.: Addison-Wesley, in press.

8

FROM HAWTHORNE TO TOPEKA AND KALMAR*

Richard E. Walton
Harvard University

INTRODUCTION

The present symposium is a reminder that 1924 was the year when researchers in the Hawthorne Works of Western Electric embarked on the series of experiments which have helped to drastically revise general assumptions about human behavior in the work place.

Fifty years later, in 1974, after gaining experience in existing plants, managers of Volvo opened a revolutionary automobile plant in Kalmar, Sweden. Kalmar is a practical experiment which both reflects and contributes to advancements in knowledge. Another similarly innovative plant was started by General Foods in Topeka, Kansas a few years earlier in January 1971.

In today's language, some "work restructuring" took place in all three experiments. The Hawthorne investigators specifically treated the variables of lighting, rest pauses and payment systems, and they recognized the importance of supervision, informal groups, and the motivational effects of belonging to a unique and special project. Simarly the Kalmar and Topeka experiments included the design of supervision, group structure, reward systems, and physical environment. But while the Hawthorne investigators paid little or no attention to the design of the tasks themselves, the Topeka and Kalmar innovators took the design of work tasks as their points of departure.

It was a premise of these two recent experiments, as it was a conclusion of the

*Prepared for a commemorative symposium celebrating the 50th Anniversary of the Hawthorne Studies, November 11–13, 1974, Oakbrook, Illinois. I wish to acknowledge the helpful comments on an earlier draft by Chris Argyris, Max Hall, George Lombard, and Renato Tagiuri; and the support for this research provided by the Ford Foundation and The Division of Research, Harvard Graduate School of Business Administration.

Hawthorne studies, that one cannot assess the appropriateness of one factor in the work situation—such as job enrichment—except as a part of the totality.

Thus, I use the term "work restructuring" in a very broad sense to include any and all of many types of change in the work situation. My normative stance is that work restructuring efforts should consider all aspects of work with the aim of creating an internally consistent work culture—one which ideally enlarges workers' scope for self-management, enhances their opportunity for learning new abilities, increases their identification with the product and the production process, and promotes their sense of dignity and self-worth. Of course, the extent to which any particular work situation can be restructured depends upon the type of technology, the skills and predispositions of the work force, and economic factors.

This chapter will analyze and compare Hawthorne, Topeka, and Kalmar as one small way of taking stock of the growing inventory of knowledge about human behavior and the extent to which it is being applied in the practical affairs of man.* The purpose is to answer the following two questions: In what ways has the knowledge generated by the Hawthorne studies been acted on in the design of the Topeka and Kalmar plants, and how do the designs of these recent plants go beyond the implications derived for the Hawthorne studies?

Knowledge which was generated by the Hawthorne studies and which also influenced the design of the Topeka and Kalmar plants is not necessarily clearly traceable from the pages of the Hawthorne reports to the heads of those who designed the plants. Rather, these are ideas, traceable or not, which were inputs to these later experiments and which were similar to ideas which were outcomes of the earlier experiments at Hawthorne.

Indeed, no attempt will be made here to trace the development and refinement of the ideas over the intervening years after the thoughts of Elton Mayo, F. J. Roethlisberger, and William J. Dickson had reached the printed page in the 1930's.** It should at least be mentioned, however, that such an exploration would touch upon the innovative work of Tavistock Institute of Human Relations in the United Kingdom during the 1950's and The Industrial Democracy Projects led by the Work Research Institute in Norway during the 1960's. One would certainly have to evaluate the contribution of the Eric Trist, Fred Emery, and Einar Thorsrud to these two European developments. One would also have to turn to the United States and the contributions of Kurt Lewin, Douglas MacGregor, Rensis Likert, Chris Argyris, Abraham Maslow, and Fredrich Herzberg.

---

*I do not offer myself as a strictly unbiased observer. Specifically, I was deeply involved in the design effort of the Topeka plant. Moreover, generally I am committed to encouraging and improving upon innovations such as those at Topeka and Kalmar.
**F. J. Roethlisberger and William J. Dickson, *Management and The Worker*, Harvard University Press, Cambridge, Mass. 1939.

The Kalmar and Topeka plants are radical departures from our prevailing work organization, but they are not isolated instances. They are leading examples of a pattern of social and technical innovation that has become increasingly important in the early 1970's. I have chosen to review Topeka, in particular, for convenience. I am more familiar with Topeka than the strikingly similar experiments in Procter and Gamble's plant in Lima, Ohio; Alcan's cold rolling mill in Quebec; Shell's refinery in Teesport, England; and Norsk Hydro's fertilizer plant in Porsgrunn, Norway. Other experiments have occurred or are underway in many other leading U.S. firms including AT&T, General Electric, Mead Corp., Cummins Engine, General Motors, Corning, and TRW. The Volvo plant at Kalmar has many similarities with all those cases and also has had a unique impact on the design of technology. Topeka and Kalmar have been publicized and described in considerable detail elsewhere.*

THE TOPEKA PLANT

This plant, in which General Foods produces pet food, has been in operation since January 1971.** To date this experiment in work restructuring has more than met the objectives of the designers in terms of productivity and human satisfaction with the quality of work-life. The effectiveness of the Topeka plant results from a number of features which combine to create an internally consistent work culture.

Self-managing work teams assume collective responsibility for large segments of the production process. The teams have from seven to fourteen members. They are large enough to embrace a set of interrelated tasks and small enough to allow effective face-to-face meetings for decision making and coordination.

Activities typically performed by functional units—that is, by departments of maintenance, quality control, industrial engineering and personnel—were built into the operating team's responsibilities. For example, team members perform what is normally a personnel function when they screen job applicants for replacements in their own team.

An attempt was made to design every set of tasks in a way that would include functions requiring higher human abilities and responsibilities, such as planning, diagnosing mechanical problems, and liaison work. The aim was to make all sets of tasks equally challenging although each set would comprise unique skill demands. Consistent with this aim was a single job classification for all operators, with pay increases geared to mastering an increasing number of jobs, first

---

*See for example, R. E. Walton, "How to Counter Alienation in the Plant," *Harvard Business Review*, Nov.–Dec. 1972; and "The Volvo Kalmar Plant," a 16 page pamphlet prepared by A.B. Volvo Company in 1974.
**My latest information on the Topeka plant is based on a visit in October 1973 and more recent discussions with plant management.

within the team and then in the total plant. Because there were no limits on how many team members could qualify for higher pay brackets, employees were encouraged to teach each other. Within several years nearly half of the employees had earned the top rate for mastering all of the jobs in the plant.

In lieu of a "foreman" whose responsibilities typically are to plan, direct, and control subordinates, a "team leader" position was created with the responsibility for facilitating team development and decision making. After several years, the self-management capacities of teams were sufficiently well-developed that these team leader positions had become unnecessary and were being eliminated.

Operators were provided information and decision rules that enabled them to make production decisions ordinarily made by higher levels of supervision. Management refrained from specifying in advance any plant rules. Rather, rules have evolved over time from collective experience.

Differential status symbols that characterize traditional work organizations were minimized—for example, by a single office-plant entrance and a common decor throughout office, cafeteria and locker room. The technology and architecture were designed to facilitate rather than discourage the congregating of workers during working hours. These ad hoc gatherings not only have afforded enjoyable exchanges but also have provided opportunities to coordinate work and to learn about other jobs.

The initial work force of 70 was selected from among more than 600 applicants. Thus management was able to hire a relatively qualified work force. More important than the actual selectivity permitted, however, was the social and psychological effect of the rigorous screening and orientation activities. They helped create a sense of excitement about the new plant culture.

Employees generally praise the variety, dignity, and influence which they enjoy; and they like the team spirit, open communication, and mastery of new skills which are fostered by the work organization. They certainly don't see the work system as without imperfections; for example, the pay scheme has been a matter of concern and is still evolving, but they are satisfied that the work system as a whole is better than any other they know about.

Plant management reports favorably on the capacities and sense of responsibilities that the work force has developed. The plant has been manned with 35% fewer employees than if the work had been organized along traditional lines. Even more important economic benefits include improved yields, minimum waste, avoidance of shutdowns, lower absenteeism, and lower turnover.

Some managers at higher levels in the corporation have mixed feelings about Topeka. Generally they are favorably impressed with results, but they observe that a plant as deviant as Topeka creates some new tensions in the corporation affecting both central staff groups and superiors in the line organization. Nevertheless, Topeka has inspired efforts in many forms within the corporation to diffuse the restructuring of work. The eventual success of the diffusion effort as well as the long-run viability of Topeka itself remains to be seen.

THE KALMAR PLANT

Volvo's experiments in work restructuring began in the late 1960's in existing truck and car plants near Gothenberg.* At the outset the program was intended primarily to make auto work more attractive and thereby reverse an upward trend in the turnover rate which could have been fatal to the auto industry in Sweden. The results from the Gothenberg program claimed by Volvo include not only lower labor turnover, but also more employee satisfaction, improved quality and fewer final adjustments. Manpower levels and output along the assembly line, however, have not varied because they are fixed by agreement with the union.

The Kalmar plant utilized the lessons from these earlier experiments at Gothenberg. In designing the plant, management consulted with a wide range of parties—current employees and prospective employees from the Kalmar area, trade union officials, psychologists and sociologists, as well as a full array of managerial and technical specialists. An undated A.B. Volvo press release describes the principal lines for the work organization, layout and work environment of the Kalmar plant:

"Instead of spreading out the work units along a line with regard only to technical matters, jobs which have some kind of relationship between them are brought together, and a group of workers is given the task to take the responsibility for a complete function or component of the car. Thus we have teams comprising 15 to 29 operators which are each responsible for special items such as electrical system, instrumentation, upholstery, engine compartment, wheels and brakes, etc. Altogether there are about 17 such items."

"Each team has at its disposal a shop floor area permitting an average of six car bodies to be worked upon simultaneously. As the production rate is one new car every three minutes, it means that the team can keep each car within its working area for about 18 minutes."

"It is up to the team members to decide how they want to distribute the job between them. Our ambition is that all members of the team—after a period of training—shall know each other's jobs. When all members of a team of 20 operators know each other's jobs, each individual has widened his scope of work from three minutes to one hour."

"In order to reduce the need for strict adherence to the clock—which is inevitable in connection with conventional lines—there is floor space for buffer storages of car bodies between the different team areas which allow variations in working rhythm and create possibilities for work breaks."

"The car bodies are transported through the factory on battery-driven self-

---

*My information on Volvo is based on visits to the two Gothenberg plants in November, 1973, numerous discussions with Volvo managers before and after that visit, and the written material Volvo has released on its program. Generally I found their actual work restructuring activities consistent with their published reports.

powered vehicle carriers which make it possible for the team to decide if it prefers to work on moving or stationary cars."

"By these arrangements we are aiming at creating good conditions for job identification, a wider range of working knowledge, flexibility in working rhythm, communications between fellow-workers and with foremen and engineers, increased job satisfaction and motivation."

Other elements in the design are described in another company report published in 1974:

"Apart from the assembly work, the employees are directly responsible for material supplies within their own team area and they play an active part in continuous quality inspection work."

"The activities of the foreman have been modified. His major function has moved towards comprehensive planning and activity coordination. . ."

"Great attention has been devoted to the acoustic environment of the factory. The goal has been to reach a noise level which makes possible conversation at normal level—average value about 65 decibels. . . In cases of workplaces near primary sources of noise, which are essential for production, the goal has been set at 80–85 db, that is to say, a value which does not make necessary the use of hearing protection."

"Assembly hand tools have been chosen with high output at low speeds, this implying a marked reduction of noise. Walls and screens . . . together with a roof noise absorber system, provides the necessary conditions for a fine working environment."

"The work places are light and airy and are mainly located along the outer walls with large windows to provide contact with the outside world."

"Separate entries lead directly to the respective team areas."

"Personnel accomodations consist of "coffee corners" as well as changing rooms with washing facilities, showers, saunas, toilets, drying cabinets, wardrobes and cupboards for clothes. The coffee corners have a heater cabinet, a refrigerator, a coffee-making machine, a pantry, and also wall-to-wall carpeting."

The plant size is comparatively small—about 600 employees—a factor which encouraged the company to choose Kalmar for advanced ideas. The cost of Kalmar is greater than the cost of a plant designed for a traditional work organization, requiring more land, building space, special tools, work-in-process inventories, etc. However, the president of Volvo has stated as a condition of the experiment that the "efficiency of the new plant must not fall below the level of conventional units in operation." Whether the president's condition will be met is an open question.

TOPEKA AND KALMAR AGAINST THE HAWTHORNE BACKDROP

The general lesson derived from the Hawthorne Studies was that the work organization should be viewed as a social system. The new viewpoint had profound implications for management actions, even though many of the specific implications were not immediately apparent. This "discovery" of the social system, with its elaborate group norms, rituals, status structure, influence processes, membership requirements, and so on, stood in sharp contrast to the mechanistic approach of Frederick W. Taylor and the scientific management movement which was gaining influence throughout the 1920's and the next several decades.

The Hawthorne Studies and the "human relations" school they produced led to a greater appreciation of the relationships between the social system and employee morale and between morale and productivity. When management acted on this knowledge, the actions typically took the form of supervisory training, more considerate management practices, and the provision of personnel counsellors.

Values

There are interesting differences of orientation between the Hawthorne experiments and the recent ones. The underlying values were not quite the same. The Hawthorne studies sought to discover variables which affected productivity. For example, the question was whether increased (or decreased) light improved productivity, and not whether the change also enhanced or degraded human satisfaction in the process. Not that the investigators were unconcerned about human satisfaction, but their focus was on productivity. The question was more whether fatigue and monotony affected output than how much these conditions depressed the human spirit and therefore raised the social costs of production. Later, when the Hawthorne experimenters discovered human attitudes were a key variable in mediating productivity, generally these human factors were treated primarily as means, and not also as ends. In contrast, the goals of the Topeka and Kalmar experiments included a more explicit concern for improving the quality of working life as well as productivity.

Certainly both Topeka and Kalmar were prompted by compelling business considerations. The Topeka experiment was partly in reaction to conditions in another pet food plant in which negative attitudes were demonstrably costly in terms of productivity. Kalmar was motivated by turnover considerations. However, the Topeka designers generally were committed to incorporate work structures and procedures which also promised to enhance the quality of human experience. Similarly, Volvo unions and management viewed Kalmar as a means for the "deepening of corporate democracy," a goal to which they were mutually committed by national trade union agreements. Thus both Topeka and Kalmar reflected a shift in values in their larger societies whereby "quality of life" in broad terms was being given increased priority relative to productivity, technology, and growth—the core values of industrial societies.

The point of contrast here is not so much between the experimenters in these several cases as it is between prevalent social values in the decades of the 1920's and the 1960's. With respect to values, the management at Hawthorne and those at Topeka and Kalmar were current with or only slightly ahead of their time. The dual motives of the Topeka and Volvo experiments—business success and quality of life—are not merely an interesting point of contrast with Hawthorne. This duality of motives is in itself a characteristic of fundamental importance— essential to the long-term durability of these innovations. If either goal is clearly subordinated to the other, these innovations will not long endure.

Openness

In their early studies of lighting the Hawthorne experimenters manipulated conditions without informing workers of the changes, the measures to be taken, the purpose of the experiment and the results. In later Hawthorne experiments, workers were given some information and occasionally even consulted about changes in their working conditions.

Topeka and Kalmar have greatly extended that trend. The innovators there tried to be completely candid and to make the experiments subject to a high level of influence by participants. Because the plants were new, however, the initial designs were established before workers were recruited. Even so, in the case of Kalmar, Volvo had involved existing and prospective employees of the company as well as trade unionists, in the design process. In Topeka, great effort was made to give applicants full information about the way work was to be structured and about the underlying rationale. Once the plant started, mechanisms permitted workers to modify work structures.

Thus, in a very important sense, the participants in these work systems become experimenters. This trend to blur the roles of experimenters and participants is even more clearly reflected in other work restructuring projects today in which workers in existing plants participate in the decisions whether or not to restructure their work and, if so, how.

Groups

A very important continuity between the findings of the Hawthorne Studies and the design of Topeka and Kalmar has to do with the strategic role of groups as an emergent phenomenon in Hawthorne and as a guiding design principle in the division of labor in Topeka and Kalmar.

The Hawthorne researchers found that individual performance often is strongly influenced by informal groups: their leadership, norms, sanctions, and clique structure. These groups were found to serve purposes for their members, such as resisting change or neutralizing management controls. But group purposes were observed to be not always at variance with organizational objectives.

Going beyond these Hawthorne insights, a basic principle of the Topeka and Kalmar designers established a principle of *quid pro quo*. Workers can be expected to become aligned with goals of the organization only if the organization is reasonably aligned with workers' career goals and is responsive to other human needs.

The Topeka and Kalmar designers anticipated the group in the formal structure of work teams. The team structure was designed to play an integral role not only in promoting the development of norms favorable to productivity, and in creating a social fabric—two types of functions which were discovered in Hawthorne—but also in exercising legitimate influence upward in the organization, in planning and coordinating tasks, and in providing for teaching-learning exchanges. Work teams became the basic units of the work organizations. The informal groupings tended to relate closely to the formal team membership because of the effect of certain other principles built into the division of labor.

Whole Tasks

One such principle of work design was that of "whole tasks." Work that has been split into simple operations is organized into more meaningful wholes that require more operator knowledge and skill. At a higher level of aggregation, individual tasks that are interdependent are brought together and assigned to teams. Functions previously performed by service or control units, such as inspection and maintenance, are assumed by the operating work groups.

The "whole task" principle of work design was not derived from Hawthorne, although interestingly the seed for this development could be found in the account of one group of Hawthorne employees. Two inspectors in the Bank Wiring Observation Room were formally assigned to a separate quality control department but took contrasting approaches to their roles. One inspector was aloof and controlling and his judgements were resisted and his work sabotaged by operators. The other joined the informal group and took a cooperative stance in ensuring quality output, an approach contrary to the formal rules. The Hawthorne observers recorded this fact, but did not derive any implication about how inspection and other support work should be structured. The fact that the Topeka and Kalmar designers were aware of similar phenomena in General Foods and Volvo plants led them to give operating groups formal responsibility for the inspection of their own work in process.

Flexibility

Equal in importance to the principle of "whole tasks" is the principle of flexibility. In the design of Topeka and Kalmar flexibility is manifested in one or more of a variety of ways: a temporary redivision of work to handle different manning levels; progressive mastery of an increasing proportion of work in a team; rotation to relieve monotony. Movement is controlled or influenced by the team. Such forms of flexibility allow more effective use of available manpower, permit more personal freedom, promote the development of skills, and provide relief from repetitive tasks. Cross-training helps promote coordination and team-wide planning.

Significantly, "flexibility" combines with the other design tendencies discussed above ("teams" and "whole tasks") to create an internally consistent scheme for the division of labor. Each element of the design reinforces the others. To cite a few examples: Identification with the team's "whole task" provides a rationale for learning all of the interrelated jobs. The flexibility options, in turn, provide an immediate decision task for cohesive self-managing teams.

Again the emergent behavior observed in one of the Hawthorne work groups contained the seeds for the development of the flexibility principle. Workers traded jobs although it was forbidden. The Hawthorne researchers noted the social function of job trading, but not the larger potential of flexibility which was realized in the Topeka and Kalmar designs.

Leadership

The Hawthorne Studies included many observations about supervisory and worker behavior and how the two behaviors were related. In the experiments involving Hawthorne's Relay Assembly Test Room, responsibility for supervising work was divided between the inside research observer, who was present continuously, and the regular foreman, who remained responsible for rate revision and promotion but was seldom physically present in the work situation. The observer-supervisor attempted to maintain a friendly atmosphere and to approach problems by paying attention to the women's fears rather than the logic of the situation. In response, the women cited "absence of bosses" and "greater freedom" in explaining their high productivity. The informal leadership which emerged in the group helped maintain cooperative task and social activity.

A different pattern was observed in another Hawthorne group. In this case the research observers remained more aloof and avoided any supervisory functions. The first line superivsor of the group being studied was closely aligned with workers' sentiments and was accepted by the workers. He did not enforce the rules and the group provided him with an acceptable level of output. When, as a result of a general reduction in force, he was replaced by a more authoritarian group chief, the workers did not change their behavior but simply concealed more things from him, as they had always concealed them from higher management. Here, as in the Relay Assembly Test Room, there was a well-articulated influence system within the work group.

The insights contained in these observations were taken further and their implications incorporated in the Topeka and Kalmar design. The self-management capabilities of the well developed group make traditional superivsory roles redundant, provided there is an alignment between organizational and individual goals. Therefore, the initial supervisors at Topeka ("team leaders") were expected to develop the self-management capacities of their groups, providing the requisite direction and control until the groups became self-sufficient. As a result supervision became a decreasing part-time assignment, and eventually supervisory positions were eliminated. The supervisors were aided in discharging their responsibilities by training which increased their ability to listen at the level of underlying feelings—much like the observer in the Relay Assembly Test Room. This ability to listen has diffused throughout the Topeka plant so that it is no longer associated with either supervisory or specialist roles.

The self-management potential of work groups goes far beyond that even hinted by the Hawthorne Studies. The responsibilities of groups either at Topeka or Kalmar include scheduling, solving production problems, screening new employees, and meeting outside vendors.

The Hawthorne investigators observed how workers kept close track of their own output and that of fellow workers, and how they often would distort the information made available to management in order to obscure actual differences between individuals and variations over time. No conclusions however, were drawn about alternative information systems.

At Topeka and Kalmar the devising of new information systems was an integral part of the work design. The information system at Topeka was designed to provide operating information to workers rather than merely report on them. The increased scope of operators' responsibilities required that they know the economic consequences of various factors such as in-process inventory levels, equipment down-time, long versus short runs, and the like. To utilize these data effectively, they also needed analytical skills. At Kalmar the computerized feedback system on quality provides each team with timely information. The computer is a tool used by operators to diagnose the source of quality problems.

Rewards

Hawthorne researchers concluded that while the design of incentive pay schemes were important, other factors had an equal or greater influence on performance. This insight is not inconsistent with the assumptions about human behavior which underlay the Topeka system. But the Topeka assumptions are more complicated.

At Topeka, pay incentives were not conceived as an inducement for people to perform in ways in which they would not otherwise want to perform. It was assumed that if starting pay levels were in line with the community, then the challenge of the work itself (groups, whole tasks, flexibility, autonomy, and information) would elicit the performance that a person was readily capable of. However, it was considered essential that pay be adjusted to achieve equity, matching the increases in value of the individual to the organization. Thus, although learning was assumed to be intrinsically gratifying, pay was based on the mastery of skills which increased flexibility and self-management capabilities.

This pay concept has been perceived as a just one by Topeka members, but the implementation of pay decisions has not always been so perceived. Moreover, there is growing interest in some additional mechanism for sharing the fruits of increased productivity. Although a productivity or profit bonus may not have been necessary to induce very high performance, I believe that some such scheme will become necessary in order to preserve a sense of equity.

Kalmar has not established any innovative pay provisions, probably because on this score the union and management wish to conform to industry patterns in Sweden. To date Volvo has relied upon the intrinsic gains in worker satisfaction rather than pay incentives to make effective their work restructuring in existing plants.

Selection and Orientation

Another support system for work organization is the selection and orientation of personnel. In the Relay Assembly Test Room experiment, in which productivity subsequently increased, the initial selection and orientation were probably significant. Two experienced operators, who were good friends, were asked to choose the remaining four members of the experimental group. The work staisfaction and high productivity records of these six operators appeared to be related to the solidarity which developed among them. This solidarity, in turn, was related to the selection process and the orientation which operators received.

Although the originators of the Topeka system were not directly familiar with the above aspect of one of the Hawthorne experiments, the organization-forming processes used in the two cases have a few striking similarities. The Topeka manager was selected first. He was an experienced and innovative engineer and production manager. He in turn selected his immediate subordinate group of three managers with whom he had worked previously and with whom he had rapport. All appreciated that they were embarking on a potentially significant experiment. This group of four managers screened applicants for the six team-leader positions (first-line supervisors), narrowing the field to about 12 by conventional methods. Then these candidates were invited to a weekend session in which they participated in role play, simulations, and case discussions in order that their approach to human problems and their interpersonal skill could be assessed. Also these experiences conveyed to candidates the values and assumptions about human behavior which the existing four managers were endeavoring to build into the new organization. Team leaders who "survived" the rigorous and anxiety-arousing selection process felt a part of an elite group embarking on a very special kind of venture.

These six team leaders, in turn, selected the rest of the work force, employing similar methods and with similar, albeit weaker, effects on the psychological set of workers. In some instances the assignment of members to teams was influenced by members' preferences for team leaders.

Later, when original team members had to be replaced, the workers took on the primary responsibility for screening and selecting new members from job applicants. Not surprisingly the screening was a rigorous one, and it conveyed to the candidate the unique characteristics of this work organization. Thus, those who were selected were already partly oriented by the time they were hired.

The work force at Kalmar too must have felt a part of a unique and important experiment. This conclusion is made unavoidable by the fact that Kalmar is a relatively small community, the new revolutionary plant was accompanied by so much publicity, and Volvo systematically consulted prospective employees and trade unionists from the Kalmar area.

The Topeka and Kalmar experiments and their participants have received enormous publicity and a steady stream of visitors. These serve to reinforce the workers' sense of the special nature of their organization. Thus, the selection and orientation processes of certainly Topeka and probably Kalmar have created what is popularly referred to as "the Hawthorne effect," namely the positive effect novelty and attention have on human motivation. This particular Hawthorne finding was one recognized and purposely utilized by the originators of the Topeka system.

To be sure, the Hawthrone effect fades eventually. Its strongest motivational force is believed to be temporary. As the new skills, habits, and work culture become established, the positive effect of novelty will decline; and as public interest shifts to other matters, the positive effect of attention will decrease. But the early period of technical start-up and of learning new patterns of social functioning is precisely the time when extra energy and involvement are needed the most. Moreover, if the "Hawthorne effect" weakens, it is expected that the other established, as well as evolving features of the work organization such as the division of labor, will continue to make the Topeka system work. So far, so good, but only time will confirm this expectation.

The significance of the Topeka selection and orientation goes beyond this popularly understood Hawthorne effect. The participation of people in selecting their subordinates and co-workers creates a widely shared commitment to the success of the persons selected. The use of the selection process to communicate the particular nature of the established or desired work culture is a way of encouraging self-selection and beginning the acculturation process. If the selection process is rigorous, the sense of being a member of a special group is promoted.

Another conclusion slightly at variance with the so-called "Hawthorne effect" is that the exhilaration of uniqueness need not be all that temporary. In fact, I believe that a feeling of uniqueness for an organization is extremely important in enabling employees to identify positively with the organization. Polaroid, Xerox, IBM, and Procter & Gamble are companies with enduring and quite different identities. I suggest that the strong identification which their members feel with these firms is due not just to the content of the firm's character but also to the members' sense that the firm is one of a kind. And at the plant level as well, it is helpful for an organization to have a unique and enduring identity. Thus, although the novelty of the Topeka system may disappear, a powerful sense of distinctive identity may continue, with positive consequences.

Context

The Hawthorne experiments produced several observations about contextual factors. First, variations in illumination within reasonable ranges had no discernible effects. Second, the physical separation of work groups appeared to promote the development of group cohesion. Third, at a more general level, it was concluded that physical conditions and other factors can significantly influence worker behavior because of their status implications. The design of Kalmar and Topeka were quite consistent with these several findings.

Careful attention was paid to lighting and noise in the Kalmar plant, less because the designers expected a direct effect on productivity (consistent with Hawthorne), but more because they wanted to enhance the internal plant ecology in a way consistent with rising worker expectations (going beyond Hawthorne). Even more impressive is the design of the Kalmar building—its layout, screening, and facilities for relaxation—which are intended to create for each work team a small workshop atmosphere and to promote group cohesion within teams.

At Topeka, the single entrance for both office and plant and many other physical factors minimized status differentials. Whereas Hawthorne sensitized managers to the well articulated and highly stratified hierarchy, Topeka is a somewhat successful, conscious effort to compress and blur traditional hierarchy.

Another contextual factor recognized as significant in Hawthorne was employment security. As the threat of unemployment increased, employees were more distrustful of management's motives and more cautious about increasing their output. This factor figures importantly in the Topeka and Kalmar experiments. Employment security is very high in Sweden because overfull employment has existed for a prolonged period, but the town of Kalmar has been an exception and has had significant unemployment. Therefore it is especially significant that output and manning standards are fixed by union and management, with the result that gains from work restructuring take the form of increased quality, lower turnover, and adaptability to change—rather than reduced manning. Moreover, employees take their gains from increased effectiveness in the form of longer periods of relaxation during working hours. Therefore employees are relatively assured that improved methods will not result in loss of jobs. The management of the Topeka plant also recognized the importance of employment security and endeavored to assure workers a high level of employment stability. But their assurance is not absolute; it lacks the solid backing of higher management in the corporation, thus leaving some uncertainty about employment security.

SIGNIFICANCE OF THE THREE EXPERIMENTS

There is important progress in the sequence of Hawthorne, Topeka, and Kalmar. The major significance of the Hawthorne Studies was stated earlier—the discovery of the social system in the work place and its importance to management. The major significance of the Topeka project and its contemporaries in the field of work restructuring is the indication that in many cases reversal is possible of the almost reflexive continuation of the trends of the industrial revolution, whereby work is increasingly fractionated, deskilled, paced by machines, and separated into its planning and implementation aspects; and whereby work organizations are increasingly stratified and dependent upon firm control systems to achieve results. These many trends have reinforced each other, sending an internally consistent set of signals to participants in the work place. The problem is, of course, that the trends are contrary to the evolving expectations of employees.

The Topeka project and similar ones today show that if one starts with certain assumptions about psychological needs and social-system requirements it is possible to design appropriate supervisory structures, compensation schemes, information systems, work teams, career patterns, authority systems, and physical environments. In brief, the total work systems can be designed to comprehend what we know about social systems and to be effective in terms of meeting output requirements.

Kalmar, of course, has similar significance to Topeka. But Kalmar went further and introduced some new production technology. To increase the autonomy of work groups, Kalmar eliminated the continuous assembly line by inventing battery operated carriers. In this respect, the Kalmar plant represents a major advance in the thinking which has occurred since the Hawthorne Studies.

Further, what I perceive as the major incremental significance of the Kalmar plant is not yet generally appreciated and has not been indicated in the publicized accounts of Kalmar, including the one quoted earlier. Kalmar pushes the design frontier back one step in another direction to the redesign of the product itself. The product redesign involves questions of internal construction, rather than appearance or functioning of the product.

To permit group assembly, the Kalmar innovators decided to assign groups to assemble entire subsystems of the car, such as the electrical system, the wheels and brakes, etc. Before this division of labor could be adopted the product had to be redesigned. To illustrate, in existing plants electrical components had been installed at many different stages of the long continuous assembly line. The electrical components, their precise placement, and their fastening devices had been designed to fit this method of assembly. Now they had to be redesigned to fit the group-assembly method.

According to an informed Volvo executive, the subsystem assembly methods imposed a large and interesting set of new constraints and opportunities for the design of the product. While some product redesign was required to permit the group assembly method to work at all, much more product redesign will occur before the full implications of group assembly have been reflected. The chain of design implications set forth above is diagrammed in the accompanying figure.

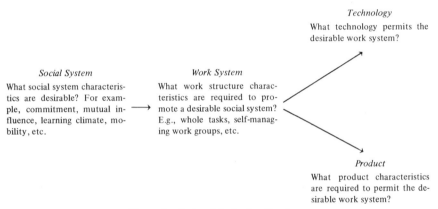

Figure 1. Chain of design implications.

Thus, whereas Hawthorne sensitized us to the social system, and Topeka and Kalmar illustrated work systems designed with full cognizance of the social-system characteristics desired, Kalmar broke new ground in redesigning both the production technology and the internal construction of the product to accommodate a desirable work system.

Several of the lessons of the Hawthorne study are incorporated and extended in Kalmar, Topeka and many other current work restructuring efforts, but unfortunately the ideas are still new ones for many managers and union officials. Consider some of these ideas:

Attributed meanings. The Hawthorne researchers found that the meaning of any particular physical, structural or procedural change will vary depending upon the circumstances surrounding the change. Further, the meaning imputed to the change will largely determine the human response to it. The Topeka and Kalmar designs reflect a keen appreciation of this idea.

Many managers and consultants continue to make changes in the work situation which completely disregard this important insight. The alternative meanings attributed to job rotation provide an example of this type of blind spot. Job rotation will often be experienced as disruptive by workers and further evidence of their powerlessness when the practice is instituted unilaterally by superiors. However, the same type of job movement may be appreciated by employees as a valuable source of variety and job knowledge when it is adopted by or controlled by the employees directly involved. Thus, in the first instance, job rotation is likely to decrease satisfaction and productivity; and in the second instance, increase them.

Interdependence among parts of the work situation.   The Hawthorne experiments resulted in an appreciation that such factors as hours of work and wage incentives are only part of a total situation and that their effects cannot be predicted apart from that total situation. As abundantly illustrated above, this idea has been greatly extended in the Topeka and Kalmar plants beyond anything contemplated in the Hawthorne Studies.

Although there is an encouraging trend toward more comprehensiveness in attempts to change the work situation, too many managers, union officials and consultants continue to think in terms of piecemeal reforms such as job enrichment, management by objectives, profit sharing schemes, participative leadership, and the team approach.

The permanent experiment.   As Hawthorne demonstrated, changes and experiments can create on the part of participants excitement and a sense of being special. These feelings can enhance the cohesion of groups affected and their levels of motivation.

This idea was used at Topeka. In fact, it takes a more dynamic form than contemplated at the time of the Hawthorne Studies. A major premise of this experiment is that learning and experience will make the "best organization" an elusive idea, and that a better way will always exist as the organization evolves. Therefore, the new organization design was not viewed as a once-and-for-all effort. A major characteristic of the Topeka organization was the trained capacity of participants to learn from experience, diagnose problems, discover opportunities, and evolve the appropriate structures, roles, and processes. The idea was that of a "permanent experiment"—an ideal which, of course, may or may not be achieved. Many practitioners and social scientists conclude too quickly that an observed "Hawthorne effect" invalidates an experiment.

The complementary roles of educational and structural interventions.   A question that has long preoccupied many social scientists and thoughtful managers is, "How can we minimize the distinction between those who manage and those who are managed, with its invidious overtones and other destructive consequences?"

The Hawthorne Studies pointed up the positive effects of consultation and consideration toward employees by supervisors. This in turn, indicated the need for skill training for supervisors. But the change achieved this way, by itself, has tended to be limited in scope to a supervisor and the small work group for which he is responsible. These changes in the culture of work groups also have tended to be transitory in nature.

The Topeka and Kalmar experiments are based on the principle that organization-wide and enduring improvement—for example, in deemphasizing the distinction between the managed and the managers—requires structural modification. It requires changes in job content and levels of supervision. The new participative structures, however, can only work if there are corresponding changes in attitudes and the acquisition of relevant skills. Hence, the need for coordinated and dual emphasis on educational and structural interventions. Unfortunately, many efforts for change still overlook the need for either structural or educational interventions.

An interesting number of threads of continuity can be found between Hawthorne and two examples of current work restructuring. The ideas that emerged from the scholarly Hawthorne Studies which have been further developed in the intervening years and which have shaped the design of Topeka and Kalmar, include the impressive capacities of face-to-face groups, the potential advantages of consultative patterns of management, the positive effects of being a member of an experimental unit, and most important, the interrelationships among many aspects of a work situation.

These threads of continuity are encouraging, looked at from either of two vantage points. First, they suggest that the phenomenon observed by the Hawthorne researchers was relatively timeless, not merely a function of social attitudes and behavior peculiar to those times. Second, they confirm that several of the assumptions underlying current work restructuring are based on evidence accumulated over many decades, not merely on theory invented to serve currently fashionable techniques.

There are also a number of important elements of recent experiments not treated in the Hawthorne Studies. These include the following design principles employed in Topeka and Kalmar: work teams collectively responsible for large segments of work, "whole tasks" that incorporate into operating jobs many service or control functions, and high manpower flexibility within and between teams. A significant advantage of these structural changes is that they help make possible changes in work cultures which are organization-wide rather than limited to a small group and are relatively permanent rather than strictly dependent upon the human relations skills of the principals involved.

The more recent recognition that the design of the task itself is a significant factor in the work situation, influencing both the quality of work life and motivation, reflects two developments. First, we have in the intervening years between Hawthorne and Topeka and Kalmar accumulated substantial additional knowledge and hypotheses about work behavior. Second, times are changing the social reality in the work place—workers' expectations about meaningful work are rising with increasing education and economic security.

Perhaps the most important developments of all are those related to the values by which work structures are judged and the ethics which are abided by in changing them.

Topeka and Kalmar are encouraging in that they increasingly give independent weight to the quality of work life broadly defined and not merely with regard to its effect on productivity. Also these two experiments indicate trends toward complete openness about the purposes and nature of a particular work restructuring project and toward a larger role for workers in deciding upon the appropriate work structure.

The positive developments from Hawthorne to Topeka and Kalmar have not come at a breathtaking rate during this half-century. Still, the rate of change is quickening and I expect the incremental lessons of Topeka and Kalmar will be diffused and improved upon much more rapidly than were the lessons of Hawthorne.

PART V

Monetary Rewards—People Do Not Work For Bread Alone, or Do They?

Perhaps one of the most controversial topics associated with human performance is the question of the influence money has on people. The scope of opinion seems to range from those who feel it has an overriding impact, to those who seem to believe that its effect tends to be minimal compared to other factors. The amount written about these positions and variations on them is substantial.

Consideration of the role of financial or monetary incentives in the reward system, factors which enhance or detract from the efficacy of this form of reward, and those aspects of monetary rewards that relate to our whole social fabric are focal points for the following presentations.

9

PAY, PARTICIPATION AND ORGANIZATIONAL CHANGE*

Edward E. Lawler III
University of Michigan

INTRODUCTION

One of the great charms of the Western Electric studies is that they seem to provide data to support almost any conclusion about employee behavior. It has been frequently claimed that they show the important influence employee attitudes, participative management, group cohesiveness, and knowledge of results have on behavior in organizations. In fact, one wise observer of the field of organizational behavior, after noting that the studies are cited as playing a seminal role in many areas of research, has commented that if the studies hadn't been done, we would have to invent them. This statement is a fitting tribute to the richness of the data that are contained in *Management and the Worker* (Roethlisberger and Dickson, 1939).

Despite the great deal of attention given the Western Electric studies it is rarely pointed out that they provide important evidence on how pay incentive plans effect motivation and performance. When pay is mentioned in connection with the studies, it is usually pointed out that the studies show the relative unimportance of pay in comparison to such thing as interpersonal rewards and group norms. This conclusion is wrong and it is unfortunate that it has been so widely accepted, since it has obscured the important lessons the studies have to teach us about pay incentive systems. These lessons are still important and indeed, when combined with the results of some recent research, lead to some interesting conclusions about the role pay can play in organizations.

*Partial support for the preparation of this paper was provided by a grant for the manpower administration of the U.S. Department of Labor.

RESULTS OF THE WESTERN ELECTRIC STUDIES

What then do the studies show about the impact of pay on motivation and performance? First, they provide evidence that when employees perceive pay and performance are related, they are motivated to perform well. The results from the original Relay Assembly Test Room suggest this conclusion and the results from the Second Relay Assembly Test Room and the Mica Splitting Test Room strongly support it (Carey, 1967; Lawler, 1971). At least part of the performance increase in the Relay Assembly Test Room and all of it in the Second Relay Assembly Test Room (12.6%) seem to have been due to the pay incentive plans that were operating there. In both these rooms the employees seemed to feel that if they performed better they would receive more money and as a result they performed better, as would be predicted by most modern motivation theories (Lawler, 1973).

The studies also show that pay incentive plans do not always produce higher motivation. The results of the Bank Wiring Room quite clearly show that under some conditions the installation of a pay incentive system may lead to production restriction, goldbricking and the reporting of false production data. Although the studies don't conclusively establish why pay incentive systems sometimes lead to these counterproductive behaviors, they do provide some interesting leads. They show, for example, that counterproductive behaviors often are supported by an elaborate system of informal norms and social sanctions. In the Bank Wiring Room, for example, failure to restrict production resulted in workers receiving interpersonal and physical abuse.

It is often concluded from the effectiveness of the sanctions that were brought to bear on the "rate busters" in the Bank Wiring Room that pay is relatively unimportant in comparison to social and interpersonal rewards, since people seem to be willing to give up money in order to be accepted by other workers and to avoid interpersonal sanctions. This conclusion, although widely accepted and correctly emphasizing the importance of nonfinancial rewards, is dangerously incomplete because it ignores the issue of why group norms and behavior develop which support counterproductive behaviors. Although the Western Electric studies provide only some answers as to why this happens, a number of later studies (see Lawler, 1971 for a review of these) provide a rather clear picture of why it occurs. As is illustrated in Figure 1, when employees do not trust management, instead of believing that good performance will lead to higher pay they believe that it will lead to higher standards, the abandonment of the incentive plan or some other "management" trick to keep pay down even though performance increases. Thus, in order to protect themselves from having to work harder in order to make the same amount of money, employees develop norms against high production, punish good performers, and provide management with false data about their performance.

Apparently, the kind of counterproductive norms which develop in groups

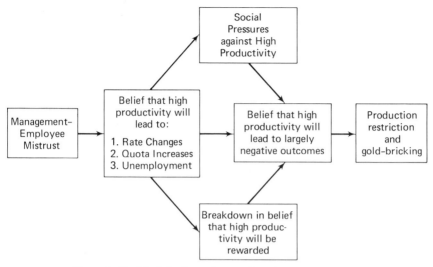

Figure 1. Model of the determinants of production restriction.

come about because of the nature of the pay system as viewed by employees. This means that the existence of antiproductivity norms, rather than showing that social rewards are more important than financial rewards, shows that pay systems can have a strong influence on the type of social systems which develop in groups. This conclusion is congruent with the data from the studies which show that pay can motivate good performance when it is tied to performance, since both argue that pay is an important influence on behavior, and that people will alter their behavior in ways that they perceive will result in the mixture of financial and other rewards they prefer. Thus, an organization that desires to use pay as an incentive is presented with a rather tantalizing conclusion: Pay can be an effective incentive if employees believe pay and performance are related. They are also presented with a warning: Often incentive plans that are designed to produce this belief don't.

The interview part of the Western Electric studies showed that employees have strong feelings of satisfaction and dissatisfaction about their jobs, and they suggest that these feelings strongly affect their behavior. Later research has shown that feelings of satisfaction have an important impact on employees' absenteeism and turnover behavior and that feelings of pay satisfaction are particularly important determinants of absenteeism and turnover (Lawler, 1971; Porter and Steers, 1973). It also shows that feelings of pay satisfaction occur when employees believe and indeed trust that they are paid fairly in comparison to others doing the same kind of work (Adams, 1965).

In summary, over the last fifty years a great deal of research has been done which supports the view that pay is an important influence on behavior. As suggested by the Western Electric studies, it shows that perceptions of the relationship between pay and performance influence motivation and that feelings of satisfaction are important determinants of absenteeism and turnover.

APPROACHES TO PAY SYSTEM DESIGN

During the last fifty years, a great deal of effort has gone into improving the design of pay plans in the hope that the solution to the problems of pay dissatisfaction, counterproductive behavior and workers' doubts that pay and performance are related can be found in the policies, procedures, and mechanics of pay plans. An incredible variety of pay plans has been designed and put into practice during the last fifty years. The majority of these plans are designed primarily to deal with the problem of pay satisfaction by determining what pay rates different jobs should have, although many are designed to relate pay to performance in order to motivate employees to perform better. Each year the avalanche of "new" approaches continues and the debates about the relative advantages of the different approaches get more complex and obscure.

There are an infinite variety of potential systems that can be used to administer pay and some are superior to others in certain respects. Some, for example, tie pay more closely to performance than others, and some more equitably distribute pay than others. It seems, however, that there has been and continues to be an over-concern with the mechanical aspects of pay administration. It is very clear that none of the present pay plans are perfect, but it is equally clear that little progress is being made toward developing the perfect pay plan. In fact, in developing new techniques of pay administration, the point of diminishing returns may have been reached. As evidence for this point, during the last ten years only two new approaches to pay administration have been suggested and tried: cafeteria-style fringe benefit programs which allow employees to pick their own fringe benefits, and skill-based evaluation plans which instead of basing pay rates on an evaluation of a job, base it on an evaluation of what the persons can do. This suggests that the time has come to direct some attention away from such mechanics as how the point system of job evaluation and profit sharing formulas can be improved. Undoubtedly improvements can be made in these, but are they the best place to focus so much attention to improve the behavioral impact of pay programs? I think not.

To make a significant improvement in the effectiveness of pay programs, two other areas need attention: the process side of pay administration and the fit of pay plans with the rest of the management systems in the organization. As far as the process side is concerned, attention needs to be focused on who should be involved in decisions concerning the design and administration of pay plans and what kind of communication structure should exist with respect to pay policies and rates. As far as fit is concerned, the type of pay plan which is used and how decisions are made about it should be congruent with such things as the design of jobs and how decisions in other areas are made. The fit issue will return later in the chapter. For the moment, I want to focus on why I think it is crucial that more attention be paid to the process issues that are involved in pay administration.

THE PROCESS OF PAY ADMINISTRATION

There is a growing body of research literature which suggests that the process side of pay programs is at least as important as is the mechanical side. This is not to say that good process can make up for a poorly designed plan or low pay, but it is to say that bad process can ruin a technically sound plan. The reason for this can be found in the basic point that people respond to the world as they perceive it, not as it exists. How pay is actually administered is an important determinant of people's perceptions concerning pay, but the technical details of the plans and the amount of money they distribute cannot explain all the variance in people's perceptions, because people often misperceive situations where pay is involved. This point is made by the Western Electric studies and by many more recent ones. For example, a series of studies have shown that managers often misperceive the pay of other managers in ways that make their pay look worse than it is. Thus, managers often report pay dissatisfaction when according to their actual pay rates, it shouldn't exist (Lawler, 1967).

Two studies provide good examples of how the same pay plan can produce very different behavioral results. In the first, two work groups were studied; in one, productivity was very high and had continued to go up for over ten years (Cammann and Lawler, 1973; Lawler and Cammann, 1972). In the other group, productivity was low and had remained relatively stable for years. Both groups did the same kinds of jobs and both had similar pay incentive plans. In the second study, identical incentive plans designed to motivate attendance were installed in a number of work groups (Lawler and Hackman, 1969; Scheflen, Lawler, and Hackman, 1971). In some of these groups the plan was highly successful in reducing absenteeism, in others it was only moderately successful.

To understand why in these cases the same pay plans worked in one situation but not another, one should look at who was involved in designing the pay plans in the situations. In the Lawler and Hackman (1969) study, the one characteristic which distinguished the groups where the plan worked from those where it didn't was decision-making. The plan was designed and developed by the employee groups where it worked. It was imposed on those groups where it didn't work. In the case of the two groups studied by Cammann and Lawler (1973) in the group where the plan worked the employees had a long history of participating in decision-making, and they had actually voted on the plan when it was put into effect years earlier. In the other group, no history of participation existed, and the plan had simply been designed by management and imposed upon the employees.

Thus, here is evidence that participation in the design of a pay incentive system can influence its effectiveness. This raises the question of why participation makes a difference. In some cases it may lead to the design of a better plan, but in the studies cited above this cannot account for the differences, since plans produced different results. Other research shows that participation contributes to the amount of information employees have about what is occurring and to their feelings of control over and commitment to what is decided (Vroom, 1964). In the case of the two studies mentioned above, these factors probably did contribute to the success of the plans in the participative groups. In the attendance bonus study the employees in the groups that developed the plans did seem to feel a sense of commitment to the plan that was not present in the others. In the production bonus study the group which increased in production clearly seemed to have more commitment to the plan, to have a clearer perception of how it operated, and to feel more control over it.

For incentive pay plans to work employees must see a relationship between pay and performance. This is a delicate perception in the sense that it is a prediction about the future that has to be based on a feeling of trust in the future. One possibility is that when workers participate in the design and administration of a system, they are more likely to trust it for two clear reasons: one, they have more information about it and two, they perceive they have control over what happens in the organization. Thus, they are in a position to correct any inequities. In summary, one reason the incentive plans worked so well in the studies where participation took place seems to be that the employees trusted they would in fact be rewarded for their performance because they participated in the design of them. Although these studies did not involve employees making day-to-day decisions, it seems that this too could have a positive effect on the behavioral impact of a pay incentive plan. This line of reasoning is summarized in Figure 2. It also shows that under some conditions participation leads to higher quality decisions, and that this in turn leads to favorable pay perceptions.

So far the emphasis has been on the effect of participation on pay incentive systems. However, the same kind of thinking would seem to be applicable with respect to systems that are designed to set salary levels and to influence pay satisfaction, absenteeism, and turnover. In order to test this out, Jenkins and Lawler have been conducting a study in a small manufacturing plant. As a part of this study, the employees were asked to design a pay system for their plant. This was handled by a committee of workers who did considerable research on different kinds of job evaluation plans and gathered salary survey data. They ended up developing a plan that gave control of salaries to the employees themselves. This plan was put into effect, and the employees set each other's salary.

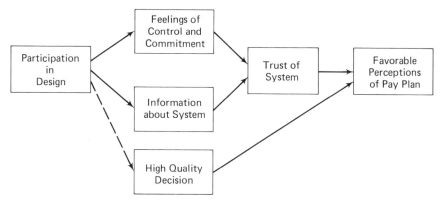

Figure 2. The effects of participation on perceptions of pay.

The results of the new pay program was a small increase in the organization's salary cost (about 8%) and a significant realignment of employee salaries. On first glance it may seem surprising that the employees gave themselves such a small raise. This didn't come about because they were highly paid already; rather it came about because they decided to behave responsibly and set their wages at the 50th percentile of their labor market. These are other evidences of workers behaving responsibly when they are asked to set wages. Lawler and Hackman note that the employees asked for a very small bonus in their study. Gillespie (1948) has reported on a study where workers were allowed to participate in setting rates. According to him (p. 95):

> "When a new job was to be quoted, the job description was sent to the shop and the men got together and worked out methods, times, and prices; the result went back via the foremen to the sales department in order that a quotation could be sent. I was, as said above, surprised and horrified at this unplanned, nonspecialized and dishonesty-provoking procedure and set out to improve organization and method. As I went deeper into the study of department economics I found:
>
> a. The group's estimates were intelligent.
> b. The estimates were honest and enabled the men, working consistently at a good speed, to earn a figure *less than that common to similar shops on organized piecework.*
> c. The overhead costs were lower than they would have been if the shop was run on modern lines."

Thus, it seems that when employees are given responsibility for something important like pay, they behave responsibly and make responsible requests. This is, of course, in contrast to how people behave when they are placed in an advisory relationship as employees are in most union-management negotiations.

A survey of the company six months after the new system went into effect showed significant improvements in turnover, job satisfaction, and satisfaction with pay and its administration. Why did this occur? The workers seemed to feel better about their pay because the additional information they received gave them a clearer, more accurate picture of how it compared with wages of others. Further, the participation led to feelings of ownership of the plan and led to a plan where the actual pay decisions were made by their peers. These factors led to feelings that it was fair and trustworthy. It also seemed that the new pay rates themselves were more in line with the workers' perceptions of what was fair and that pay satisfaction would have increased somewhat even if the employees hadn't developed commitment to the plan. This is not surprising, of course, since what constitutes fair pay exists only in the cognition of the person who perceives the situation, and in this situation the plan allowed the people with the relevant feelings to control the pay rates directly. Thus, in this case not only did employee participation lead to more understanding and commitment, it led to better decisions.

Similar findings have come from a recent study by Lawler and Jenkins of the Topeka Gaines Dog Food plant where pay rates are based on the skill of the employees and other employees openly decide when the skill has been acquired (Walton, 1972). In this situation, pay satisfaction is high and turnover is practically nonexistent. It is interesting to contrast the situations in this plant and those in the plant previously discussed with the way pay is handled for managers in most organizations. The process is almost entirely different. Pay rates are always set by supervisors so the individual has little control. Further, pay rates of all employees are kept secret as are the results of salary surveys, so that the individual has little information on what others are paid. Given the situation, it is hardly surprising that managers often don't have any commitment to the pay plan and don't trust company statements to the effect that they are fairly paid.

In summary, data are accumulating to support the thinking represented in Figure 2. Participation in pay decision-making does seem to increase pay satisfaction and motivation when pay systems are designed adequately. It has this effect because it increases trust and commitment and assures that employees will have accurate information about how pay is administered. In the case of pay satisfaction, it also seems to help assure that pay will actually be allocated in ways that fit the employees' perceptions of equity.

At this point a great deal more research is needed on what kind of participation is appropriate. There are a number of different kinds of participation in pay decision-making that are possible. In the area of pay, decisions need to be made about system design, about where individuals should fall in the system, and about what individual salaries should be. In other words, decisions need to be made about how big the pie will be, what procedure will be used to divide it up, and what size piece each person will get. Further, there are, as many have pointed out, different levels of participation, ranging from consultation to full participation where the employees make the final decision (Vroom and Yetton, 1973). In two of the studies mentioned earlier (Lawler and Jenkins; Lawler and Hackman, 1969), the employees were asked to make all the pay decisions, but were told that their recommendations with respect to amount of pay were subject to veto. This approach seemed to work well in these situations. The employees worked hard and made responsible recommendations that management considered conservative. It is quite possible, however, that research will show that this approach cannot be used in many situations, and that the type of participation which is appropriate actually depends upon a number of situational factors. For example, unionized situations would seem to require a different strategy because of the advisory relationship that exists over the issue of total amount of pay. It is possible, however, that in unionized situations decisions concerned with type of pay system and the pay of individuals could be made jointly by the union and management outside of the normal adversary relationship.

PAY AND ORGANIZATION DEVELOPMENT

The apparent relationship between participation in pay system design and trust has some interesting implications for organization development. Many organization development (O.D.) theorists argue that participation can increase trust and satisfaction, but few suggest that participation *start* in or even include the area of pay. Quite to the contrary, it is seen as a difficult area to work in and one that is frequently dealt with only after a spirit of trust and participation have been established, if at all (Likert, 1961, 1967). For example, a recent book on the Scanlon Plan suggests that if a climate of participation and trust exists, then it should be installed, because it is likely to be successful (Frost, Wakeley and Ruh, 1974). The reasoning in this paper suggests that quite a different strategy can be used. It does not disagree with the point that pay can be handled after a spirit of trust and participation have been established. In fact, it agrees with it, and indeed some of the studies cited earlier support it in the sense that the pay system changes were made easier, because a good climate already existed (e.g., Lawler and Cammann, 1972). However, it suggests the possibility of starting organization development efforts with participation in pay administration precisely because it is so important and difficult to deal with. This approach is consistent with the literature which suggests that participation is likely to be meaningful only when it involves decisions that are important to employees (Vroom, 1964). It also seems likely to lead to organization-wide changes because of the importance of the pay area. Success here can strongly reinforce a more participative style of management, and thus, lead to experimentation elsewhere. Finally, pay system changes are highly visible in organizations and as such can produce rapid change. What better indication of the seriousness of an O. D. effort and of the trustworthiness of management is there than for them to turn over pay administration to employees. It can provide dramatic proof to employees that management is "for real" when it talks about participation, and that it trusts them to handle a very important facet of the organization's existence.

Some evidence in support of beginning an O. D. effort with pay changes is provided by the results we obtained in the plant where the employees were asked to design their own pay system. Prior to this, the plant was run in a very traditional way and trust of management and satisfaction were low while turnover was high. After the experience with designing the pay system, trust, job involvement and job satisfaction all went up dramatically in a manner that indicates the experience impacted upon other areas of the relationship between the employees and the company. One reason for this seems to have been that the participative skills and effects which were generated in dealing with the pay issue generalized to other organizational issues. This was clearly illustrated by the events which followed the pay plan changes. The same process was effectively used to set company policies in other areas (e.g., terminations and layoffs) and to develop a pay incentive plan. The experience of many Scanlon Plan companies also suggests that organization change efforts can begin with pay system changes. Lesieur (1968) argues quite convincingly that it often leads to a high level of worker involvement in decision making, and that when this happens, it is most effective.

A case can be made for the view that the spread of participation from pay to other areas of decision-making is not only a logical consequence of its success in the pay area, but a necessary one if the pay system is to continue to work well. Earlier it was mentioned that one important determinant of how well the pay system operates may be the congruence between how it and the other systems in the organization are run. It is frequently pointed out in the literature on organization change that organizations have multiple systems, and that in order to have an affective organization, all the systems must be congruent; often, of course, this calls for introducing multiple changes in organizations (Katz and Kahn, 1966; Leavitt, 1965). The reason for this is that when incongruence exists, a role conflict situation is set up and employees receive conflicting messages about what behavior is expected of them and how the organization regards them. Although employees are capable of a certain degree of compartmentalization, it is difficult and uncomfortable for them to do this for a long period in an area which is as important as pay (Kahn et. al., 1964). Thus, systems usually head toward balance, and this often leads them to reject the changes which have been introduced.

Unfortunately, there is relatively little research which has looked at the issue of what constitutes system congruence or symmetry in the area of pay. Thus, little can be said about it based upon empirical evidence, but a few observations can be made. Briefly stated, it would seem that congruence must exist within and between two areas: decision making process and system design or structure. As far as decision making process is concerned, congruence would seem to mean that decisions about such things as rate of production, product quality, new employee selection, and purchasing are made in the same way as decisions about pay. As far as design or structure is concerned, congruence would mean that the type of job evaluation plan (e.g., skill bonus versus point method) and the type of incentive plan which is used (e.g., group, individual) are supportive in a measurement and reward sense with the way jobs are designed and decisions are made. Specifically, the pay system needs to measure and reward those things that are critical in making the job and organization design work (e.g., cooperation, skill acquisition), and it needs to measure behavior at the same level (e.g., individual, group or department) as the job design emphasizes.

The importance of structural congruence has often been overlooked by people who take job enrichment and participative management approaches to organization development. I have come across a number of cases where either a traditional job enrichment approach was tried or an autonomous work-group approach was tried, and nothing was done to change the structure of the pay system. The result in almost every instance was problems caused by a misfit between the structural design of the pay system and the new job designs. For example, in several instances job enrichment and job rotation were done, but a traditional job evaluation was left in place. The result was employee demands for higher pay because they now had more responsibility. Management had trouble answering this demand because the job evaluation was designed for situations where employees did not rotate and acquire new skills. In one plant a woman who was asked to take notes at team meetings asked for a raise because she had taken on secretarial duties. It is interesting to note that in the Topeka plant where both job enrichment and a skill-based evaluation plan was installed, these problems are not present because the evaluation approach is supportive of people changing jobs and acquiring new skills; in fact it rewards them for it (Walton, 1972).

In another case, a large airline recently tried an autonomous work group experiment with its maintenance employees that failed because the pay system was not changed. In this case the employees were not on an incentive plan, but they had come over the years to expect large amounts of overtime. In effect, since harder work didn't get them more money and slow work did (it got overtime), they had decided to work overtime in order to earn more money. In this situation the establishment of an autonomous work group did not increase performance, because it was against the best economic interests of the employees.

Lindholm (1974) has reported on a Swedish case that emphasizes what can happen when a pay system does not fit the structure of jobs and organizations. In this case a piecework system was abandoned in favor of an hourly wage, and the jobs of the employees were enriched. The result was a failure, performance went down and turnover went up, apparently because the financial incentive to perform well was gone as was the positive effect which the system had on scheduling. Two years later a plant-wide incentive system was added and suddenly productivity went up 45%, and turnover dropped to a lower level than before the piece rate plan was dropped. This pay plan seemed to fit just perfectly with the new organization design. It provided motivation through tying pay to performance, and since it rewarded plant performance it encouraged cooperation and teamwork which was needed to make the new approach to job and organization design work effectively.

It is interesting to note that in the example given by Lindholm as well as in many of the other successful Scandinavian experiments in job and organization, redesigned pay incentive plans have been used (see e.g., Jenkins, 1972). However, the plans have never rewarded individual performance, rather they have focused on group, department, or plant-wide performance. These experiments seem to point to the same conclusion that the research mentioned earlier on the Scanlon Plan does, namely that certain kinds of pay incentive plans can be very effective in an organization that uses participative management, autonomous work groups, and job enrichment. In some ways, this is an ironical conclusion, since the proponents of these approaches often argue that they are powerful motivators on their own, and, as a result, make pay incentives unnecessary. It is also rather ironical that traditionally-run organizations usually are in a poor position to use pay as an incentive because the trust level is low, yet these are just the organizations that would seem to need to use pay as a motivator the most.

This discussion suggests some interesting conclusions about what constitutes congruence between some process and structural areas in organizations. Participative decision-making with respect to pay, openness about pay, group and plant-wide incentives, and skill-based bonus plans are congruent with such new approaches to organization design as autonomous work groups and job enrichment. In addition, standard job evaluation plans, piece rate incentive or no incentive at all are congruent with the more traditional top-down approach to management.

SUMMARY

In summary, this chapter began by pointing out that a large number of studies, including the Western Electric studies, showed that for a pay system to operate effectively a high level of trust must be present. It was further pointed out that there are a number of ways to establish trust, but that openness about information and some power-sharing are particularly effective. Traditional wisdom often suggests that openness and power sharing can best start in areas other than pay and indeed it often ignores changing the pay system. The data reviewed in the chapter suggest that this is a particularly dangerous view, because it rules out a potentially effective change strategy, beginning with changing pay procedures, and because it often leads to the creation of organization structures and processes that are out of phase with each other.

REFERENCES

Adams, J. S.   Injustice in Social Exchange.   In Berkowitz (ed.) *Advances in experimental social psychology.* Vol. 2, New York: Academic Press, 1965, 267–299.

Cammann, C. and Lawler, E. E.   Employee reactions to a pay incentive plan. *Journal of Applied Psychology*, 1973, **58**: 163–172.

Carey, A.   The Hawthorne Studies: A radical criticism. *American Sociological Review*, 1967, **33**: 403–416.

Frost, C. F., Wakeley, J. H. and Ruh, R. A.   *The Scanlon Plan for Organizational Development: Identity, Participation and Equity.*   East Lansing: Michigan State University Press, 1974.

Gillespie, J. J.   *Free Expression in Industry.*   London: Pilot Press, 1948.

Jenkins, D.   *Job Power.*   New York: Doubleday & Company, 1973.

Katz, D. and Kahn, R. L.   *The Social Psychology of Organizations.*   New York: Wiley, 1966.

Kohn, R. L., Wolfe, D. M., Quinn, R. P. and Snoek, J. D.   *Organizational Stress: Studies in Role Conflict and Ambiguity.*   New York: Wiley, 1964.

Lawler, E. E. III   Secrecy about management compensation: Are there hidden costs? *Organizational Behavior and Human Performance*, 1967, **2**: 182–189.

Lawler, E. E. III   *Pay and Organizational Effectiveness: A Psychological View.*   New York, McGraw-Hill, 1971.

Lawler, E. E. III   *Motivation in Work Organizations.*   Monterey, Calif.: Brooks/Cole, 1973.

Lawler E. E. III and Cammann C.   What makes a work group successful?   Chapter in A. J. Marrow (ed.) *The Failure of Success.*   New York: Amacom, 1972. 122–130.

Lawler, E. E. III and Hackman, J. R.   The impact of employee participation in the development of pay incentive plans: A field experiment. *Journal of Applied Psychology*, 1969, **53**: 467–471.

Leavitt, H. J.   Applied Organizational Change in Industry: Structural, technological and humanistic approaches.   Chapter in J. G. March (ed.) *Handbook of Organizations.* Chicago: Rand McNally, 1965, pp. 1144–1170.

Lesieur, F. G.   *The Scanlon Plan.*   New York: Wiley, 1958.

Likert, R.   *New patterns of management.*   New York: McGraw-Hill, 1961.

Likert, R.   *The Human Organization.*   New York, McGraw-Hill, 1967.

Lindholm, R.   *Payment by results—Leading system in production development.*   Paper presented at EFPS-EAPM Conference, Amsterdam, October, 1974.

Porter, L. W. and Steers, R. M.   Organizational work and personal factors in employee turnover and absenteeism. *Psychological Bulletin*, 1973, **80**: 151–176.

Roethlisberger, F. J. and Dickson, W. J.   *Management and the Worker.*   Cambridge: Harvard University Press, 1939.

Scheflen, K. C., Lawler, E. E. and Hackman, R. J.   Long-Term Impact of Employee Participation in the Development of Pay Incentive Plans: A Field Experiment Revisited. *Journal of Applied Psychology*, 1971, **55**: 182–186.

Vroom, V. H.   *Work and Motivation.*   New York: Wiley, 1964.

Vroom, V. H. and Yetton, P. W.   *Leadership and Decision-making.*   Pittsburgh: University of Pittsburgh Press, 1973.

Walton, R. E.   How to counter alienation in the plant. *Harvard Business Review*, 1972, **50**(6): 70–81.

10
THE CONCEPTUAL CONTEXT FOR COMPENSATION

Harry Levinson
President, Levinson Institute

INTRODUCTION

Much has been said in the management literature about money as a motivator. Money is important to everyone but it has variable significance, depending on the context or the configuration of variables of which it is a part.

This configuration of variables is usually thought of as related solely to the personality structure of the individual. However, given the concept of the psychological contract (Levinson, et al. 1962), it is no longer possible to think of the individual alone. When one speaks of such a context, one must also speak of the organization. Some effort has been made to define organizational climate as one way of describing the organizational component of the psychological contract (Litwin and Stringer, 1968). A more significant contribution has been made by Roger Harrison, who delineates four general organization characters built around organizational ideologies (Harrison, 1972).

Harrison's contribution provides a platform on which to begin refining the concept of organizational character and differentiating its varied configurations and components. By so doing, a context can be defined for understanding the varying meanings of motivational techniques in organizations. In addition a mode is developed of viewing organizational character development, the problems and necessary processes in effecting organizational change, and for differentiating components of an organization whose structure should be varied according to the character of the components (Lawrence and Lorsch, 1967).

ORGANIZATIONAL CHARACTER

Harrison postulates four organizational ideologies: (1) power orientation; (2) role orientation; (3) task orientation; and (4) person orientation. These are not pure types, but each tends to be the central thrust of an organization.

As Harrison defines it, a power-oriented organization attempts to dominate its environment and vanquish all opposition. It is competitive and jealous, exploitative and dominating. Ruthless competition prevails both inside and outside, sometimes masked by paternalism.

A role-oriented organization is preoccupied with legality, legitimacy, and responsibility. Indeed, often in reaction to a previous power orientation, competition and conflict are regulated or replaced by agreements, rules, and procedures. Rights and privileges are carefully defined and adhered to. Hierarchy and status are modulated by commitment to legitimacy and legality. Harrison differentiates power and role orientations to authority by comparing the two to dictatorship and a constitutional monarchy. Stability, respectability, and predictability of behavior are highly valued and change comes slowly. Many banks, insurance companies, public utilities, and social work organizations are illustrative.

In the task-oriented organization, achievement of a superordinate goal is the highest value. Structure, functions, and activities are all evaluated in terms of their contribution to the superordinate goal, and nothing is allowed to get in the way of accomplishing the task. Personal needs are suppressed in the interest of getting the job done. Authority is considered legitimate only if it is based on knowledge and competence, and structure is changed to serve task accomplishment. Task forces, project teams, associations of people to accomplish a social or business goal are illustrative.

The person-oriented organization exists primarily to serve those needs of its members which they cannot meet by themselves. The organization is a tool for each of its members—to evaluate, to use or to dispose of if it no longer serves their purpose. Individuals are expected to influence each other, and authority, when it exists, is on the basis of task competence. Consensus methods of decision-making tend to prevail and roles fit personal preference and personal needs. Small groups of scientists or technicians or consultants may be examples. Harrison notes that there seems to be increasing pressure on members of modern industrial organizations to move toward a person orientation. I would extend the concept of person-oriented organizations to include some components of power- and role-oriented organizations like research and development or creative advertising.

Neither the power-oriented nor the role-oriented organization is able to adapt easily to rapid external changes. However, when the power-oriented organization decides to change course, it can attack the environment vigorously and often take high risks, but both the power-oriented and the person-oriented organizations take longer to respond to change. The task-oriented organization can change easily. The power-oriented organization is more aggressive in its collective response, while the person-oriented organization has difficulty responding in unison.

Neither the power- nor role-oriented organization, according to Harrison, provide for the development and utilization of internal commitment, initiative, and independent judgment except at the highest levels. The power-oriented organization exercises tight internal control and integration and copes well with problems that can be solved by a few intelligent leaders. Despite the policing, most people have little security in it unless they accept its word that it is paternalistic. However, with size, controls tend to break down and role-orientation with its greater long-term security creeps in. Some organizations attempt to cope with the breakdown of controls by combining some features of the task-orientation in a matrix structure, but there is no security in a task-oriented organization when the need for one's task is over.

Extrapolating from Harrison's conception, one can delineate further differences in such areas as organizational leadership style, the primary direction of organizational energy, organizational structures, organizational themes, organizational behavior, organizational communication patterns, distribution of power, the manner in which needs are met and skills are used, the sources from which roles are derived, models of interdependence, significant losses, value systems, myths, elaborations or ideologies, foci of competitive effort, and underlying assumptions about individual motivation, including the role of compensation.

Since the days when the Hawthorne Studies resulted in qualifying the basic conceptions of economic man with a new conception of social man (Roethlisberger and Dickson, 1939), more refined conceptions of man have evolved: self-actualizing man (Maslow, 1954) and psychological man (Levinson, 1973). These need to be integrated, given the psychological contract, with conceptions of organizational character.

POWER ORIENTATION

From my point of view, a power orientation is characteristically also an entrepreneurial orientation. The entrepreneur builds a big organization or obtains a corner on a market or vanquishes competitors. By whatever mode suits him best he starts the organization, builds it, and makes it succeed, thereby acquiring power himself. The entrepreneur is notably authoritarian in his mode and his business is an extension of himself. The organization is clearly his property and essentially his to do with as he wishes. Leadership is by command or direction, however well that process might be masked.

The entrepreneur's powers may be inherited, literally, or they may be acquired by those who, having identified with the entrepreneur or on becoming "favorite sons," inherit the mantle of power or, surviving combat, take over. The leadership theme in such an organization is "Do what I say." The boss' rules are primary and paramount. Therefore, as a guide to behavior, what the boss says is more important than what the roles demand.

Controls are provided by the systems established by the leader, as well as by direction and the threat of punishment. Both by verbal direction and published exhortation, the boss usually pounds into the subordinate what it is that he wants, the way to achieve it, and the penalties and rewards for behavior. There tends to be resigned acceptance of the leader's power and an inability to displace him, to do better than he, or even to contradict him. Frequently there is an overvaluation of his power, which is reflected in the identification with the aggressor in an attempt to act towards subordinates as one experiences the leader acting towards one's self.

Using Greiner's terms, Phase I is when the organization is preoccupied with creating both a product and a market, which frequent and immediate communication among employees enhances (Greiner, 1972). After this creative stage the leadership problem becomes the need for formal management, which usually means bringing in a technically competent and strong manager. This manager takes the organization into Phase 2, a period of sustained growth and direction, and introduces a functional structure: Accounting, budgetary and work standards, goals, and more formal direction. This produces an autonomy crisis with respect to leadership, which in turn requires greater delegation as the organization grows. The greater delegation then runs into problems because lower level managers are not accustomed to making their own decisions.

The typical power-oriented organization is characterized by a pyramidal organizational structure and is held together by a centripetal force which compels people to stay. Employees may feel they can't get a job elsewhere, or be overly dependent, or feel compelled to respond to the needs of a paternalistic leader. Whatever the reason, they feel attached to the organization and required to obey its commands. The characteristic mode of trust, if it exists at all, derives from the ancient concept of noblesse oblige. One owes fealty to his lord and in return the lord has certain obligations to his servants: he will defend, protect and care for them. Paternalism is another variant of this concept. There is a certain interdependence in such a relationship, but the primary experience is one of dependency—one does what one is told. The employee depends most heavily on the leader himself and to a lesser extent on the structure. The structure is less stable than that in a role-oriented organization because it depends heavily on the whims and moods of the leader.

The purpose or goal of the organization is fundamentally that of the boss. That is, the whole organization is an instrument for the fulfillment of the ego ideal of the leader (Levinson, 1968). Everyone else in the organization becomes an instrument of the leader to achieve his own purpose and goal. Usually he wants to lead, to control, to be on top, and to leave a monument behind. That is often why such men, coming to the close of their careers, seem to be compelled to build big buildings.

Communication is almost altogether downward. There may be mechanistic attempts at upward communication, as in attitude surveys and morale studies, which frequently are used as weapons to whip middle managements into shape, but the primary communication is downward.

Power is distributed by the head of the organization in accordance with his own whims and wishes. It is less likely allocated by formal job descriptions, delegation, and other methods which can be trusted consistently. When power is decentralized and lower level managers are able to act more quickly and flexibly, the organization has come to the end of its developmental Phase 3, and management seeks to regain control over the total company with systems (Greiner, op. cit.). However, as Greiner points out, experts usually fail because of the scope of the organization's operations, which in turn sets the conditions for subsequent phases (4 and 5) of coordination and collaboration.

In my terms, the power-oriented organization meets ministration needs. It sometimes meets mastery needs if there are allocations of role and function to people who have charge of the organization (Levinson, 1968). In Maslow's terms, it meets physiological and safety needs, although frequently social needs and needs for love are also met if members of the organization are mutually supportive and if the organization exercises paternal concern (Maslow, op. cit.). There tend to be relatively fixed tracks of movement. Who learns what skills is frequently determined by assignment from the boss or his representatives. Unless a person happens to be employed for fixed skills or can assume sufficient initiative to find an appropriate niche for himself, someone else decides his place and position, indeed his occupational direction. This heightens the possibility of occupational obsolescence and the risk of being summarily rejected. That risk extends to the highest level executives.

The view of the leader by those who are subjected to his power is often one of fancied omnipotence. In fact, such a leader, particularly if he has rescued the organization several times, frequently becomes legendary. He is often viewed as paternal, whether good or bad, but nevertheless the founder or inheritor of the organization. If he is entrepreneurial, his subordinates usually see him as having unique talents that none of his followers (who have been chosen because they are relatively incapable of rivalling him) have.

Where leaders are so powerful, the most significant loss is that of the leader himself. All kinds of organizations, from kingdoms to companies, fall with change of leadership, particularly charismatic or authoritative leadership, which leaves people feeling helpless to do anything about the inadequate adaptive efforts of the organization.

Hughes and Flowers (1973), building on a theory of Clare Graves (1970), have delineated seven value systems. Determination of which value systems people hold makes it possible to evolve styles of management, organization structures and organizational processes which fit the needs of people who hold these diverse value structures.

The value system behavior of a power-oriented organization is in many cases reactive. That is, it is a primitive response to physiological needs, particularly in developing countries where work is extremely scarce. It is sometimes tribalistic, most often conforming and frequently manipulative. Thus money and supervisory direction are important. While in the entrepreneurial stage, many people work long and hard hours, for which they usually expect some considerable financial gain when the market has been dominated or the product developed and sold (Harrison, op. cit.). Frequently that expectation comes to the fore when the entrepreneurial leader sells his organization and fails to give his loyal servants what they believe to be their due. If the organization is not in an intrepreneurial or creative phase, then money becomes an important indication of power and position, a reflection of how much one is loved by the boss and how much power one can exert over others. It is also a reflection of one's own batting average or position in the competitive swim. Sometimes, but less often, it is a device for the appeasement of the leader's guilt for having to bypass, abandon or demote a loyal servant.

The major channels of affection and aggression have significantly different routes in the power-oriented organization. The organization itself demands obeisance, loyalty, and regard, as does the leader. Aggression presumably is directed primarily to the task, but significantly in protecting one's self and in competition against one's fellows, as well as in acting on behalf of the organization to attack whatever external enemies there may be. The ego ideals of individuals of such an organization revolve significantly around being liked, in simple form, "for being a good boy" and making no waves.

The political ideology, at least initially, of the power-oriented organization revolves around the issue of private property because the entrepreneur owns the organization (Lodge, 1970). Sometimes it may be related to state property, as when one develops a public agency in which there is great pride (the FBI and NASA are examples).

There is a great tendency for people in the power-oriented organization, already viewing themselves as inadequate in the face of a more powerful competent leader, to tend to feel themselves constantly accused of something without quite knowing what. They always seem to feel "under the gun" and never adequate to the role demands, since they are rarely praised except in a paternalistic way, and vulnerable to repetitive criticism. They often feel themselves too driven and manipulated to a production or sales target held aloft by the boss or his representatives.

Planning is done at the top and often by the entrepreneur himself. In large organizations which have moved into Greiner's Phase 2, it may be done by headquarters staff but it is likely to be highly centralized.

The prevailing myth is that of a Horatio Alger character. Most often the entrepreneur has risen from rags to riches, the organization from a basement, garage, shack, or other business equivalent of the log cabin to great plants and significant financial resources. The organization's successes are exhibited in oil paintings or photographic equivalents. One has only to think of Henry Ford or Thomas Edison as the prototypes of such heroes. The morality of the organization therefore tends to be essentially the Protestant ethic, namely hard work. Sometimes morality is honored more in the breach, as when such an organization exploits people or the environment or unfairly destroys its competition. However, even in such cases, that behavior is cloaked with a rationale of righteousness.

Individualism prevails, according to this ethos, since each employee presumably is for himself an individual entrepreneur. As a matter of fact, as George C. Lodge notes, this is an atomistic notion in which the community is no more than the sum of the individuals in it, and the fulfillment lies in survival of the fittest (Lodge, 1974). However, in the political order in this country, he points out, individualism evolved into interest group pluralism which became the preferred method of directing society. The community is more than the sum of the individuals in it. This makes for basic conflict between the individual who seeks to fulfill his many psychological needs in the organization, and the power-oriented organization which denies it has any responsibility other than to provide security in return for service (even it if does that) and "a good day's pay for a good day's work." The power-oriented organization feels that it must compete ruthlessly with other organizations outside its control and in its market place, so it assumes that people within the organization must compete with each other for their individual share of the market or level of power. The power-oriented organization also assumes an economic man, motivational model. It may foster secondarily a social man orientation as in the "one big family" concept.

ROLE-ORIENTED ORGANIZATION

The role orientation of an organization may evolve out of the transition from the power-oriented organization through Greiner's first three phases and into Phase 4, coordination. Greiner sees this evolutionary period as characterized by two things: 1) use of formal systems for achieving greater coordination, and 2) top executives taking responsibility for the initiation and administration of these new systems. In business organization, decentralized units are merged into product groups. In addition, there are formal planning procedures, intensive reviews, larger staffs and centralized services to carry out the coordinated effort. This fits with the rational and orderly format of the role orientation.

Nonbusiness organizations, such as hospitals, universities, and similar institutions made up of people drawn together from and for a variety of roles, may be role-oriented from the beginning, although some entrepreneurial person starts such an organization and exerts a significant influence over it. Some business organizations are role-oriented from the beginning, e.g., accounting firms, banks, utilities.

A role organization is usually administered rather than commanded or directed. Whoever heads such an organization, characteristically, has not founded it or given it its basic function or its original functional activities. These usually have derived from the service to be performed. Such a leader presides over a body of rules and a set of roles directed to the performance of a service or a social role. His task is to see that the rules of role performance are followed. The hospital director who must maintain the hospital's accreditation and legal responsibility is an example. The unwritten motto of such an orientation is, "Follow the rules." There may be a compelling quality about joining a role-oriented organization. This may derive in part from whatever dependency there may be in the people so employed, in part because of the limited sites in which one can perform a professional role, and in part because of specialization. People who are nurses or biologists or professors of archaeology usually require organizational settings for their work.

The compelling quality of the role organizations tend to proliferate in the form of many rules and regulations, on the one hand, and multiple role obligations, on the other. For example, the members of a hospital staff are compelled not only by the value system of the hospital but also by the demands, ethical and professional, of the respective roles. Physicians, nurses, and aides have certain well-defined tasks which can be done only in that setting. In the power-oriented organization the compulsion is more in the exercise of someone else's power over one, or at times of environmental forces, while in the role-oriented organization it is more in terms of assuming certain types of roles and the social obligations that go with them.

The role-oriented organization is similarly pyramidal, except that the role demands may be more qualified and have greater stability because of their origin in ethical, professional, or occupational standards outside the organization. By both law and the standards of their professions, a nurse, an engineer, and an accountant can do only certain kinds of things and not others, no matter what a superior says.

Given such well-defined roles and social obligations, one trusts the system. There are rules and regulations governing both the roles and their interrelationships and the service or activity which is supposed to derive from the practice of those roles. Institutions frequently have formal obligations to those who are in certain roles, as in the tenure system in colleges and the ratio of personnel to patients in hospitals. In such settings there are also formal professional routes of appeal and modes by which the role holders in formal associations exert influence on the organization.

The goal is the activity itself, whether patient care or technical performance of another kind. The outcome of the service of the function is the purpose, e.g., to conserve funds, to advance education. The mode of communication tends to be formal, often in the third person in written communications, and in language that is best described as abstract-professionalese. Such language is typically found in letters from federal officials. The communication of one professional to another in the form of certain kinds of memos, and particularly communication across disciplines, tends to have a certain formality about the way it is done. As in the power-oriented organization, because there is considerable difference in the power wielded by people in different roles, there tends to be considerable negative conformity, and other hostile acts. As a result, in both forms of organization structure, there is a powerful informal communications network through which the work actually gets done. The greater the disparity between the informal structure and the formal structure, the more the organization is undermined.

Power tends to be allocated by function and the social importance of the function, as well as functional responsibility. In a hospital a physician has more power than a nurse because he has greater knowledge and legal responsibility. Within a given function or service, power may be exercised much as it is in power-oriented organizations or by bureaucratic administrators. However, in the role-oriented organization the professions' roles, ethics, and codes of conduct dominate so long as these are supplemented by idiosyncratic rules for a given institution, formulated by a board or by a manager on behalf of a board. Also, there are usually avenues of appeal from the arbitrary exercise of power.

The role-organization usually meets ministration needs and, depending on the role, also maturation and mastery needs. That is, people have the opportunity to grow within their roles and to become highly skilled professionals in their areas. Certainly the role-oriented organization meets physiological and safety needs, but needs for social relationships and love tend to be met within a given discipline, except where disciplines may operate on a team basis in which case they tend to move towards a task orientation.

Dependency needs are gratified largely by formal professional role performance, which in turn depends upon a repertoire of professional behaviors allocated to that role, as well as on the general guidance and integration which the profession's set of rules offers. It is complemented by identification with the institution and dependency on it. The role-oriented organization in turn is heavily dependent on its people for they, rather than machines or financial resources, carry out the functions of the organization. Usually skills are relatively fixed, depending upon the profession or role, but there is some possibility that people may refine and update these skills in on-the-job and professional training programs.

Issues of role conflict, role stress, and role ambiguity are far more pressing in role-oriented organizations than in those that are power-oriented because of the impulsive and arbitrary definition of roles in the latter. The role-orientation makes for dual loyalty to profession and institution, and sometimes conflict results.

In the role-oriented organization the major potential loss is that of professional esteem, whether loss of accreditation, loss of reputation, or loss of regard by one's peers and the supporting community.

The leader is viewed as a servant of those who carry out the roles, and frequently is the first among equals. This is particularly true if he too is a professional. If he is not a professional, but a manager or administrator, then he may not be regarded even as the first among equals. This is the problem of hospital administrators who are not themselves professionals in health care. Such a view of the leader may not hold with equal validity in business organizations, particularly those which identify with a more power-oriented direction and have a more power-oriented structure.

The value system of a role-oriented organization may be tribalistic but also sociocentric. Higher pay is often sacrificed for the social value of the organization and because of its nonprofit orientation. Also, organizations of this kind, which can offer greater security and long-term employment, are likely to do so in lieu of competitive pay scales. Thus, money is important over the long term for its relation to security but is subordinate to identification with the organization and its goal of service.

Affection in such an organization is channelled in two ways: 1) in, on, and through the role, and one's view of one's self in that role; and 2) onto people whom one serves and activities related to that service. Aggression is channelled primarily into work and secondarily into organizational problem solving. The ego ideal revolves significantly around the professional image of the person and the organization. Usually, people in role-oriented organizations will not be able to remain comfortably in such organizations if they do not have high standards and maintain them. Role-oriented organizations are significantly superego-oriented in the sense that one tends to be more conscience-driven or conscience-guided than in many other kinds of organizations.

The ideology of the role-oriented organization is primarily role ideology and the role ethics, together with the overall ideology which has to do with the service the organization renders. That is, what people do occupationally serves as the core of the value system they practice and the rules by which they relate to others. There will be a heavy emphasis on the concept of membership both within an association of people who have similar roles and in the organization.

Superior-subordinate relationships tend to be primarily of a mutually supportive kind inasmuch as it is more difficult to transcend the role boundaries. Within the role structure itself, the person more proficient in role performance is likely to be given more administrative responsibility; but the administrative head of the organization, not being able to relate to the professional roles, and not being proficient in them, is more dependent on role performers for organizational achievement and attainment of organizational goals, and they, in turn, are dependent on him for financial support, support services, budgeting, and similar managerial activities. Under such circumstances there is often grudging tolerance of the administrator and the tendency to depreciate his importance. Professional people often feel grudgingly accepted by the leadership, as if the leader is rivalrous with them and resents their role-derived power. One sees this phenomenon frequently both in college faculties and in hospitals.

Planning is frequently limited and often to such things as buildings and anticipated statistics, like numbers of students enrolled and numbers of beds required or patients discharged or dollars paid out in benefits. Rarely is planning focused around the conceptual development of the organization, which is one of the reasons such organizations find themselves obsolete, as frequently schools and universities do. Medical services, for instance, are no longer determined by hospitals but by lay committees in behalf of states and areas, and the service functions which used to be offered by banks increasingly were taken over by credit card companies and similar organizations. As Harrison has pointed out, such organizations do not manage the change process well.

The superego orientation, resulting in greater attention to role performance than in relationship to the outside world, more often has a Florence Nightingale or Horace Mann type of myth to typify its person-to-person service orientation. Not long ago, newspaper and magazine ads trumpeted the insurance agent as a financial advisor. However, the fact that such agents were paid to sell—and to sell certain kinds of policies—and that what they had to offer was limited to the offerings of the organizations they represented, undermined the attempt to define that role as part of a role-oriented organization. The heavy-power orientation, with its emphasis on money, simply did not fit the role-orientation.

Morality is usually built around the ethics of the respective professions and the ethical reputation of the institutions for whom and in whom the roles are performed. Thus, morality may well have to do with the freedom of ideas and the preservation of life. A typical moral conflict arises for doctors and nurses who are trying to preserve life when issues of abortion and euthanasia arise.

In the role-oriented organization with its heavy emphasis on function, controls are significantly part of professional role requirements, as well as institutional role requirements. Frequently there are also the requirements of governmental or accrediting bodies or both. Such controls are relatively independent of those in authority, as contrasted with the power-oriented organization, and sometimes are even more powerful than the established role norms. Thus, for example, physicians are now required to be reviewed by Professional Service Review organizations. Often, as in the power-oriented organization, the usual accounting and inventory controls are also necessary and these tend to be formulated by managerial staff who, as adults, frequently decide how the professional role is to be practiced by their allocation of funds and controls over spending.

As contrasted with the power-oriented organization, there tends to be greater attention to social responsibility, although in some service organizations this may merely be a mask for rationalizing personal gain, as in the previous example of the insurance companies or in some medical institutions run for private profit. The primary focus of competitive effort is the problem to be solved. Death or disease is the enemy to be vanquished by a hospital staff. Such organizations also compete with similar institutions but unless one is dealing with a company which is competing for a share of the market, the essential orientation is service and solving problems for people.

Here too there are subtleties which must be examined. For example, churches, which presumably render service, often covertly compete for parishioners and funds. Colleges and universities must certainly compete with other such institutions. There is also competition for power, but this competition tends to be masked behind service rationalizations and is less acceptable than it is in power-oriented organizations. The acquisition of power does not necessarily carry with it greater return in personal or organizational wealth. More often it has to do with the influence of a given discipline or orientation within the institution.

The implied motivational assumption in such an organization is that of the professional person striving to meet a professional ego ideal. Sometimes that assumption is in conflict with reality. An example of this is when a noted surgeon, a member of a medical association committee sent to study medicine in China, returns with the observation that he would not have believed such good medical and surgical care could have been rendered to people without a profit motive. This conflict between power-orientation and role-orientation has been extremely disruptive to medical practice in the United States and has caused physicians to lose both public esteem and the freedom to make major power decisions about health care.

The inability of the role-oriented organization to respond to change because of its structure is compounded even more by what Greiner calls the red tape crisis. The proliferation of systems, programs and controls makes the organization increasingly sluggish, increasingly bound internally and, in effect, psychologically constipated. Conflicts arise between line and staff in business organizations and between administrators and professionals in others. In Greiner's words, both groups criticize the bureaucratic paper system where procedures take precedence over problems and innovation is dampened. This then creates the conditions for Phase 5 collaboration.

TASK-ORIENTED ORGANIZATION

The task-oriented organization's greatest strength is dealing with conflicts in changing environments. Its flexible use of temporary systems for emergency problem-solving denotes that the task force leader was selected for his combination of technical expertise and ability to manage a small group in an egalitarian manner. According to Greiner's Phase 5, the task-oriented organization emphasizes greater spontaneity in management action through teams and the skillful confrontation of interpersonal differences. The focus, he says, is on solving problems quickly through team action, with teams usually combined in a matrix type structure across functions supported, but not directed, by staff services. Thus, characteristically, a task-oriented organization is managed. That is, someone has to mobilize the resources, organize them, allocate them, and guide their use. The manager is not an entrepreneur nor is he mainly an administrator. The central theme for such an organization is, "Let's lick the problem."

There is a shift from centripetal forces to centrifugal forces. That is, there are tasks to be accomplished and teams are organized around tasks. The core of the organization is the attraction of people to the tasks, rather than compelling power or role performance requirements. Further, energies are directed less to controlling and policing people, to reinforcing roles and rules, and more to the interchange of task roles. Energies tend to be more outwardly directed, as it were, rather than inwardly directed.

Such a differentiation may be seen among different units of the same organizations. For example, those employees of a petroleum company who are scattered in different parts of the world and have the immediate task demands of finding oil tend to be far more preoccupied with that task than with what goes on in the organizational structure back home. Furthermore, they are less rigidly controlled and directed and more mutually supportive.

There is a great deal more flexibility in the task-oriented organization because the roles may not necessarily be so uniquely qualified and defined. Roles may be interchangeable, depending on competence, information or skill. When tasks are imposed on a role organization which require mobilization of task forces or teams of people who readily can be assigned to and discharged from tasks, then a matrix organization arises. People may be based in functional units, but carry out activities in groups or teams organized around cadres of managers. To illustrate, an engineering construction company constructing a refinery in Egypt may be also building a pipeline in Norway and a subway in Montreal. Other projects may evolve requiring the services of some of those who are presently on these projects. Later they may go somewhere else, bringing their specialties with them from one task to another. However, as Greiner points out, such an orientation is especially difficult for those who identify with power or role orientations. Furthermore, as Harrison notes, the matrix system often suffers from attempts of the role-oriented functions to overcontrol the task-oriented functions. The resulting conflict is usually won by the former, which has greater permanence and resources. Thus, he observes, role-oriented people cannot be plugged into a task-oriented system without conflict. The dual loyalty issue raises its head, especially if the loyalty to task accomplishment or to the leader is not adequately internalized. The matrix organization, thus, is not necessarily a panacea and not without its problems.

While there is less compulsion, either from a formal structure or from roles, greater attention must be given to creating integrative devices or psychological bonds in both the task-oriented and person-oriented organizations. The greater the differentiation of role and task, the more difficult the integrative task and the more complex the leadership role. That is, the more specialized people are, the less readily they can shift into egalitarian and complementary activities and the more difficult it will be to make a task force out of them and to maintain their cohesion.

Greiner points out that social control and self-discipline in a collaborative organization take over from formal control. One implication is that people in such an organization have to trust each other. In a team of people with different skills and competences, one has to take for granted that the skill and competence is valid until demonstrated otherwise. If a shift in role is necessary, a basic trust in the initiative and complementary support of the other is required. Thus, goal and purpose are essentially identical with the task accomplishment and serve as the basis for group cohesion. Task accomplishment is the end-all for which the team exists. That end must therefore have psychological meaning for all of the team members.

Communication is around problems to be solved and it tends to be both inter-disciplinary and intrateam. Of course, there needs to be considerable bridging effort by persons who are familiar with the range of disciplines involved on the team. Power is shifted according to what may be needed at any given time to accomplish the task. In a matrix organization it may be managed collectively. The leader of such an organization is in effect a chairman who has the delegated authority his group gives him in addition to that which his superiors allocate by charging him with task accomplishment.

The rules are limited largely to disciplinary requirements of each of the team members and the overall design of the project, if there is a design. Beyond that and budget requirements, anything is possible if it helps get the job done. A task-oriented organization may meet ministration, maturation, and mastery needs in relatively equal proportions, as contrasted with the dominance of ministration need fulfillment in the role organization, and even more so in the power organization.

There tends to be flexible interchange of skills to the extent to which specialization is not required. In such an organization one depends heavily on one's own skill, on the outcome of the collective effort, and on the achievement, so that there is a great deal of interdependence among the members of the task force. Nevertheless, as Harrison notes, the task-oriented organization may exploit the individual because he is expected to step aside when he is no longer necessary or when someone else is more qualified. Status and recognition depend almost entirely on contribution to the task. An adaptive orientation is necessary which may make an individual who was valued under one set of circumstances lose both his financial advantage and work satisfaction.

Depending on the nature of the organization, money may be quite incidental to the task at hand, as for example, a task force within an organization or one created to deal with an emergency on behalf of an organization. However, with heavy emphasis on expedient accomplishment by a temporary team (e.g., the construction of the Alaska pipeline or military bases in distant countries), money in significant amounts would be a major attraction to compensate for the predictable gaps in employment. In such instances it is frequently used on an incentive basis as a device to facilitate task accomplishment in a minimum of time. It might be said that the stronger the identification with the task accomplishment and the goal, the less likely money need be used as an incentive.

The greatest potential loss in a task-oriented organization is the failure to accomplish the task—the inability to win, as it were. The petroleum exploration team which again and again drills dry holes becomes demoralized. A team building a nuclear power generating station which runs into repetitive delays and technical problems will begin to lose its momentum. Sometimes the loss of the leader, if he is a key factor in integration, could be the critical loss. In such an organization the leader is generally its captain. He is simultaneously a protector and a supporter and often rides herd on the operation. Rarely is he an entrepreneur or a chairman.

The value system is likely to be tribalistic, sociocentric, egocentric, and also existential to a certain extent. Which of these views is dominant will depend on the nature of the task to be accomplished. Each conceivably could be under certain circumstances. The degree to which egocentric value system behavior holds is the degree to which money will be important as a motivator.

Affection is significantly directed to one's fellows and peers as well as to the goal, and aggression mainly to task accomplishment. Aggression diverted from task accomplishment usually reverberates throughout the task force or diverts energies to noncontributory activities. The ego ideal revolves around winning and mastering the problem as well as the technical proficiency one contributes to that mastery. The ideology has to do largely with the collective good of the team in its task mastery. If compensation is based on team accomplishment, it has even more motivating power.

In an organization where there is free exchange of support and information, there is also a recognized need for the leader, and how much he is esteemed depends on his competence as an integrating force which moves the team towards accomplishment. The participants feel that they are needed by the leader and by each other. They share a mutual need with the leader, namely victory.

Despite its flexibility, the task organization often operates by well-defined plans, even to the point of blueprints. Frequently, also, it develops step-by-step processes, as for example PERT charts and other management devices for task accomplishment. It frequently operates on a well-defined schedule also, where the outcome is a product or structure.

The myth of the task-oriented organization, especially with a good leader, is one of being champions and solvers of social problems or creators of the technical necessities of an industrial world. Those who invented the atomic bomb or evolved the space flights saw themselves as an elite group at the frontiers of science and the future.

Given the freedom they have and the importance of the task, inevitably those associated with it must feel themselves to have an elite status. During wartime, crews of bombers or naval vessels who spent long hours within the confines of their crafts disregarded rank and status and operated on an egalitarian basis. They gave unique names to their vehicles and kept score of their victories. Legends grew up around such crews and in some cases motion pictures were made of their adventures. In World War II, General Patton achieved notoriety by breaking the formal military rules and roles and turning his army into a major task force, expelling those who could not or would not operate that way.

The morality of such an organization has as its foundation stone the concept that ends justify the means. Often people engaged in such tasks do not think of the consequences. This, for example, is what happened after the atomic bomb was created in the Manhattan Project. Only later were there reactive feelings on the part of those who had constructed the bomb.

Time limits, money limits, and limits of persons and material, as well as the strictures of design or task requirements serve as the boundaries for behavior in the task-oriented organization. Often there are subsidiary disciplinary boundaries with their own requirements as well. This is especially true if some of the participants in the task are members of unions. However, the ethos is task responsibility and competition is directed to the task to be finished and mastered. Such an organization assumes a social man willing to share with others in a common task.

Although the task-oriented organization may well grow out of a previous stage as a role-oriented organization or be a temporary device used by a power-oriented organization, it may also arise spontaneously out of a specific need, such as the Manhattan Project or NASA. A task-oriented organization can ultimately be frozen into a role-oriented organization once its task is accomplished and the subsidiary or secondary task is that of continued management of the project. Usually such an organization, now dominated by those in functional roles, loses some of the innovative momentum it had as a task-oriented organization and acquires some of the psycho-social limits of the role-oriented organization. Greiner notes that sometimes people involved in such task forces acquire "psychological saturation" and are additionally physically exhausted by the intensity of the work and the heavy pressure for innovative solutions.

PERSON-ORIENTED ORGANIZATION

In Harrison's terminology, the person-oriented organization is used as a tool by those who are in it as contrasted to their being used an instruments for higher authority or higher purpose.

Despite this self-centeredness, leadership is a critical issue, for such an organization is led rather than commanded, administered, or managed. The leader of a person-oriented organization must create conditions where he himself is his basic instrument for leadership, for he cannot command nor does he have the structure to control. He usually does not have either functional role definitions to police or tasks around which to organize. He himself must therefore be the psychological glue which holds the organization together and gives it that kind of direction which in turn gives meaning to the work of those who are part of it. While this issue may be less important for a group of artists gathered to display and sell their paintings than for a research laboratory whose task it is to develop new products or solve basic technical problems, to the extent to which there are fixed internal demands to be met by the organization, whether in a larger organization or with respect to the outside world, leadership is of critical importance.

There may be elements of each of the styles of leadership I have mentioned so far in organizations that have different basic orientations and are led predominantly with a different style. These styles are not necessarily mutually exclusive any more than individual people, despite their vast individual differences, are totally different from everybody else. Power-oriented leaders may at times defer to those with technical expertise. On the other hand, administrators of role-oriented organizations and managers of task-oriented organizations may at times resort to power methods.

In the person-oriented organization, the central theme is "innovate." Centrifugal forces proliferate in this kind of organization because there are many individual and different self-demands. Researchers, artists, and writers, for instance, may be going in different individual directions, thus making it more difficult to integrate and to guide them. Often such an organization will tend to have some form of matrix structure, but the structure will vary considerably with the people and with the task. Some people will function alone, some perhaps in small groups, and some in more stable teams. Thus, the person-oriented organization can approach a task-oriented one, depending on how much freedom people within the organization have to move from one task to another, including self-directed tasks.

In such an organization trust is placed in the leader but in a different way than in a power-oriented organization. An organization member must believe the leader has an understanding of what he is trying to do and that the leader will support that activity. He must also trust that the leader will integrate what he is doing with what others are doing and that he will protect the group from external influences, as well as internal differences and conflicts. This is frequently the function of a head of a research laboratory, for example.

There is a heavier element of voluntary commitment to the leader in person-oriented organizations. That voluntary commitment, of course, implies that there is also a greater capacity for withdrawal. If the particular person-oriented organization does have some collective purpose, as often such laboratories do, then those who are in it usually must have some commitment to their collective purpose, even if they have a broad range of freedom within which to approach it. A physicist, for example, in a corporate research laboratory may have a wide range of freedom to approach product innovation, but usually he is not free to undertake basic research—though sometimes such a distinction does not make a significant difference. However, in such an organization, the achievement of some kind of creative or innovative end is intended. Sometimes the creative or innovative end may also be a service function orientation, as in the contribution of research institutions to the resolution of social problems.

In the more diffused organization, geared to innovation, the communication will tend to be diffused because of the limitations of formal structure and even of informal structure. Since people tend to work in a more autonomous fashion, perhaps even unrelated to one another at the levels at which they are operating, the problems of leadership proliferate because the leader must devote much of his time and effort within the organization to sustain continued communication. However, with respect to political decisions in the structure, there may tend to be more open sanction for political alliances and coalitions among members of the organization because consensus is more important in collective purpose. At times such communication may be more angry and militant than in the structures which are oriented to power, role, and task. With greater functional freedom usually goes greater freedom for emotional expression, including anger.

In such an organization the group may evolve its own rules for cohesive effort, although it may also be partially governed by the rules of the respective disciplines and modes of professional, scientific, or other creative behavior.

In the person-oriented organization, mastery needs are met primarily, and ministration and maturation needs probably less so, unless there are people in apprenticeship positions within such an organization. The organization may provide certain kinds of logistical support and protection against illness and loss of income for individuals, but by and large they tend to operate as competent authorities with their own skills. Seen in another way, Maslow's self-actualization needs would be more likely to be met in a person-oriented organization, perhaps somewhat less in a task-oriented organization, but with a heavier emphasis in the latter on social needs and love.

Skills are idiosyncratic in the person-oriented organization, and people are free to use them, develop new ones, and abandon old ones. They may even shift their disciplinary orientation. Frequently one finds researchers becoming masters of two different disciplines as they find their research problems crossing disciplinary lines and requiring multidisciplinary skills. It is not unusual, for example, to hear someone say, "I started out as a biologist, but I don't know what I would be called now." Role conflict, role definition, and role ambiguity take on correspondingly less importance than in power-oriented and role-oriented organizations. A major task of the person-oriented organization is continuously to recreate the standards and ethics of the organization as it encounters new problems in evolving new modes of behavior, action, research, or new basic information. A contemporary issue of that kind involves ethics in research on human beings and implications in research on creating life.

In the person-oriented organization one depends most heavily on oneself. In fact, there are likely to be many counterdependent people in a person-oriented organization. When one leans most heavily on one's own ideals and creativity, one must necessarily have a tolerance for ambiguity strong enough to allow ideas to flow. Frequently dependency needs can be met in laboratories or other kinds of organizations which are part of larger organizations oriented in a different way. For example, a power-oriented organization might have provisions for tenure, seniority, pensions, and so on which would be equally available to those who might be in a person-oriented component. Indeed, it is often the freedom from being concerned about personal financial security that enables some people to be more innovative. Scholarships and grants for the support of individuals such as artists, writers, composers, and others testify to this necessity.

In this kind of organization, the most significant loss is likely to be the failure of the person to create, innovate, discover, or whatever the organizational charge may be. Failure, then, is extremely personal. Although, to a lesser extent, the failure to accomplish the task may be felt very personally in the task-oriented organization, there is no question about personal responsibility. In such an organization the major guide is one's personal ego ideal, what one expects of oneself.

The leader in this kind of organization, as already noted, is viewed more as an integrator, a quarterback, a provider, and a person who, in an avuncular, supportive way, brings people together, eases conflict, and creates conditions under which creativity can flower with a minimum of interference. The value system orientation is primarily existential and secondarily egocentric. Money for such people will often carry the connotation of public recognition of creative genius and, for many, will assure continued security when their creative impetus wanes.

Aggression and affection are largely directed to the service of the ego ideal. Energies are invested primarily in creative accomplishment. However, there may also be a great degree of affection narcissistically invested in the individuals themselves, as is required in order to be able to trust that one will evolve creative ideas. Reaching for a high ego ideal, such people often need great support for their self-images, particularly in the absence of success over an extended period of time. They have no support themselves psychologically in a self-centered fashion, which often makes others feel that they are temperamental and insensitive to their relationships with others. Leaders of such groups frequently need a great deal of tolerance and patience and must do much hand-holding. The product of personal creativity is the end to be attained.

With greater social good as the basis for the ideology of such an organization, the people usually see what they are doing both as a contribution to the civilizing aspects of society and as a new way of viewing phenomena or solving problems. Property is usually not an issue except for copyright and patent issues, and frequently the organization may seem to others to be anarchic because of its lack of concern for material values. For example, some corporate presidents became angry with the staffs of their research laboratories who seemed to feel that they should continue to follow their own noses regardless of what it will cost the organization as a whole. Many researchers operating under grants have asserted that research should be supported for science's sake because ultimately that is what is important to society.

In the person-oriented organization, the relationships among people are for the most part ad lib and ad hoc. The leader will lead by affirmation or, in effect, by the permission of the followers and is viewed both as their instrument and as the nexus of their collective effort. Leadership is frequently regarded with great ambivalence; nevertheless it is required and is less readily replaceable than in the task-oriented organization.

There tends to be little planning in people-oriented organizations unless the organization is a research laboratory dependent on others for research contracts and therefore must shift its focus and orientation with changing trends in its field or with the need to support itself. Harrison notes that these organizations are less likely than organizations based on other ideologies to be effective in a changing external environment because it is difficult for the members of such organizations to act in unison. On the other hand, they do have the advantage of commitment.

Initially, the dominant myth in these organizations has to do with creativity. This mythology frequently reflects itself in the temperamental qualities that sometimes are found in such settings because such people often assume that they have a divine right to be temperamental, that such freedom of temperament is necessary for creativity, and that other people should let them get away with impulsive behavior. Such a myth usually fades in organizations which are more than temporary. In advertising agencies, for example, the brash impulsiveness of some creative people is sometimes very upsetting to a more formal structure and frequently is destructive to the rest of the organization. The leadership fears that to interfere with such behavior, to exert controls normally expected of other people, will hamper creativity. However, when the leader learns not to accept such a myth, creative people manage to be creative without also being destructive to others.

There is also a certain amorality in such organizations, as people tend to go their respective ways and are less bound by group standards. Controls tend to be loose and may be limited to simple financial controls or those broadly defining the area in which the organization focuses its efforts. The ethos is individualism tempered by the concept of giving some kind of creative gift to society. The competition usually is directed to the problem to be solved by the innovative or creative contribution, but sometimes it is directed toward others in the field who are to be shown up. The person-oriented organization assumes psychological man striving independently to meet the demands of his own ego ideal.

Given the movement of some organizations in the direction of task orientation and person orientation and the evolution of other organizations that are directed from the beginning toward either one of those two orientations, many people are likely to be required to make a greater investment in their work. Greiner suggests that new structures and programs will be required which will allow employees to rest periodically and revitalize themselves. He speculates that companies will develop dual organizational structures: a "habit" structure for getting daily work done, and a "reflective" structure for stimulating perspective and personal enrichment. People could move back and forth between these two structures as they may need to do so.

Compensation for person- and task-oriented groups may well move in the direction of the time span of responsibility concept proposed by Elliott Jaques (1956) and Wilfred Brown (1972) as it becomes increasingly difficult to gauge individual salaries on the basis of fixed standards more appropriate to power- or role-oriented organizations. In order to evolve more effective modes of compensation, more of the appraisal process will have to be carried on by peers. One research-consultant firm already does this informally by allowing project leaders to choose their own team members. Those who remain consecutively or frequently unchosen not only get paid less but quickly get the message and look elsewhere for employment.

CONCLUSIONS AND OBSERVATIONS

All of these dimensions of organizational character, while seemingly pedantic differentiations, nevertheless help us see the many-faceted themes of an organization. It is imperative that one recognize these dimensions as organizations change, or as one is involved in changing organizations because, to the degree to which entire configurations are not changed to new equilibria, the organizational change process and outcome will be laden with conflict.

As George Lodge points out, businessmen operating primarily power-oriented organizations are experiencing an erosion of old values without being fully aware of it (Lodge, 1970). Since an ideology is the connective tissue of an organization, he notes, organizations as a consequence are beginning to come apart at the seams. He outlines five elements of ideology which are eroding. The first of these is the concept of individualism. He notes that individualism is yielding to individual fulfillment through participation in an organic process. The second, property rights, is giving way to rights of membership in the organization, that is, the right of employees to survive, enjoy income, health, and other rights associated with citizenship. Furthermore, shareholders do not really have an effective property right influence on the corporations in which they presumably hold ownership so the concept no longer means what it was originally intended to mean. Third, the idea of open competition is yielding to the community need to satisfy consumer desires. Fourth, the concept of the limited state, that government which governs least is best, is yielding to the inevitably expanding role of government as it becomes the "setter of our sights and the arbiter of community needs." Fifth, scientific specialization and fragmentation is now giving way to the required perception of whole systems, not merely the parts. These changes are crucial because values are what people live and die for; what people appreciate. They are the basis for people's perceptions of their environment and, therefore, for their actions.

Such a shift in values means inevitably that the power-oriented organization is not likely to be continued in its historic mode, the pyramidal structure, even when, pressured by role demands, it shifts to a predominantly role-oriented organization. Increasingly, organizations become configurations of resources which may be used in many different ways. They are not limited to single product lines or to continuing in the same service directions. They must be ready to change with changing market circumstances.

Furthermore, although the country needs entrepreneurs to start organizations, it increasingly will be unable to afford to let entrepreneurs abuse their organizations by not being able to develop successors. Left to their own devices, entrepreneurs will build dependent organizations and will have inadequate succession. The cost to employees, society, stockholders, and financing agencies becomes increasingly high when organizations fail. We have seen from recent events that the federal government cannot let major businesses fail because they upset the whole national economy.

There is a tendency for power-oriented organizations to become role organizations in the second generation. When the powerful figure is gone, those who are left behind tend to form alliances and sub-empires. Such a charismatic leader inevitably makes others fearful of his power, and when he is gone they will bureaucratize the organization by creating a set of rules that govern relationships; a form of Magna Carta for an incoming president who may then be limited to being an administrator. Of course, the more an organization is bureaucratized, the more it is paralyzed, and ultimately it must move from the bureaucratic or role-oriented structure to a task orientation. In some cases that may mean a matrix organization; in other cases it may mean decentralization into task groups. The more diversified the organization, the greater the demand for managers.

This problem in seen particularly in large banks, many of which were started by charismatic leaders. These leaders were followed inevitably by weaker leaders who were promptly outflanked by organizations offering many innovative techniques such as credit cards and other ways of handling money. In response, they recruited young business school graduates who were well-trained technical specialists and could handle loans and other technical aspects of money. The banks then began to expand in many different directions, and the more they expanded the more they needed managers who were not the same people who were expert at lending and manipulating money. A number of large banks are presently in the bind of having many knowledgeable technical specialists but too few managers for their diversification. The greater the differentiation of the marketplace, the more the organization is required to be decentralized, calling either for a matrix organization or one broken down into smaller units. In either case, the greater the number of substructures, the greater the need for management and less for administration.

When the marketplace becomes sufficiently differentiated that it accelerates the need for new products to stay ahead of proliferating competition, greater innovation is required. Products become obsolete quickly, patents run out, techniques that are the property of a given organization may become the property of others, so that competitive advantage depends heavily on continuous innovation. That in turn calls for a more person-oriented organization that can innovate. Organizations which have not developed people who can act managerially, relatively independently, or innovatively are then at a very painful disadvantage.

One can see a pattern of organizations as they move from power orientation to role orientation to task orientation and closer to person orientation. Some organizations will never move from a power orientation, and others will perhaps not stray far from a role orientation. Still others may stop at matrix or task orientation and some may move on to more creative activity. An organization may differentiate itself so that some components remain power-oriented, as in a manufacturing assembly line, some aspects of it may be role-oriented, as in staff functions for that manufacturing process, some components may be task-oriented for resolving special problems and some, like a research department, may be person-oriented.

One can look at this another way, namely, to see the direction in which organizations as a whole are going. In this country, with the proliferation of smaller units which devote themselves to the development of highly technical products, as happened in the electronics industry, we probably will see a more rapid growth of person-oriented organizations.

It is necessary to observe that this way of looking at what happens to organizations and their continuity is gross oversimplification. No doubt there is much overlap among these various organizational characters and there are many aspects of organizational character which neither Harrison nor I have touched on at all. In time, perhaps, we will learn to define organizational character in a much more accurate and vivid way. There are problems, however, in moving from one organization structure to another and in changing an organization's character, because one has to do more than change structure. One has to change values, needs, satisfactions, compensation modes, and all the other requirements touched on above. One is essentially changing networks or configurations of forces. One also changes the balance of trust, as can be seen from what I have already outlined. In the power-oriented organization, one presumably trusts the boss. In the role-oriented organization, one trusts the rules, and one may not feel very comfortable about that unless he has had considerable experience with rules. In the power-oriented organization, one will have learned how to play the game of getting along; but the rules are different in a role-oriented organization, and they certainly are significantly different in a task organization. People in a task organization certainly cannot be promised a job for life, nor can they resolve the task by some set of rules. The only trust lies in trusting one's own skills and the integrity of the next person. The closer one moves toward a person-oriented organization, the heavier the emphasis on the leadership and the more people must be able to trust the leader.

Each of these turns and twists in organizational evolution gives a different meaning to money as a motivator. To fully examine its meaning, a given set of organizational circumstances must be defined, and the configurations described here must be analyzed together with a weighing of the multiple components. A regression equation for doing so may yet be evolved.

REFERENCES

Brown, Wilfred. *The Earnings Conflict*. London: Heinemann, 1972.

Graves, Clare. Levels of Existence: An Open System Theory of Values. *Journal of Humanistic Psychology*, **10 (2)**: 131-155, Fall, 1970.

Greiner, Larry E. Evolution and Revolution as Organizations Grow. *Harvard Business Review*, **50 (4)**: 37-46, July-August, 1972.

Harrison, Roger. Understanding your Organization's Character. *Harvard Business Review*, **50 (3)**: 119-129, May-June, 1972.

Hughes, Charles S. and Vincent S. Flowers. Shaping Personnel Strategies to Disparate Value Systems. *Personnel*, **50 (2)**: 8-23, March-April, 1973.

Jaques, Elliott. *Measurement of Responsibility*. Cambridge, Mass.: Harvard, 1956.

Lawrence, Paul R. and Jay W. Lorsch. *Organization and Environment*. Boston: Harvard Business School, 1967.

Levinson, Harry, Charlton R. Price, Kenneth J. Munden, Harold J. Mandl and Charles M. Solley. *Men, Management and Mental Health*. Cambridge, Mass.: Harvard, 1962.

Levinson, Harry. *The Exceptional Executive*. Cambridge, Mass.: Harvard, 1968.

Levinson, Harry. *The Great Jackass Fallacy*. Cambridge, Mass.: Harvard, 1973.

Litwin, George H. and R. A. Stringer, Jr. *Motivation and Organizational Climate*. Boston: Harvard Business School, 1968.

Lodge, George C. Top Priority: Renovating Our Ideology. *Harvard Business Review*, **48 (5)**: 43-55, September-October, 1970.

Lodge, George C. Business and the Changing Society. *Harvard Business Review*, **52 (2)**: 59-72, March-April, 1974.

Maslow, Abraham H. *Motivation and Personality*. New York: Harper & Row, 1954.

Roethlisberger, F. J. and W. J. Dickson. *Management and the Worker*. Cambridge, Mass.: Harvard, 1939.

PART VI

Personal Adjustment—Coping, Feeling and Being;
Where are the Satisfactions?

One underlying tenet of the original studies was that what happened to the worker outside the work place affected how he performed while at work. With this idea in mind, detailed information was collected on many aspects of the worker's personal life. More recently, attention has been directed in the other direction. This reversed viewpoint suggests that what happens to the person while at work greatly affects his or her family, social and political life and may lead one to drug/alcohol dependency, psychosomatic ailments, etc.

The following presentations involve consideration of the causability relationship between personal adjustment and mental health, on the one hand, and the job, social and organizational factors in the work environment, on the other.

11

OCCUPATIONAL STRESSORS

Alan McLean

New York Hospital-Cornell Medical Center

INTRODUCTION

The principal work of this chapter is to assess the relationship between job stressors and the individual worker. More specifically, it is an assessment of the individual who reacts to something in his or her job setting with disability; in particular with mental disorder. What are these symptom-producing events? In what contexts are they most apt to produce symptoms? What seems to sensitize the individual and make him or her more susceptible?

A brief review of the historical meaning of work will provide a frame of reference from which to address these complex issues. Next, a consideration of the contributions from the Hawthorne research will provide a better understanding of adaptation to work. Then, as a frame of reference, a mechanism will be presented through which stressors produce symptoms. Once some specific stressors are described, it would seem worthwhile to conclude with some recommendations on how individuals can better cope and how work organizations can better assist in that coping process.

WORK

Many have pointed out that the most primitive societies knew no word for work; that there was no distinction between work and nonwork, between labor and leisure.

But by the time of Grecian civilization, a separation between "work" and "life" had evolved (Mosse, 1969). Leisure and idleness were goals to which every gentleman aspired and "labor . . . appeared as a sentence to which no redeeming value was attached."

During the Middle Ages work regained a measure of respectability. It became fully honorable and even a "gateway to spirituality." Paul's stern admonition, "If any would not work, neither should he eat," was interpreted by Thomas Aquinas as meaning exactly that.

Protestantism fostered the development of capitalism (Jenkins, 1973) "through its benevolent view of commercial activity in general and the money-making side of it in particular. Catholicism previously had taken (officially at least) a dim view of excessive profit."

Martin Luther increasingly leaned toward the opinion that worldly duties were a necessity in the eyes of God, thus coming even closer to an outright commercial opinion. Building on the base created by Luther, Calvin added a vital link: asceticism. With this key connection, work *and* money-making could be made fully legitimate—as long as you were careful not to enjoy either.

These Calvinist-capitalist ideas of work were most convenient for the leaders of the Industrial Revolution in England in the late 18th century (Jenkins, 1973). For the first time the worker became one small, relatively insignificant facet in a mechanical complex. There was no freedom of movement in the planned production process. As Adam Smith commented, "The man whose life is spent in performing a few simple operations . . . has no occasion to exert his understanding or to exercise his invention in finding out expedients for removing difficulties which never occur . . . and generally becomes as stupid and ignorant as it is possible for a human creature to become." "And all the nobler parts of the human character may be, in a great measure, obliterated and extinguished in the great body of the people."

David Jenkins, however, disagreed with Adam Smith; "It was not at that early stage of industrial capitalism that the worker became 'stupid and ignorant.' A subsequent step would not only bring work closer to being a punishment but would call forth even greater resources of stupidity and ignorance. This invention was to be known as 'scientific management' and was without a doubt (in Jenkins mind) the most significant method of dehumanizing work ever devised."

The basic concept of Frederick Taylor's scientific management was a single "one best way" for performing every job. This way could be scientifically established and every worker could most efficiently do his job by adhering to this rigid pre-established pattern.

1924

Interestingly enough, Elton Mayo's work at the Western Electric plant at Hawthorne, Illinois was originally designed to refine some of Taylor's concepts. Employee morale was said to be at a low level in 1924 and Mayo wanted to find out why and how improvements could be brought about. Omitting here a description of the years of work and the multitude of conclusions reached, it can be said that Mayo formulated a new interpretation of work in which a job's social aspects were considered to be as important as the physical working conditions; that worker needs for recognition and satisfaction can be decisive, and that informal groups shaped by the workers themselves can be more significant than a formal organization chart. Further, a principle was clearly established that there was a direct connection between job satisfaction (which was largely determined by satisfying social experience) and productivity.

The "human relations" concept of management was thus born. One perhaps should say concepts since there have been many interpretations and refinements of the work at Hawthorne. There were those, for example, who made the interpretation that all one need do is add an element of human kindness to Taylorism, giving employees a feeling of importance (generally quite artificial). One must agree that the uses to which this concept of human relations were put were of questionable merit and doubtful ethical acceptability. Indeed, this might be termed the manipulative school of human relations and many of its naive adherents were seriously disappointed since there seemed an inconsistent relationship between productivity and their manufactured happiness.

A second human relations school or concept was both more sophisticated and more successful. In this case, legitimate work needs (physical, social and psychological) were perceived and met by management. They were identified by techniques that included measurement, observation, participant observation, interviews and questionnaires. For example, employee needs for broader participation in the control of their work were noted. At times the needs were subtle, at times simply met. At times they were complex and only the reasons why they could *not* be met were explained to employees (but they were at least explained). In this frame of reference needs were always seen as legitimate by both the individual and management, and the "happiness doctrine" was ignored. This approach could be called the legitimate human relations school. The ramifications of this set of concepts to behavioral sciences and to management continue today as the soundest approach to the fundamentals of administration.

1974

The growing interest in psychosocial aspects of work received considerable recent stimulus from the release of the conclusions of Secretary Elliott L. Richardson's "Task Force" on *Work in America* in December 1972. With the commercial publication and the widespread distribution of the report months later, reaction seemed to polarize. It was not easy for many reviewers, particularly in management, to accept that the organization of work adversely affects both the mental and physical health of many Americans, which were ideas strongly suggested by Mayo so many years before.

For months the debate flourished. Rekindled were old arguments about job enlargement, job enrichment, team building and the relationship between morale and productivity. Many criticized the report itself. Its sweeping conclusions, they said, could not be supported by much of the material presented; its omissions were grievous.

In the report to the Secretary, considerable attention was focused on issues concerned with the quality of working life in the early 1970s. Although thought by some to be peripheral to the health of workers, others (I among them) felt that aspects of the work environment which encourage healthy behavior or which moderate feelings of anxiety or depression are a very real interest. The *Work in America* authors concluded that improvements in the quality of working life hold out opportunities for avoiding physical and mental illness.

The task force also believed that various aspects of work account for many factors associated with heart disease, hypertension, high cholesterol, elevated blood sugar, etc. Work problems also correlate highly with symptoms of mental disorder (they included low self-esteem but not major mental illness such as schizophrenia).

The task force further observed that, although we are largely ignorant of causal factors, the correlational, case history and anecdotal evidence relating work conditions to both mental and physical health problems are too convincing to dismiss. One of the most interesting findings in this regard is that workers who are motivated by extrinsic rewards such as pay and security are more likely to have heart disease than those motivated by intrinsic rewards such as job challenge and self-actualization.

The summary chapter of the report states, "Because work is central to the lives of so many Americans, either the absence of work or employment in meaningless work is creating an increasingly intolerable situation. The human costs of this state of affairs are manifested in worker alienation, alcoholism, drug addiction and other symptoms of poor mental health. Moreover, much of our tax money is expended in an effort to compensate for problems with at least a part of their genesis in the world of work. A large part of the staggering national bill in areas of crime and delinquency, mental and physical health, manpower and welfare are generated in our national policies and attitude toward work. Likewise, industry is paying for a continued attachment to Tayloristic practices through low worker productivity and high rates of sabotage, absenteeism, and turnover. Unions are paying through the faltering loyalty of a young membership that is increasingly concerned about the occurrent disinterest of its leadership in problems of job satisfaction. Most important, there are high costs of lost opportunities to encourage citizen participation: the discontent of women, minorities, blue collar workers, youth, and older adults would be considerably less were these Americans to have an active role in the decisions in the work place that most directly affect their lives."

Since the report was published (O'Toole, 1974), Secretary Elliot L. Richardson has written that: "The findings of *Work in America* came as a shock to many readers . . . The approaches to meeting these problems that the task force advocated were long-term, indirect, and would impose the need for short-term sacrifice on the parts of management, unions, and school officials, among others. It is easy to see why the report was not universally praised . . . This report is a beginning, not a conclusion."

REACTIONS TO HAWTHORNE AND *WORK IN AMERICA*

In their textbook, *Industrial Sociology*, Miller and Form (1951) summarized the criticism of the work of Mayo and his research group, of which there was a great deal. Daniel Bell, as outspoken in the 1940s as he is today, felt there was a paucity of conclusions drawn from the mass of material collected. He criticized the researchers for simply "psychologizing" rather than testing hypotheses. He and others pointed out that Mayo did not acknowledge the dynamic changes going on in the status of workers in the United States during the period of study.

Mary B. Gilson criticized the report of the Western Electric research for its absence of references to organized labor. She said, "The interviewers who engaged in 'counseling' service subsequent to the interviewing experiment of 1928-31 surely must have had some echoes of dissatisfaction due to a lack of recognition of unions . . . We wonder whether the interviewers have the proper technique for revealing the cause of what Mr. Mayo terms 'futile strife and hatreds.' We are also surprised that in twenty thousand interviews the workers are reported to have criticized the company in no instance."

Much other criticism was leveled. The work was attacked for a pro-management bias and for clinical bias. It was criticized for a lack of theoretical framework as well as its research methodology.

Negative reactions to the *Work in America* study were also numerous and parallels may easily be drawn. The more recent project stimulated several conferences and at least two published volumes of critique. In a paper that criticizes *Work in America* for giving short shrift to the human relations approach to management, with overemphasis on what he considers to be uneconomic job redesign, Howard Hess (1974) bluntly states: "The study tends to turn off business leaders because it is so completely negative. From beginning to end it is a symphony with one theme, work in America stinks . . . A book written hopefully with the expectation of influencing the business community to improve the quality of American jobs has instead tended to make it angry at and hostile toward the social science professionals that produced it."

Along the same line, Michael Kami (1974) commented that "The top corporate viewpoint regarding the subject of work is still, unfortunately distorted and unreal. The larger the corporation, the bigger the isolation of the executive suite from the realities of life. The chief executive is protected from 'problems' by an impressive array of assistants—expensive water boys—and lives in a rarified atmosphere of the ivory tower, often compared to the never-never land of Disney World." He suggested that the study simply did not get to them and was therefore unsuccessful; that volumes such as *Work in America* should clearly demonstrate the relationship between enhanced working conditions and improved productivity, which *Work in America* did not.

Many critics said the evidence described by the task force was insufficient to support the conclusions they reached. This was a common theme in several reviews.

SPECIFIC STRESSORS

The tendency to hold the world of work responsible for enormous emotional discomfort should, I believe, be examined critically. I have no quarrel with the carefully developed standards associated with exposure to noise or the criteria used for safe exposure to toxic substances. I recognize that much remains to be done—and with some urgency—to determine what those substances are and what those criteria should be.

The Hawthorne Studies and the vast body of data which followed and which owe allegiance to them focused on psychosocial issues. *Work in America* similarly identified principally those aspects of work which are intellectually and emotionally disruptive, which is the concern of this chapter. To discuss coping with psychosocial stressors, it is vitally important to clearly define the issues, in this case, in terms of health and disease.

Most people adjust with varying degrees of success to unpleasant aspects of work. Even the safest anthracite coal mine is not an ideal work environment. Commuting several hours each day can be uncomfortable. The physical exertion of long hours in a hot, humid sugar cane field hardly describes ideal working conditions.

The volumes by Harvey Swados, Studs Turkel and so many others point to much that is wrong with work in America today—low wages, unemployment, long hours, physical and emotional discomforts. These and many other variables are often indicted and yet I submit they rarely produce disability or clearly disordered health. Strangely, it is more often situations of a more subtle nature which command our attention. It is these emotionally noxious stressors rather than the blatant and obvious ones which trigger disability.

Stressors have been categorized in many ways and called many things, largely based upon the theoretical background of the observer. Role stress, role ambiguity, overload, threats to self-esteem, disparity between ego ideal and reality, are all events which trigger anxiety and depression. Or one can speak both in terms of stressors or in terms of individual reactions and resultant suffering.

For the purposes of this discussion however the *specific stressors* I have in mind are those which produce at least some degree of physical or emotional disability in the exposed individual—stressors which make coping difficult or impossible and, of equal importance, which interfere with adjustment off the job as well as on. For it is these reactions to aspects of work which must be dealt with in occupational medicine. They range from every nonorganically produced emotional, intellectual and psychophysiological disability listed in the International Classification of Diseases to some reactions which defy any diagnostic categorization and which would be more generally described (for instance, a pattern of increasing dependence on others, or of withdrawal from active social and occupational activity). Other reactions to such stressors might include anger and frustration, disordered interpersonal relationships, excessive drinking (though not necessarily to the point of alcoholism). From the viewpoint of an employer, reduced productivity, diminished morale, high absenteeism and accidents may all be by-products of individual reactions to both subtle and grossly overt stressors.

What produces these reactions? Very often disruptive change, disordered leadership and inappropriate job placement. There are others as well, such as disordered relationships with fellow workers.

CONTEXT, VULNERABILITY AND SYMPTOMS

Two factors help to determine if a specific stressor will produce symptoms. First is the context in which an interaction takes place. Even more important is the particular vulnerability of the individual at the time.

The context may be as wide as an economy or as small as a family unit. A context may be industry-wide or limited to a single work organization or a plant within it. A context is set too by a management policy or practice. There are also the contexts of the community with its churches, schools, formal and informal, social and athletic activities (Figure 1). During an economic recession with loss of employment for example, stressors may be much more significant

Figure 1.

than they would be when one's economic security is not threatened. If a factory or industry closes there is obviously vast disruption. The changing life and activity of the family unit can also be a supporting or distracting contextual entity.

Individual vulnerability to specific stressors vary widely and are even more important than contexts in determining reaction to factors in a work environment. Certainly the enduring personality characteristics of a person are major factors. Therefore both genetic and developmental influences must be recognized which stamp each person uniquely. At the same time, these characteristics will in turn vary as other factors change (Figure 2). One's vulnerability alters with

VULNERABILITY
Internal
Personality
Age
Occupation
Education

Figure 2.

age, occupation, occupational level, and education. Predisposition to react to a specific stressor may be enhanced by unfulfilled occupational expectations. High educational achievement in a person with a low-skilled job can increase susceptibility to stressors. So can work requirements which do not meet personal biological rhythms.

Psychosocial stressors in this scheme tend to be defined in terms of producing symptoms of disability when context and vulnerability are ripe (Figure 3). It is therefore difficult to categorize or present a nosology of such factors. They are quite literally defined in terms of the vulnerability and context. All appear to involve change in some way. The stressor, for instance, may be a factor in the work environment which has not itself changed but which becomes productive of symptoms when vulnerability is increased. The change is often one of a supervisor, a task or a comfortable routine. Illustrative examples appear in the section which follows.

One way to illustrate the relationship between context, vulnerability, stressors and symptoms is through the use of Venn diagrams. All three circles may overlap to some extent with time. One represents context, one vulnerability and the third specific stressors. The area where all three overlap may be thought of as the individual's symptomatic response.

Figure 3.

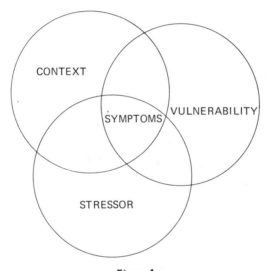

Figure 4.

As one views the illustration (Figure 4) bear in mind that each circle moves away from or toward the others dependent upon the importance of each of the three groups of variables. They are in constant and fluid motion. Each for that matter may symbolically vary in size. If the symbol of vulnerability has shifted to the right so there is no overlap, there are obviously no symptoms. It takes a degree of vulnerability for a specific stressor to act. The same of course is true with context and with stressors interacting. One can clearly withstand otherwise destructive stressors if the context is appropriate and the vulnerability is low (Figures 5, 6, 7).

Figure 5.

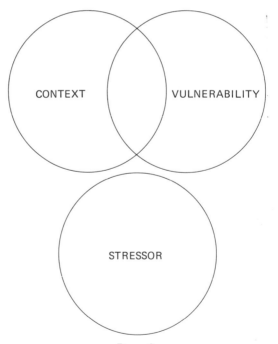

Figure 6.

Figure 7.

STRESSORS AND ADAPTATION

The interviewing program at Hawthorne clearly demonstrated two significant phenomena. (1) To develop meaningful information about employees' perceptions and feelings about work, one should, very simply, ask them. By the end of 1930, twenty-one thousand employees had been interviewed. Specific complaints were classified and many rectified. (2) More important, a psychological phenomenon was demonstrated which today is commonplace. Many complaints simply could not be taken at face value. You may recall the example of the employee who complained of his boss as a bully. If the boss gave him an order, he felt he was abusing his responsibility. If the boss said nothing to him, he felt slighted and ignored. During the interviews, as the talk turned to his past experiences, he spoke of his father, an overbearing, domineering man whose authority could not be challenged without a rage reaction. Gradually the interviewer saw that the employee's dissatisfaction was rooted in his attitude toward authority, developed during early childhood. He tended to hate everyone in power positions in the same way he hated his father. The investigators began to realize that to understand what was involved in an employee's complaint it was often necessary to understand the background of the employee and his or her personal situation. The complaint in itself might be largely a symptom of a personal situation which needed to be explored.

It is the second point which must be kept in mind as we reconsider the conclusions of the *Work in America* project discussed earlier. A reaction to stressors at work with symptoms of emotional disability does not necessarily prove a one-to-one cause and effect relationship. Nor does the fact that an individual is coping unsuccessfully with personal problems mean that he is necessarily more susceptible to stressors on the job. That said, however, it is important to recognize that data exists which supports the contention that there are such relationships in many instances. This now extends beyond anecdotal case histories. Two previously unreported studies will illustrate the point.

OCCUPATIONAL STRESS AND ANXIETY

Several years ago, eight hundred sixty-five individuals at three levels of management in one company completed a confidential questionnaire which asked, among other things, about their satisfaction with work. It further inquired about the perceived stressfulness of their tasks and about specific physical and emotional disabilities. Some twenty questions also inquired as to anxiety level. Each of these questions referred to the present time and a period three years in the past.

In relating increase and decrease in symptoms of anxiety to other items on the questionnaire, it was determined that there was no correlation between a shift in anxiety and the degree of satisfaction with salary, with the number of hours worked or with the number of hours traveled away from home. Very simply, this says one cannot buy a reduction in symptoms of anxiety by salary increases, by arbitrary reductions in the work week, or by restricting work travel.

A correlation did show up between increase or decrease in anxiety and the individual's perception of the stressfulness of his job, with his satisfaction with his work and with reported physical or health problems. This is shown in Table 1.

Men who felt less anxious than they did three years before also saw their job and the company as less stressful. They derived more satisfaction from their work and experienced fewer health problems. Just the reverse was the case with managers who had an increase in symptoms of anxiety over the previous three years. They perceived their job as more stressful, their company as more stress-

TABLE 1.

Men with Increased Symptoms of Anxiety		Men with Decreased Symptoms of Anxiety
More	Perceived Job Stress	Less
Less	Job Satisfaction	More
More	Amount of Health Problems	Less
More	Increase in Health Problems	Less

ful, their job as less satisfying and experienced both more health problems and an increase in health problems over three years prior.

These data are highly suggestive of a relationship between perceived job stress and levels of anxiety and health problems which permeate an individual's life off the job as well as on. Further, it illustrates a technique which can and has been elaborated upon for the study of these relationships in greater depth. Space does not permit the presentation of more details. It does illustrate what one can obtain by simply asking.

OFF-THE-JOB STRESSORS

Various changes at work have been blamed for psychiatric disability. Included among others are promotions, demotions, transfers, new management and new processes. Technological change and obsolescing skills have commonly been accused.

Over the past twenty years a colleague and I have collected a series of cases where severe emotional reactions were apparently precipitated by such change in the work environment. Individuals were included in this sample when they met two criteria: (1) Psychiatric illness which necessitated work absence, and (2) Change at work immediately prior to the onset of symptoms. Some thirty-six patients met these qualifications and were included. Dr. Eugene T. Hupalowsky and I saw a great many other patients over this time span who also met these criteria but who were not included for various reasons. This is not rigorous research but relatively "soft" clinical data.

Nonetheless there were some remarkable similarities among the cases. Although these individuals worked for seven different employers and although occupations ranged from skilled craftsman to corporate officials, there were common characteristics in the employee-employer relationships, which could best be described as one of mutual dependency. The patients presented unusually strong basic dependency needs. They were the sort of people who seemed to require rather firm leadership but who were able to make adequate adjustment and many were quite successful. As best as we could determine, none of the patients had a past history of psychiatric disorder. The average age was in the late forties.

The occupational changes which appeared to trigger the emotional disability ranged from retirement without an anticipated preretirement promotion, to promotion itself. Demotion triggered some psychiatric illness as did a change in supervision to a manager with a sharply different administrative style. The displacement of valued skills also produced several cases of disability.

While the emotional reactions occurred in a setting of occupational change, they invariably developed at a time when the individual was adjusting to an unrelated personal stress. The length of time between these associated extrinsic factors and the time of the change which triggered psychiatric illness was generally less than three months.   Apparently, external influences had strained the individual's ability to adapt.   The patient then turned for greater emotional support to his close relationship with the company and when that was disrupted by change, he was no longer able to cope successfully.

This abstract of a more complex study suggests the complex interrelationships between one's life off the job and at work.   I am equally sure that psychiatrists working away from occupational settings could point to a similar pattern with "sensitizing" factors at work setting up an individual for changes at home which in turn precipitate psychiatric disability.

THE REINFORCEMENT OF COPING

From the foregoing it is clear that if one can reduce a stressor and cut the vulnerability or somehow improve the factors which make up context, no symptoms would occur.   The circles of the Venn diagram would not even touch, let alone overlap.   Obviously it is much easier to manipulate stressors than it is vulnerability or context.   On the other hand, if one treats symptoms directly (through the use of medication or psychotherapy for instance) one presumably modifies vulnerability to some degree.   As time brings about change, these too alter.

The main point here is that there are several ways to assist the individual to cope with stressors on the job.   These range from efforts to change the political and economic climate of the country or the community to specific therapeutic programs within the work organization itself (occupational health and counseling programs for example).   To illustrate the varying levels and quality of activity in the support of occupational mental health, a concluding discussion follows of four broad categories of such aid: (1) policy considerations, (2) legislative considerations, (3) considerations related to education and training, and, (4) clinical designs to support the individual employee in forestalling or alleviating specific symptoms.

Policy considerations.   Broad policy considerations may be highlighted in several intriguing areas.   The first relates to the social concern of work organizations.   What does one do when an industry or plant becomes obsolete and an employer plans to build a new plant elsewhere?   What are the responsibilities of the employer?   This suggests that techniques should be imposed to force an employer to exert social responsibility for the health and the lives of those he may be tempted to abandon.   The same may be suggested when productivity can be advanced through major technological changes which displace highly valued skills and cause serious employee maladaptation.

The whole question of leadership is dealt with in a separate seminar.   Yet much that supports successful coping on the job relates to the exercise of authority both at the first-line level and at the top of the hierarchy. Underlying policy considerations include the need for the work organization to recognize the role of familial authority figures in the work community—usually the role of a father. Once the general characteristics of the successful father in that subculture are identified, one may select for first-line supervision individuals with such personalities. In general such a person offers a most successful model as foreman and usually he understands that leadership role well. The selection, placement, training and education of those in supervisory positions is equally important to the background and context in which he leads.

Related to the broad issues of leadership are convincing studies which tie productivity to the worker's attitude toward his immediate supervisor. Gerstenfeld (1969) studied absenteeism, correlating it with many variables. He found no relationship between any variable other than style of management. Those workers who felt their boss was frequently unfair are generally the same workers with poor attendance records. In effect, the supervisor was found to be far more important than the job itself.

Many agencies have responsibility for the work setting—the individual employer of course, but also federal agencies, academic centers (which provide knowledge of matters relating to health and safety standards) and professional and standards associations. It should be possible to build into such responsible agencies techniques to take advantage of existing scientific knowledge; of having expert information available to the work organization leadership. This would include the improvement of communication within and among those in specific specialties, such as economists, managers, union leaders and physicians. Other techniques for collecting and disseminating such knowledge must be stimulated at a multinational level.

Legislation.   There appears to be an international trend toward the corporate employer as a public trust with greater public and employee representation at policy-making levels. Public trusts encourage greater public control and therefore more legislative mandates and sanctions at the federal, state and community level. One legislative approach which may foster the coping mechanisms of the individual and enhance the ability of the employer to support them would specifically include the requirement of social indicators as part of the monitoring process of a work organization.

This is relatively easy to do with a statement of concern for the psychosocial work factors as a part of employer responsiblity. Such legislation could charge a capable agency with the development of indicators of job satisfaction as well as the development of techniques to evaluate the effectiveness of those measures. Measures of job satisfaction and the psychosocial climate of an organization would in turn be ultimately related to specific standards. The mechanisms will take time to develop but the model in operation in several countries for assessing the physical environment can be modified to evaluate the psychological factors as well.

Legislation is also required in many countries to effect change in the use of various economic means to foster increased choice for employees. For example, corporate benefit plans are often quite rigid and uniquely individual. Programs for retirement, sickness absence, holidays, health and life insurance often tie people to unrewarding tasks; force them to remain with an employer who no longer can provide stimulating work just so the employee can, for instance, have a pension. Through "portable" benefit plans of uniform character and with vesting in such programs outside the specific work organization, greater freedom to seek more fulfilling work would become possible.

Education—Training. An international conference recently concluded that there should be much greater flexibility and imagination in the educational system to prepare youngsters for careers. The ideal model suggested was that there be a broad, basic education for all, with work organizations subsequently assuming responsibility for specific "applications education" probably to be repeated several times during a lifetime as career changes become desirable or technology alters. Greater effort should be provided in every country to expose children from about years twelve to sixteen to various work experiences so that a more intelligent choice can be made of one's first career.

There should also be lifetime guidance systems—career centers to aid in initial occupational choice and subsequent career change as well as with individual retirement programs. Finally, the education system of any country should stimulate greater awareness of the psychosocial work factors by industrial engineers, occupational health professionals, and general community physicians, and should also expose social scientists and occupational health people to the study of management techniques.

Programs of individual support. Examples of specific programs designed to provide clinical support for more successful coping with occupational stressors are many and have often been described. They include occupational health and counseling programs which focus on both preventive and therapeutic activities, the education of supervisory personnel about specific mental health principles and the techniques of individual referral to such programs (Warshaw and Phillips, 1970). Employment practices designed to foster healthy behavior on the part of employees have also been elaborated elsewhere (Kahn and Quinn, 1970; McLean and DeCarlo, 1972). This broad range of illustrations of legislation, policy and practice in support of reduced job stress clearly has roots in *Management and The Worker*. The underlying theme that a job should provide for participation by the employee in its structure and function came indirectly from Hawthorne. Relief from leadership clearly came from the first Relay Assembly Group Study.

Greatly enhanced understanding of employees' legitimate occupational needs came from the interviewing program, and the relationship between productivity and the more sophisticated human relations applications owes its allegiance in later years to that earlier work of fifty years ago. I am hopeful it will not take another fifty years to implement the lessons which Elton Mayo and his associates taught and which subsequent behavioral scientists have elaborated.

REFERENCES

Gerstenfeld, A. Employee absenteeism: new insights. *Business Horizons.* October, 1969, 12 (5): 51-57.

Hess, H. *Journal of Occupational Medicine.* November, 1974, 16(11).

Jenkins, D. *Job Power.* New York, Doubleday, 1973.

Kahn, R. and Quinn, R. Role Stress: A Framework for Analysis. *Mental Health and Work Organizations.* Rand McNally and Co., Chicago, 1970.

Kami, M. *Journal of Occupational Medicine*, November, 1974, 16(11).

McLean, A. and DeCarlo, C. The changing concept of work. *Innovation.* April, 1972, pp. 38-49.

Miller, D. and Form, W. *Industrial Sociology.* New York, Harper Bros., 1951.

Mosse, C. *The Ancient World of Work.* London, Chatto and Windus, 1961, p. 1.

O'Tolle, J. Work in America and the great job satisfaction controversy. *Journal of Occupational Medicine.* November, 1974, 16(11).

Roethlisberger, F. and Dickson, W. *Management and the Worker.* Harvard University Press, Cambridge, Mass., 1939.

Roethlisberger, F. and Dickson, W. Task Force of Secretary of Health, Education and Welfare, Elliot L. Richardson. Report of *Work in American.* MIT Press, Cambridge, Mass., 1973.

Warshaw, L. and Phillips, B. Mental Health Programs in Occupational Settings. *Mental Health and Work Organizations.* Rand McNally and Co., Chicago, 1970.

12

THE POWER OF EMOTIONS; THE ROLE OF FEELINGS

W. Walter Menninger
Topeka State Hospital

INTRODUCTION

This anniversary symposium is indeed impressive, with some powerfully rational dissertations about man and work which discuss motivation, participative management, groups, etc. Inevitably, much of the rational dissertation seems dull and without feeling. What seems to be missing is an acknowledgement of the power of emotions, and the role of feelings in work.

There is no question that mankind and womankind have been able to accomplish incredible mastery over the environment by virtue of the opposable thumb and a remarkable, unique forebrain. The forebrain, particularly, has permitted homo sapiens the capacity for rational thought—the ability to translate experience into symbols called speech, to develop language, and further to create additional symbols to preserve our communication in writing or printing. Thereby, knowledge and experience can be accumulated, stored and passed on to new generations through the written word.

However, despite the intellectual capacity and an ostensible commitment to rational functioning, careful observation of human behavior notes that all too often it is not rational. Indeed, in situations where rational principles encounter emotional pressures, it is the emotional pressures that consistently carry the day. This is evident in a host of examples, past and present, whether in conflicts over school desegregation, voting rights, school textbook content, etc.

Sigmund Freud put it this way:

"Students of human nature and philosophers have long taught us that we are mistaken in regarding our intelligence as an independent force, and in overlooking its dependence on the emotional life. Our intelligence can function reliably only when it is removed from the influences of strong emotional impulses; otherwise it behaves merely as an instrument of the will, and delivers the inference which the will requires."

> —Freud, S. *Civilisation, War and Death*
> Selections from five works, edited by
> John Rickman, London: Hogarth Press, 1939. p 13.
> (Freud's paper on "Thoughts for the Times on
> War and Death"–1915)

Emotions are the complicating factors in life. They are powerful influences and they are not necessarily rational! Therefore as one approaches consideration of satisfaction in work, one must search for the feelings, the emotional pressures, and the psychological-feeling needs to be satisfied.

One other introductory observation may also be in order. There is a human tendency to study something by establishing contrasts and looking at extremes in either/or–all or nothing terms. Thus one may tend to see workers as good/ bad, trustworthy/untrustworthy, dedicated/indolent. In reality, there is a range from one extreme to the other, and the potential for the whole range may exist in every individual. How the individual performs will result from the combination of life experiences and inner emotional pressures. Further, the outcome may be significantly affected by the expectations in a given life or work situation, with a potential for the so-called "self-fulfilling prophecy."

PSYCHOLOGICAL FUNCTION OF WORK

It is well to begin with a consideration of the function of work in the psychological life of the normal individual. If one conceptualizes the human personality as being motivated by some powerful emotional drives, drives which are constantly seeking expression, then work is one life activity which provides an opportunity for the expression of these drives. Indeed, work is a significant life activity where there is the playing out of both aggressive and libidinal (or pleasure-seeking) drives.

In his early formulations about personality functioning, Freud focused on the drive theory and emphasized especially the need for individuals to have socially acceptable outlets for sexual energies. As he came to consider more the aggressive drive, Freud identified it, too, as being sublimated or transformed into socially acceptable behavior in work. In his discussion on "Civilization and Its Discontents," he put it this way:

"The task [of the personality] is . . . one of transferring the instinctual aims into such directions that they cannot be frustrated by the outer world. Sublimation of the instincts lends an aid in this. Its success is greatest when a man knows how to heighten sufficiently his capacity for obtaining pleasure from mental and intellectual work."

(—ibid p 32)

Freud went on to observe:

"Work is no less valuable for the opportunity it and the human relations connected with it provide for a very considerable discharge of libidinal component impulses, narcissistic, aggressive, and even erotic; than because it is indispensable for subsistence and justifies existence in a society."

(—ibid p 33)

Certainly, as Freud outlined, an important psychological function of work is its role as an activity in which basic emotional drives can be expressed in a socially acceptable manner; at the same time, it is a means by which an individual can earn a subsistence. Further, work can play an important role in providing a justification for existence, a "raison d'etre" for an individual. This function of work serves to sustain one's self-esteem in a meaningful and positive manner. Somewhat parallel is yet another function of work, namely an achievement of "mastery" by the individual which likewise elevates self-esteem and self-worth.

However, work is but one of a number of life activity areas in which the individual may seek opportunities to express aggressive and libidinal strivings; and in which one may seek to find a sense of self-worth, mastery, and a raison d'etre. Other areas include recreation, social relationships with others, and relationships within the family. To say that one or another of these life areas is pre-eminent is unrealistic. Indeed, it is a manifestation of the aforementioned tendency to think in either/or, all or nothing terms to assume we must place a greater importance on one area than on another. In reality, life represents a complex interaction of the individual with all the life areas; and the final result is a function of the law of mass action, with a shifting back and forth in response to changing pressures.

On one day, the significant pressures affecting an individual might well be related to events developing in the home and family, e.g. some unexpected serious illness or an especially painful argument. The emotional set prompted by the home event carries over and affects the worker's functioning on the job. In the same way, an event at work, either positive or negative in impact, will prompt an emotional response which spills over into life areas outside work.

One may diagram this formulation, placing the individual (I) in the center, constantly interacting with various life activity areas. (See Figure 1.) There is the constant expression of aggressive energy (A) and of positive or libidinal drive (L) in each of the areas, and a simultaneous feedback. Generally work is an area

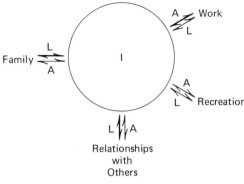

Figure 1.

where the aggressive drives can be expressed more directly and freely, though this is certainly not always so. Definitely, the aggressive energies can be directed in work activity far more than in social relationships with others; for to be too aggressive in relationships with others is to discourage friendships.

At work, when one experiences more frustration than satisfaction (1), an outlet for the frustrated emotional pressures may be sought in another life area, e.g. through physical activity or recreation (2). (See Figure 2.) Or one may carry the frustration home, kick the dog, swear at the children, deaden the pain with a few drinks, or in other ways pass on the aggressive mood toward the family (3). Hopefully, one's spouse will be sensitive to distress and respond with loving attention that will compensate and neutralize some of the wrath (4).

Certainly, the impact of what happens at work is substantial because such a significant part of waking life is spent in a work setting. But the complexity in assessing the role of work in life adjustment was recognized by the Hawthorne

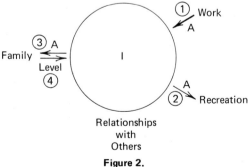

Figure 2.

investigators. They noted the problem of sorting out complaints and personal equilibrium and identifying what is cause and what is effect. Thus, in one case cited (operator M_5) they could identify five significant factors, part at work, part outside, and part related to the individual personality; and they could not say which was cause and which was effect:

1) Situation at home.
2) The nature of her social relations with fellow workers and supervisor.
3) Preoccupations of futility.
4) Frequent complaints about headaches.
5) Irregular and low output.

> —Roethlisberger, F. J. and Dickson, W.J.
> *Management and the Worker*
> Cambridge: Harvard Univ. Press, 1939, 1967. p 326.

Roethlisberger and Dickson also observed:

". . . it was evident that the supervisor in his daily duties was frequently to take account of many factors in a complex human situation . . . , the general consequence of which was unsatisfactory to some one of his subordinates. Inasmuch as in most cases the worker could not adequately specify the locus of his dissatisfaction, it was important that the supervisor be alert to interferences of many types and kinds, those arising from within as well as from without the immediate working environment."

(—ibid p 328)

That last observation is a point of no small significance, namely, that it is a difficult challenge to specify the "locus" of the problem.

IDENTIFYING THE PROBLEM—A CRITICAL STEP

Problems abound in human relationships, and generally the sticky problems are a function of emotional reactions between individuals or within an individual. Indeed, if it were not for emotions, people could probably get along rather well with one another; but life would also be rather dull. To express emotions is to find satisfaction, feeling and being, along with problems. All too often, one is unaware of the manner in which emotional pressures provoke problems.

It is a commonly observed phenomenon in medicine that the presenting problem of a patient, identified as a "chief complaint," is accompanied by a hidden agenda or a hidden parallel chief complaint. Characteristically the stated "chief complaint" is a physical symptom, and the hidden chief complaint is an emotional issue. Often the emotional chief complaint is not particularly rational or logical; and it may be kept "hidden" to the patient because it is in some way unacceptable to his conscious self. Until that hidden issue can be identified and dealt with, however, the patient is likely to continue to have a problem.

The parallel of this medical analogy to the work situation should be obvious. An important responsibility of the work supervisor is to tune into the hidden agenda items of his supervisees; and the degree to which he can do this may have a lot to do with the satisfaction his subordinates experience in working with and for him. As noted by Roethlisberger and Dickson, this is no easy task; but it is complicated by yet a further factor which impinges on the supervisor-supervisee relationship, a factor we would label "transference." The essence of transference is that subordinates will "lay on" to the supervisor emotional expectations which are displaced from the supervisee's early-life encounters with authority figures, especially parents. This is a process which occurs spontaneously and unconsciously, and which is not necessarily rational. Unless the supervisor has some appreciation of this process, he will find it difficult to understand some of the attitudes and behaviors of his subordinates.

TRANSFERENCE—THE RESULT OF PROGRAMMING

For the most part, life is focused in the here and now; assumptions about human behavior are made on the basis of a simple theory of causality that places the greatest emphasis on recent events to explain why something is as it is. Yet, the human brain which controls our personality functioning is the most complex computer ever created, with something like 10^{13} associational connections. Further, we know that as the central nervous system matures and the associational network expands correspondingly, there is constant activity taking place in the brain, reflected in electroencephalographic patterns of electrical activity. Finally it is clear that throughout our life, there is a constant input and sorting of outside stimuli into the brain, with life experiences serving as a kind of "programming" of the "computer."

One of the difficulties with which all must live is that this programming takes place in the early years in life, at a time when the computer (central nervous system) is yet immature. For that reason, as well as because of the overall immaturity and physical limitations of the child, distortions are built into the system. For example, the capacity for abstract thinking does not develop fully until adolescence and yet the child must attempt to explain complex and abstract life experiences long before that time when concepts like death, sex differences, are understandable. Extrapolations must be made by the child which may or may not be accurate, and which require repeated testing.

If, for example, a child's parents are loving and consistent in their attention and concern and can be trusted to respond to cries of pain and discomfort, the child will then have a basic expectation that people are like that. But if, instead, the child has parents who are more concerned about themselves, who see their children only as extensions of themselves to be "used" in some way to enhance their (the parents') life, and who are inconsistent in their degree of concern and sensitivity, the child will have a far different view of people and what he or she may expect from others. Because exposure to parents is so intense and generally unchallenged for such a long period of time—four or five years—these persons become the pre-eminent examples of people. They leave powerful early impressions of what to expect from others "like" them.

To illustrate this situation with another analogy, when traveling to another country which has an entirely different and unfamiliar culture and language, one seeks assistance from a native of that country to help him get oriented. It may take a while to fully realize what is happening in that situation. A discovery that his host is taking advantage of him would lead one to develop a profound skepticism not only for the host, but for others like him, namely other citizens of the country. He would assume that the host is typical and the prototype for others like him. He will proceed to test out his impressions in contact with others, but will do so with the inevitable bias of the initial experience.

The child is constantly seeking to explain the world in terms that are understandable in his limited mental capacity. When he encounters a problem that is not readily solved, the child will repeatedly return to the problem and tussle with it to find some solution. The child seeks to gain mastery over the world, but not all things can be mastered; and thus not all problems get resolved. Adults may continue to approach certain life situations in a manner which suggests they are still trying to work out an unresolved frustration of childhood.

To return to the computer model, when an error is programmed into a computer, it is well-nigh impossible to get it out. This concept is equally valid for the distortions and errors and early life impressions which are recorded in the central nervous system computer.

THE WORK SITUATION—A SCENARIO FOR TRANSFERENCE

What does all this discussion have to do with Hawthorne and with satisfaction from work? Simply stated, the work situation represents a life activity where the individual can play out again and again any unresolved life struggles with a range of issues: relationships to authority, achieving mastery, being worthwhile, giving and receiving, trust, dependence vs. independence, autonomy. In the process, the other individuals in the work situation become unwitting participants in the "scenario," and the supervisor is a key participant in the drama.

Insofar as an individual has achieved some sense of peace and resolution in earlier life encounters, there is less pressure to recreate the struggle in the present situation, wherever it is. However, there are always a significant number of persons who have not resolved some of the earlier life struggles, and they manage to plague the work situation with their continued efforts. Theirs is all too often a frustrated and frustrating struggle to solve past problems in today's environment. One of the special problems in dealing with such individuals is that one is rarely aware of their past; therefore one tends to approach them only in terms of the here-and-now situation.

The Hawthorne interviewers became acutely aware of this kind of problem, as exemplified in the case report of "Mrs. Black" who had been identified by her supervisor as a "chronic kicker . . . a problem case." The interviewer, as the supervisor had predicted to him, "got a lot out of her." The interview culminated with Mrs. Black's observation:

"You know, I think the reason I can't stand [my supervisor] is because every time I look at him he reminds me of my stepfather."

(—ibid p 307–310.)

In this clear instance of the transference phenomenon, the worker's reaction to the supervisor was not a function of the supervisor's personality per se, but rather a function of feelings within the worker originally experienced toward another significant person in her life and displaced onto the supervisor.

The capacity of the supervisor to help Mrs. Black achieve job satisfaction was obviously impaired by the mental "set" Mrs. Black had for him, putting into him feelings and motives that were not really his. The supervisor would be expected to have continued difficulty in trying to deal with Mrs. Black as long as he responded only in terms of the "here and now" and was completely unaware of his similarity to an emotionally-loaded figure in her life.

ROLE OF THE LEADER/SUPERVISOR IN ENHANCING JOB SATISFACTION

While certain aspects of leadership are addressed in another part of this symposium, it is well to look at some elements of leadership or supervisory functioning which affect job satisfaction and morale. Obviously, one element is the sensitivity of the leader to how his subordinates see him, including some awareness of the concept of transference. The effective leader is also alert to other irrational expectations of his subordinates, and to the fact that most will feel ambivalently toward the leader—at times positive, and at times envious and negative. Further, the leader acknowledges that subordinates have difficulty in approaching their superiors and talking freely. Yet, people want a leader who will listen to them and tune in to their concerns.

Listening is a critical element and perhaps is also one of the most important findings of the Hawthorne Studies, when one identifies factors contributing to job satisfaction. It is the professional commitment of the psychiatrist to listen to others; but an unfortunate reality in life is that most people aren't really interested in listening. They want to talk. If they do listen, they listen only for what they want to hear. The sensitive, thoughtful, active listener is a rare individual. Many who have studied worker satisfaction, including other distinguished contributors to this symposium, have cited the ability to listen as a critical factor.

Another role of the leader is in his impact on the morale of the group with which he works. It is well known that a good leader can stimulate a mediocre group, and a poor leader can destroy a superior group. Of course, there are other factors besides leadership that influence both group and individual morale. They are related to the degree to which the work meets certain psychological needs of the individual to have an enhanced self-esteem and raison d'etre. To some degree, these elements parallel the concepts of Herzberg and Ford. Specifically, for a worker to maintain a high sense of commitment and good morale, he must have a sense of and identify with the goals and purposes of the organization for which he works; and then he must also have a conviction that those goals could not be accomplished without the essential contribution he makes in his work. Thus, he is something "more" because of his work by virtue of what the organization is accomplishing; and he knows that the organization needs his contribution in order to achieve its goals.

In any discussion of job satisfaction, it is important to be alert to one's perspective. One senses that some investigators in this field have developed theories emphasizing the importance of jobs which may reflect more their own investment in work, in contrast to the investment in work of a considerable part of the labor market. The reality is that for many people, jobs are not particularly satisfying; they do not feel "needed." Yet it is probably fair to say that most people would like to find their work satisfying and rewarding, and the continuing challenge of management is to help them accomplish that, and at the same time increase productivity. Another important contribution of the Hawthorne Studies was the conclusion that both greater job satisfaction for the worker and greater productivity can be achieved hand in hand.

How does it happen? In part, it is the result of recognizing workers as individuals who are worth being listened to and who can make a contribution to decision-making in the corporate structure. In most corporations, the work is carried out largely by laboring class individuals who are variously categorized as "low level" personnel. And the policy decisions and the determination of what is best for these people—and the corporation as a whole—are most often made by individuals of a different socio-economic and educational background, with different interests. All too often, the higher level personnel assume that they know what is best, and apply their value system to decisions regarding lower level personnel, without any awareness of the fallacy of their biased approach.

The only way to counteract the inevitable bias of the middle class executive in decision-making is to establish ways for the line personnel to make some input into the decision-making process. This does not mean that decisions must be expected from lower level personnel; it does mean that the organization should make a commitment to solicit and register in a meaningful way opinions from the line. Those opinions should be weighed with other data in reaching a decision. This is a concept which is given much lip service in business and industry, but its actual application is rare. Much more often, the actual corporate philosophy is "father knows best," or "don't confuse me with the facts, my mind's made up."

The Hawthorne Studies explored an approach to listening to the line, establishing a communications system that could allow the organization to listen to the employees and consider their views in the process of making decisions. The early "counseling" program developed at Western Electric in response to the Hawthorne experiments reflected one approach to structuring line personnel "input" to management. One problem in the viability of that program was the way it was organized, with counseling seen as a function outside of management, and with no provision for input to management at the supervisory level in ways to strengthen the supervisors. Indeed, it is easy to see how the counseling system undermined the supervisor, introducing a "good" representative of management who was available to listen and make no demands. An obvious split could develop, with the worker then seeing the supervisor as the "bad" representative of management, demanding, ungiving, a taskmaster.

The challenge is to develop a system that strengthens the supervisor, particularly in terms of his capacity to help the worker achieve the optimal psychological-emotional need satisfaction from work. To achieve meaningful satisfaction, the worker needs consistent and constructive "feedback" on his performance and the degree to which his efforts are meeting needs of the organization. The supervisor has no less a need himself for feedback from his superiors on his performance.

Currently there is much discussion that focussing on the group relationships will provide the answer to job satisfaction, and there is intense consideration of "participative management." What cannot be overlooked however is the continuing critical role of the leader in the work process.

CRITICAL NEED—GOOD SUPERVISORS

Part of the human condition is a wish to deny limitations. People like to believe that they can do anything and everything. Yet, they all do have limits, whether physical, intellectual, psychological, emotional or other. The commonly cited illustration of limitations is the "Peter Principle," when an individual is promoted to the level of incompetence which is beyond his capacity to effectively perform.   All people have their "level of incompetence;" and despite intense efforts to improve the technology and judgement in selection, mistakes are still made.   People are still assigned to positions beyond their capacity to perform. This is the "achilles heel" of management.

One must acknowledge that the functioning of the line supervisor and of supervision up the line is vitally important in the job satisfaction of the worker. While principles of supervision can be outlined and presented in supervisory training, regrettably not all supervisors have the capacity to carry the responsibility effectively.   The answer to this problem is not in a backup system of counseling along the lines of the now defunct Western Electric program.   But the Hawthorne Studies pointed in an important direction.   Unfortunately in the last 50 years, little has been done to meet the continuing challenge so well expressed by Roethlisberger and Dickson: to select, train and support individuals to fulfill their responsibilities as good supervisors and leaders of the line. It is still this group which has such a significant contribution to make to the job satisfaction of the vast majority of workers and to their coping, feeling and being.

PART VII

Leadership—Direct, Delegate, Dictate and Participate: How Much, When, and to Whom?

According to what one reads, there are many people who claim the single most important quality that leads to a successful organization is the caliber of its leadership. Perhaps no topic has been more researched and speculated about, whether it be at the foreman level, among middle managers, or amid the incumbents of the executive suite. It appears most appropriate that the last input section developed at the symposium be based on this concept. From the wealth of information on this topic, the presentations which follow in this section look at ways to identify, develop and assess the effectiveness of leadership.

13

NEW CONCEPTS FOR THE MANAGEMENT OF MANAGERS*

Fred E. Fiedler
University of Washington

The Hawthorne Studies ushered in a new era not only in industrial relations but also in the concept of leadership and group dynamics. The time was, of course, right for a reaction to the mechanistic approaches of scientific management and the sterile conception of Economic Man. The Hawthorne Studies acted as an important catalyst. Human relations, that is, concern for the individual employee, and a new vision of the work group as a social unit were seen by many as the basic ingredients from which to build a new industrial democracy, a system in which the leader would serve more as a growth agent and counselor than as a task master, evaluator, and disciplinarian.

This management philosophy found its most effective advocate in Douglas McGregor (1967) whose "Theory Y" was based on the assumption that employees wanted to be effective self-starters, and that they needed only the right leadership to realize their full potential for creative participation in the organizational enterprise. While this management approach has been successfully applied in some situations it has failed in many others. As even McGregor had to admit, the world was not yet ready for the utopian industrial organization which merely had to unlock the bureaucratic constraints to free the employee's creativity and to enable him to find fulfillment and self-actualization in his work. In short, while McGregor and his like-minded colleagues introduced a breath of fresh air as well as a valuable new set of assumptions into the management area, the theory now appears too simplistic to account for the various other factors which contribute to organizational performance.

*This paper is based on research performed under ARPA Order 454, Contract NOOO14-67-A-0103-0013 with the Advanced Research Projects Agency, United States Navy (Fred E. Fiedler, Principal Investigator) and Contract NR 177-472, N00014-67-A-0103-0012 with the Office of Naval Research, Department of the Navy (Fred E. Fiedler, Principal Investigator).

Having said this, where does one go from here? Clearly not back to the 1910's and 1920's when the foreman, unencumbered by union and government controls, was the absolute boss. But neither can the weight of empirical evidence be ignored which indicates a failure to find the magic leadership trait, the one best management style, or the single set of rules which assures effective organizational performance.

WHAT DO WE KNOW ABOUT LEADERSHIP?

Let me here give a brief synopsis of the leadership problem as I see it through data collected over a period of 23 years, as well as in the light of the knowledge which has accumulated in the area within the last four or five decades. Without question, leadership turns out to be a much more complex human interaction than anticipated a few decades ago. It has been of absorbing interest to mankind at least as far back as Plato's *Republic* and Confucius' *Analects.* If it were simple, the problem of leadership would surely have been solved a long time ago.

What do we know at this time?

1. Leadership is a relationship between one person and one or several others, and it is a relationship based on power and influence. It is not a trait or a characteristic of a particular individual. Rather, it is a characteristic of the relationship among people in a particular group.

2. Leadership is attained by people who have the personality, the abilities, or the resources which members of a group perceive as desirable or necessary to attain their goal. The kid with the only ball is in a strong position to emerge as a leader, as is the only electrical engineer on a problem involving electrical equipment, or the young man whose father happens to own 51% of the company's stock.

3. Effective leadership means effective and productive group performance. One cannot be called an outstanding leader if his group's performance is a disaster. An orchestra conductor is acclaimed for how well his musicians play, not for how well they like him. It has been claimed that an autocratic leader who pushes his subordinates to greater productivity will fail in the long run because he will wear out his employees, deplete their willingness to perform their jobs, and therefore bring the organization to ruin. However, at least within the limits of present-day practice there is very little empirical evidence to support this view.

4. The leaders who perform well in one group situation may or may not perform well in a different situation. This means that one really cannot talk about a "good" leader or a "poor" leader, but only about someone who performed well in one type of situation and poorly in another.

5. For this reason the prediction of leadership performance must take into

account how the personality of the leader matches the situation for which he is selected. If the organization places him properly, his performance will be good; if he is assigned to a job which does not fit his personality, then he is likely to fail.

6. Above all, leadership is a dynamic process. Leaders' personalities may change over time but as we well know, personality changes tend to be slow and uncertain. What changes rapidly are the organizational variables which determine the degree to which the leadership situation fits the leader's personality.

7. A viable leadership theory must account for the interaction between personality and leadership situation, as well as the way in which the situational changes affect leader behavior and organizational performance. The Contingency Model is one major attempt to specify in detail the nature of this interaction.

THE CONTINGENCY MODEL

The theory postulates that at least two types of individuals must be considered. There are some people who are "task-motivated," who get their major satisfaction and security from some tangible evidence of their competence. They need to accomplish their tasks before they can relax. However, when they feel sure that the task will get done they can be charming and considerate in their relations with their co-workers.

There are other types of people who are "relationship-motivated," who need the security which comes from having close interpersonal relations and the support of their coworkers. However, when the relationship-motivated leaders have these close relations with their subordinates, they tend to seek admiration and approval from their superiors and others, and they are likely to focus their attention on the task and their relations with superiors, often to the neglect of their relations with subordinates.

Note that this emphatically does not mean that the relationship or the task-motivated people always behave in the same way. On the contrary, we are talking about people who have different primary and secondary goals and needs, who will behave quite differently, depending on whether they are at the time pursuing their primary or their secondary goals. Thus, in a different context, a man may express his concern about the future by immediately going to the doctor when he is sick, and by putting money into his saving account when he is well. That is, the same goal will evoke different behaviors under various conditions.

Leadership must be considered as an interaction based on power and influence. How much power and influence the leader gets from the way his organization operates, the degree his task is structured, and the support he obtains from his group members and his superiors is therefore of special importance.

Having power and influence gives one security. It makes it possible to control and predict the consequences and outcomes of decisions. If a leader knows that his subordinates will comply with his requests and directions in letter as well as in spirit, he will feel more in control than if he never knows what they will do next. If he knows, in addition, from the blueprint or the instructions in his hand how the job is to be done, and if he can reward and punish those who work for him, he has complete control and power over the task. There is then no reason to doubt the group's acceptance of his leadership, nor that the group task will be accomplished.

If, on the other hand, he cannot be sure of his group's willingness to go along with him, or if the task is vague and unstructured, then there is no way of knowing whether a decision will be carried out, or whether the decision (e.g., to market a new product) will bring financial success or disaster. The leader obviously will be uncertain as to his success in these latter cases since he cannot control or predict the outcomes of his decisions, and his anxiety will be correspondingly high.

What does this mean? People behave differently when they are insecure or anxious than when they are self-confident, secure, and relaxed. The leader who is in complete control has nothing to worry about. Under these conditions the task-motivated leader will tend to be considerate and easy to get along with. The relationship-motivated leader can be assured of his group's esteem of him, and the strong bonds between himself and his group members. He may now also try to develop a good relationship with his boss by impressing him with his concern for the job and his attention to organizational problems, and he may pay correspondingly less attention to his relations with subordinates.

In "unfavorable" situations, in which the leader cannot rely on his group members or in which he cannot predict the outcome of the task, the relationship-motivated leader's anxiety will express itself in the need for closer relations from his group members. He may solicit their support by showing concern for their well-being, their opinions, and their good feelings toward him. The task-motivated leader who cannot be certain of success will devote his full attention to the task, if necessary, to the neglect of his group, and he will seem distant and inconsiderate. In other words, both types of leaders will seek to allay their anxiety by accomplishing or securing their primary goals. Their goals are, of course, different, and therefore, require different behaviors. These behaviors will match the requirements of the leadership situation under some conditions but they will be detrimental to the accomplishment of organizational goals in other conditions (Fiedler and Chemers, 1974).

Numerous studies have now shown that the task-motivated leaders tend to be most successful in situations in which they have either a great deal of power and influence, or else in which their control and influence is relatively slight. Relationship-motivated leaders tend to excel in situations which provide them with moderate influence and control.

This is schematically shown in Figure 1. The horizontal axis indicates the favorableness of the situation. That is, the degree to which the situation provides the leader with power, control and influence. The left side of the axis indicates a very favorable situation, the right a relatively unfavorable situation. The vertical axis shows the leader's effectiveness or performance. The performance of the relationship-motivated leader is shown by a solid line, and that of the task-motivated leader by a dashed line.

Both types of leaders should perform well under some conditions and poorly under others. This means, of course, that most people can be effective leaders provided they are placed in a situation which matches their particular leadership style, or provided they learn how to modify their situation to match their style.

It is tempting to think that the problem is now solved. Task-motivated leaders must simply work in situations in which their power and influence is either very high or relatively low, and the relationship-motivated leaders work in situations of moderate power and influence.

While this is a neat solution to all the problems in theory, it is considerably more complex in practice. First of all, even under the best of circumstances, no theory at the present time gives even close to perfect predictions. Other approaches, like those which consider bettering the organizational structure, espousing the advantages of participative management, or methods of

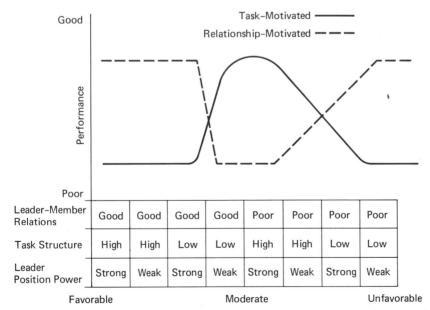

Figure 1. Schematic representation of the performance of relationship- and task-motivated leaders under varying working conditions.

improving organizational decision-making also have their contributions to make to this problem. While at least one experiment by Chemers and Skrzypek (1972) showed that the Contingency Model predicts roughly 28 per cent better than chance—a very impressive finding—it still leaves considerable room for improvement.

THE EFFECT OF ORGANIZATIONAL CHANGE

The other, more important point is that leadership situations change, and that appropriate adjustments must be made for such dynamic components. Some of these changes occur in quite obvious and dramatic form. The boss with whom one has developed a close and pleasant relationship is suddenly transferred or promoted to a new job, and one may or may not get along with the new boss, whose standards and management philosophy he may or may not share. Or the manager of a production department in Chicago is transferred by his company to a similar job in San Francisco where he must again train new subordinates in his methods and where he must develop stable relations with those who work for him and with those for whom he works. One may also get promoted to a new job, for example, from assistant to the plant manager to supervisor of engineering services.

Other changes are less dramatic but no less important. Consider the case of the new manager of a production department where everything is new and unfamiliar. Every problem requires new solutions or choices among alternatives whose outcomes are unknown. After three years on the job, he has successfully met just about every problem that is likely to come up and has worked out standard operating procedures for almost all of them. The job itself may not have changed but his ability to deal with it has. It is no longer strange and unfamiliar but rather routine and comfortable. Three years of experience have, in effect, increased his control and influence, and he now performs and behaves quite differently.

Or, one is assigned to a new supervisory position. Shortly after beginning the new job he is sent to an intensive training course which deals with all the problems likely to come up on the job, and he is now an expert in his field. He returns with more confidence as well as more expertise and therefore more control and influence to handle the situations he is likely to face. Training obviously increases control and influence. As a result, one will behave and perform differently if one is relationship-motivated rather than task-motivated.

To illustrate this rather complicated but extremely important point further, consider two hypothetical supervisors, the task-motivated Mr. Able and the relationship-motivated Mr. Baker who are equally qualified to be considered for a new managerial position. Assume further that this position is characterized by a highly structured task (e.g., production manager or supervisor of a shipping department) and has high position power, that is, the manager is able to make decisions affecting the employees' careers. He is consulted on hiring and firing, promotions, transfers, raises, and he is in charge of work assignments and evaluations of his subordinates. Moreover, relations between supervisors and subordinates historically have been good. In other words, this position will give the manager a relatively high degree of power and influence after he gets to know his job well through experience or training.

At the beginning, of course, as long as the manager lacks experience and training, he must rely on the advice of his more experienced employees and he will find it difficult to predict what the right decision will be in many situations which he has not encountered before. In other words, the situation will be only moderately favorable for the new managers. Thus, the relationship-motivated Mr. Baker is likely to perform better in the beginning than the task-motivated Mr. Able, as Figure 1 shows.

Selection

It should now be obvious, that a man cannot simply be selected for a position of leadership and be expected to remain there forever, even if his personality fits the job. This becomes a problem which requires a further decision. Is a leader wanted who will perform well immediately or rather after he learns the job or has been fully trained?

After gaining experience or becoming fully trained, be this in six months, as is likely to be true of infantry squad leaders, or six years, as we have found in a sample of college presidents, the task-motivated Mr. Able will outperform Mr. Baker who has now become less effective. Baker may have become "stale," disinterested, bored or arrogant, while Able is really involving himself in his job and continues to improve. The choice now is between immediate performance, or Baker, and long run gains, or Able. The old adage of putting the right man in the right job has to be revised, at least as far as leadership positions are concerned. The right job today may be the wrong job in a few months or a few years.

Training

Our findings also mean, of course, that leaders must be selectively trained. The task-motivated Mr. Able will perform well in the long run, and an intensive course of training will hasten the day when he will be an outstanding leader since it will provide him all the sooner with full control and influence.

The same course of training will have the opposite effect on Mr. Baker who may soon find himself in a position with very high control and influence. For him, as a relationship-motivated leader, this will tend to result in a relatively poor performance. He will be "overtrained" and would have been better off not becoming so expert. Without training, or with training which stresses participative management (which lowers his position power), he would have continued to seek good relations with his subordinates so that they will assist him in performing his managerial functions.

We have found results of this type in more than ten different analyses. The point is best illustrated by a study conducted with infantry sergeants who were assigned to brand-new squads and whose effectiveness was rated at the beginning and again at the end of the training cycle by two or more of each leader's superiors.

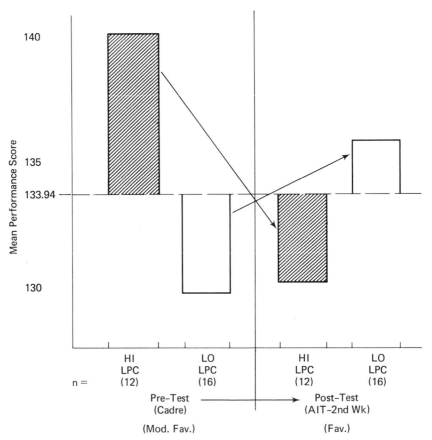

Figure 2. Change in the performance of high and low LPC leaders as a function of increased experience and more structured task assignment over five months (P. Bons & Linda Hastings, unpublished paper).

The infantry squad with its highly structured task and position power typically presents a very favorable situation for the experienced leader who has worked with his unit for some time. Figure 1 would lead one to expect better performance from the task-motivated than from the relationship-motivated leader. However, in the formative stages of the group, before the unit has had a chance to shake down and to develop routines and before the leader has learned how to handle the men in his particular squad, the situation will be only moderately favorable. Hence, a relationship-motivated leader should perform better here.

If our theory is correct it should mean that the relationship-motivated leader will then be better in the beginning, and gradually decrease in his effectiveness as he gains experience or training. In contrast, the task-motivated leader will start out poorly and gradually improve as he gains in control and influence. Figure 2 shows the average performance ratings of 19 squad leaders who were evaluated by the same officers at the beginning and at the end of their unit's training cycle. The data clearly bear out this prediction.

A second illustration of this relationship comes from a study of consumer cooperatives where the effectiveness of each company could be measured by the percent of net income and of operating costs to total sales over a three year period. For purposes of this analysis we divided the company managers on the basis of their experience in the organization and on their leader motivation score.

Again, the manager's situation was rated as favorable if he was experienced and as moderately favorable if he was relatively inexperienced. As can be seen from Figure 3, then relationship-motivated managers with high experience actually were less effective than were relationship-motivated managers with less experience. That is, they may have become bored, stale or no longer challenged by their job, while the task-motivated managers improved the performance of their organization.

Rotation and transfer

The relationship-motivated Mr. Baker as discussed above is likely to become a relatively poorly performing manager. He may have become disinterested or too cocky about his job. In other words, Baker's leadership situation has become too favorable. Relationship-motivated leaders like Baker tend to perform best in moderately favorable situations.

The contingency model now suggests a different strategy. Mr. Baker might be rotated to another job in the organization which will require that he learn new methods and that he establish himself with a new set of subordinates and superiors. The task-motivated Mr. Able, on the other hand, is just hitting his stride and definitely should not be rotated at this point. Giving Mr. Able new

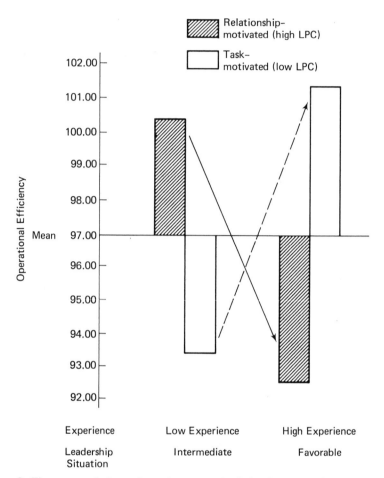

Figure 3. The presumed change in performance of relationship- and task-motivated company managers as a function of increased experience.

problems or assigning him to unstructured and creative tasks under these conditions is likely to be disfunctional.   Mr. Baker will, however, thrive on exactly such assignments.

An example of this type again comes from the study of infantry squad sergeants which shows the effect of organizational change, namely, changes in boss or job.   The new squad leaders faced a situation that was only moderately favorable and, as expected, the relationship-motivated leaders performed better than the task-motivated leaders.   However, with a change in boss or job, the situation becomes unfavorable.   Hence the task-motivated leaders should show an improvement while the relationship-motivated leaders should show a decrease in effectiveness.   The results in Figure 4 illustrate this point.

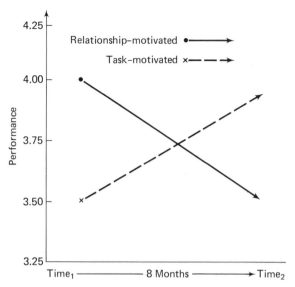

Figure 4. The effect of change in job or boss on the rated performance of relationship- and task-motivated squad leaders.

It is important to stress once more that the discussions involving the imaginary Messrs. Able and Baker as well as the infantry sergeants dealt with the managerial positions which typically are highly favorable, that is, giving the experienced and trained leaders a high degree of control and influence. A quite different set of personnel decisions would have to be made if the managerial positions were only moderate in the power, control and influence they provided the experienced managers. Thus, the director of a research unit or the chairman of a policy- or decision-making committee would be faced with a situation in which his control and power would be moderate. Here the relationship-motivated Bakers would perform best after they have become fully experienced, but the task-motivated Ables would be the better performers in the beginning. They would also be the better performers in situations of crisis and in those in which their power and influence are very low. These would be positions such as the disliked chairmen of policy committees or the rejected leaders of such groups as advertising agencies, or the leaders operating in crisis-like situations.

To conclude with an oversimplified summary:

1. The contingency model, here briefly described, has shown that the performance of a group depends on the motivational structure of the leader and the degree to which the situation is favorable, that is, to which it gives the leader control and influence.

2. We can distinguish between relationship-motivated and task-motivated

leaders, and find that they behave and perform quite differently under conditions which are relaxed and pleasant or anxiety-arousing and stressful.

3. We find that the task-motivated leaders perform best in situations which give them a high degree of power and influence, or relatively low power and

TABLE 1.   Effects of Personnel and Organizational Changes on
Leader's Control and Influence.

Personnel Strategy	Effect on Leader's Control
Selection	Leaders who perform well at first may perform less well in the long run, and those who perform poorly at first tend to improve. Hence, is leader needed immediately or in long run?
On-the-job training (experience)	The leader's control is increased as he gains experience (and if he has the capacity to learn). Some leaders will, therefore, improve; others become less effective with experience.
Training	Training is generally designed to increase leader's control and influence, especially in the area of task structure and leader-member relations. Training in participative management and similar techniques may decrease control and influence.
Rotation and transfer	While no deliberate attempt is made to change the leader's control and influence, the effect of rotation and transfer to a similar job decreases the leader's control and influence—his relations with superiors and subordinates are more uncertain and the task seems less structured (and more challenging).
Organizational Changes	
Change in superiors	Control is temporarily decreased since leader becomes less certain about his ability to satisfy superior's standards and requirements.
Change in subordinates (labor turnover)	Control is temporarily decreased since leader becomes less certain about his relations with subordinates and their support of him.
Change in task or assignment	Control over task generally is decreased since leader must learn new routines and operating procedures.

influence or control. Relationship-motivated leaders perform best with moderate influence and control.

4. Experience and training, by and large, increase the leader's power and influence. Leadership rotation, change in subordinates, and changes in superiors decrease the leader's control and influence.

5. The maintenance of an effective cadre of leaders requires a sensitive and dynamic balance of organizational interventions and personnel strategies which keep the task-motivated leaders operating in situations of high or very low power, influence and control and the relationship-motivated leaders in situations of moderate control and influence.

6. While we do not have, at this time, a cookbook or a blueprint which can guide the top manager on how to manage his leadership cadre to the organization's and to his own best advantage, we do have a rudimentary theoretical framework which permits us to predict the effects which various events in the organization's life have on leaders with particular motivational structures.

Table 1 briefly summarizes the consequences which various personnel strategies and organizational changes will have on the favorableness of the situation. Knowing which types of leaders will perform best in favorable, moderately favorable, or unfavorable situations allows us then to make decisions about selection, experience and training, rotation, and transfer. It also permits us to predict the effects which various organizational changes will have on the performance of different leaders.

It is now obvious that the same approach to all managers and leaders will be likely to have beneficial effects for some and detrimental effects for others. Since it is to the leader's own advantage to be at his best in as many situations as possible, management training as well as such other interventions as transfers and rotations should seek to provide the leader an environment in which he will be maximally effective. There is now reason to believe that the contingency model provides a basic framework for this purpose.

REFERENCES

Chemers, M. M. and Skrzypek, G. J. An experimental test of the contingency model of leadership effectiveness. *Journal of Personality and Social Psychology,* 1972, 24: 172–177.

Fiedler, F. E. and Chemers, M. M. *Leadership and Effective Management.* Glenview, Illinois: Scott, Foresman and Company, 1974.

McGregor, D. *The Human Side of Enterprise.* New York: McGraw-Hill, 1960.

14
LEADERSHIP REVISITED

Victor H. Vroom
Yale University

INTRODUCTION

A critical stage in any scientific inquiry seldom covered in textbooks is the formulation of questions or problems. Research endeavors which have uncovered problems previously overlooked or suggested new phenomena to be investigated tend to acquire a "landmark quality" not because they proved anything definitively but because they revealed rather new directions for investigation. The Hawthorne Studies are an interesting case in point. The tremendous influence which these studies have had on the emerging field of organizational behavior did not stem from their "proof" of any behavioral propositions. Rather, these studies served to bring to light a class of phenomena which had been ignored in prior research. They are remembered more for the questions they raised than for the answers they provided.

One of these questions pertained to the role of the supervisor in the dramatic increases in productivity observed in the Relay Assembly Test Room. If the effects could be attributed to the informality of the supervisor or to the frequent consultation with workers about the changes being introduced, it could have important implications for our understanding of the process of leadership.

It is not my purpose here to participate in the seemingly endless debate about what happened at Hawthorne and why, but rather to take advantage of the occasion of the 50th anniversary of the inception of these studies to review where we have come since that time in our efforts to understand the topic of leadership and to consider what appear, to this writer at least, to be some promising new directions.

RESEARCH ON LEADERSHIP TRAITS

Early research on the question of leadership had roots in the psychology of individual differences and in the personality theory of that time. The prevailing theory held that differences among people could be understood in terms of their traits—consistencies in behavior exhibited over situations. Each person could be usefully described on such dimensions as honesty-dishonesty, introversion-extroversion or masculine-feminine. In extrapolating this kind of theory to the study of leadership, it seemed natural to assume that there was such a thing as a trait of leadership, i.e., it was something that people possessed in different amounts. If such differences existed, they must be measurable in some way. As a consequence, psychologists set out, armed with a wide variety of psychological tests, to measure differences between leaders and followers. A large number of studies were conducted including comparisons of bishops with clergymen, sales managers with salesmen and railway presidents with station agents. Since occupancy of a leadership position may not be a valid reflection of the degree of leadership, other investigators pursued a different tack by looking at the relationship between personal traits of leaders and criteria for their effectiveness in carrying out their positions.

If this search for the measurable components of this universal trait of leadership had been effective, the implications for society would have been considerable. The resulting technology would have been of countless value in selecting leaders for all of our social institutions and would have eliminated errors inevitably found in the subjective assessments which typically guide this process. But the search was largely unsuccessful and the dream of its by-product—a general technology of leader selection—was unrealized. The results, which have been summarized elsewhere (Stogdill, 1948; Bass, 1960; Gibb, 1969), cast considerable doubt on the usefulness of the concept of leadership as a personality trait. They do not imply that individual differences have nothing to do with leadership, but rather that their significance must be evaluated in relation to the situation.

Written more than 25 years ago, Stogdill's conclusions seem equally applicable today:

"The pattern of personal characteristics of the leader must bear some relevant relationship to the characteristics, activities and goals of the followers . . . It becomes clear that an adequate analysis of leadership involves not only a study of leaders, but also of situations." (1948, pp. 64–65)

The study of leadership based on personality traits had been launched on an oversimplified premise. But as Stogdill's conclusions were being written, social scientists at Ohio State University and at the University of Michigan were preparing to launch another and quite different attack on the problem of leadership. In these ventures, the focus was not on personal traits but on leader behavior and leadership style. Effective and ineffective leaders may not be distinguishable by a battery of psychological tests but may be distinguished by their characteristic behavior patterns in their work roles.

RESEARCH ON EFFECTIVE LEADERSHIP METHODS

The focus on behavior of the leader rather than his personal traits was consistent with Lewin's classic dictum that behavior is a function of both person and environment (Lewin, 1951) and of growing recognition that the concept of trait provided little room for environmental or situational influences on behavior. Such a focus also envisioned a greater degree of consistency in behavior across situations than has been empirically demonstrated (Hartshorne and May 1928; Mischel, 1968; Vroom and Yetton, 1973).

If particular patterns of behavior or leadership styles were found which consistently distinguished leaders of effective and ineffective work groups, the payoff to organizations and to society would have been considerable, but of a different nature than work based on the trait approach. Such results would have less obvious implications for leader selection but would have significant import for leader development and training. Knowledge of the behavior patterns which characterize effective leaders would provide a rational basis for the design of educational programs in an attempt to instill these patterns in actual or potential leaders.

Space does not permit a detailed account of the Ohio State and Michigan research or of its offshoots in other institutions. It is fair to say, however, that the success of this line of inquiry in developing empirically based generalizations about effective leadership styles is a matter of some controversy. There are some who see in the results a consistent pattern sufficient to constitute the basis of technologies of organization design or leader development. Likert (1967), reviewing the program of research at Michigan, finds support for what he calls System 4, a participative group-based conception of management. Similarly, Blake and Mouton (1964), with their conceptual roots in the Ohio State research program, argue that the effective leader exhibits concern for both production and employees (their 9-9 style) and have constructed a viable technology of management and organization development based on that premise.

On the other hand, other social scientists including the present writer (Sales, 1966; Korman, 1966; Vroom, 1964) have reviewed the evidence resulting from these studies and commented lamentably on the variability in results and the difficulty in making from them any definitive statements about effective leader behavior without knowledge of the situation in which the behavior has been exhibited.

At first glance, these would appear to be two directly opposing interpretations of the same results, but that would probably be too strong a conclusion. The advocates of general leadership principles have stated these principles in such a way that they are difficult to refute by empirical evidence and at the same time provide considerable latitude for individual interpretation. To say that a leader should manage in such a way that personnel at all levels feel real responsibility for the attainment of the organization's goals (Likert, 1967) or alternatively that he should exhibit concern for both production and his employees (Blake and Mouton, 1964) are at best general blueprints for action rather than specific blueprints indicating how these objectives should be achieved. The need for adapting these principles to the demands of the situation is recognized by most social scientists. For example, Likert writes:

"Supervision is . . . always a relative process. To be effective and to communicate as intended, a leader must always adapt his behavior to take into account the expectations, values, and interpersonal skills of those with whom he is interacting . . . There can be no specific rules of supervision which will work well in all situations. Broad principles can be applied in the process of supervision and furnish valuable guides to behavior. These principles, however, must be applied always in a manner that takes fully into account the characteristics of the specific situation and of the people involved." (1961, p. 95)

To this writer, the search for effective methods of supervision management and leadership has come close to foundering on the same rocks as the trait approach. It too has failed to deal explicitly with differences in situational requirements for leadership. If the behavioral sciences are to make a truly viable contribution to the management of the contemporary organization, they must progress beyond an advocacy of power equalization with appropriate caveats about the need for consideration of situational differences and attempt to come to grips with the complexities of the leadership process.

INVESTIGATION ON LEADERSHIP STYLES

These convictions, whether right or wrong, provided the basis for a new approach to the investigation of leadership style—its determinants and consequences—launched about six years ago by the author and Philip Yetton, then a graduate student at Carnegie Mellon University. We set ourselves two goals: 1) to formulate a normative or prescriptive model of leader behavior which incorporated situational characteristics in an explicit manner and which was consistent with existing empirical evidence concerning the consequences of alternative approaches, and 2) to launch an empirical attack on the determinants of leader behavior which would reveal the factors both within the person and in the situation which influence leaders to behave in various ways.

In retrospect, these goals were ambitious ones and the reader will have to judge for himself the extent to which either has been achieved. We attempted to make the task more manageable by focusing on one dimension of leader behavior—the degree to which the leader encourages the participation of his subordinates in decision-making. This dimension was chosen both because it was at the core of most prescriptive approaches to leadership and because a substantial amount of research had been conducted on it.

The first step was to review that evidence in detail. No attempt will be made here to repeat that review. (The reader interested in this question may consult Vroom, 1969; Lowin, 1968; or Wood, 1974.) Instead, we will restrict our attention to a summary of the major conclusions which appeared justifiable by the evidence.

(1) Involvement of subordinates in "group decision-making" is costly in terms of time. Autocratic decision-making processes are typically faster (and thus of potential value in emergency or crisis situations) and invariably require less investment in manhours of the group in the process of decision-making than methods which provide greater opportunities for participation by subordinates, particularly those decision processes which require consensus by the group.

(2) Participation by subordinates in decision-making creates greater acceptance of decisions which in turn is reflected in better implementation. There is a wide range of circumstances under which "people support what they helped to build." Increasing the opportunity for subordinates to have a significant voice in decisions which affect them results in greater acceptance and commitment to the decisions, which will in turn be reflected in more effective and reliable implementation of the decision.

(3) The effects of increased participation by subordinates in decision-making on the quality or rationality of decisions tend to be positive, although the effects are likely to depend on several identifiable factors. Extensive research has been conducted on group and individual problem-solving. Group decisions tend to be higher in quality when the relevant information is widely distributed among group members, when the problem is unstructured and when there exists a mutual interest or common goal among group members.

(4) Involvement of subordinates in decision-making leads to growth and development of subordinates. This consequence of participation has been least researched and its assertion here is based primarily on theoretical rather than empirical grounds. It is different from the three previous factors (time, acceptance, and quality of decision) in its long-term nature.

From this general research foundation a normative model was constructed. The model utilized five decision processes which vary in the amount of opportunity afforded subordinates to participate in decision-making. These processes are shown in Table 1.

TABLE 1.   Types of Management Decision Styles.

AI	You solve the problem or make the decision yourself using information available to you at that time.
AII	You obtain necessary information from subordinate(s) and then decide on a solution to the problem yourself. You may or may not tell subordinates what the problem is in getting the information from them. The role played by your subordinates in making the decision is clearly one of providing the necessary information to you, rather than generating or evaluating alternative solutions.
CI	You share the problem with relevant subordinates individually; getting their ideas and suggestions without bringing them together as a group. Then you make the decision which may or may not reflect your subordinates' influence.
CII	You share the problem with your subordinates as a group, collectively obtaining their ideas and suggestions. Then, *you* make the decision which may or may not reflect your subordinates' influence.
GII	You share the problem with your subordinates as a group. Together you generate and evaluate alternatives and attempt to reach agreement (consensus) on a solution. Your role is much like that of chairman. You do not try to influence the group to adopt "your" solution and are willing to accept and implement any solution which has the support of the entire group.

The model to be described is a contingency model. It rests on the assumption that no one decision-making process is best under all circumstances, and that its effectiveness is dependent upon identifiable properties of the situation. However, it is different from other contingency models in the fact that the situational characteristics are attributes of the particular problem or decision rather than more general role characteristics. To distinguish this type of situational variable from others we have designated them as problem attributes. These attributes are the building blocks of the model and represent the means of diagnosing the nature of the problem or decision at hand so as to determine the optimal decision process.

The most recent form of the model is shown in Figure 1. It is expressed here in the form of a decision tree. The problem attributes are arranged along the top and are shown here in the form of yes-no questions. To use the model to determine the decision process, one starts at the left-hand side of the diagram and asks the question pertaining to attribute A. The answer (yes or no) will determine the path taken. When a second box is encountered, the question pertaining to that attribute is asked and the process continued until a terminal node is reached. At that node one will find a number (indicating problem type) and a feasible set of decision processes.

For some problem types only one decision process is shown; for others there are two, three, four or even all five processes. The particular decision processes shown are those that remain after a set of seven rules has been applied. The rules function to protect both the quality and the acceptance by eliminating

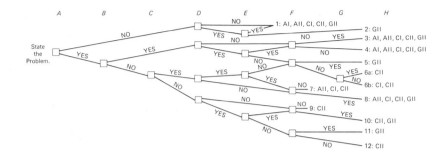

Figure 1. Decision-process flow chart for group problems.

A. Is there a quality requirement such that one solution is likely to be more rational than another?

B. Do I have sufficient info to make a high quality decision?

C. Is the problem structured?

D. Is acceptance of decision by subordinates critical to effective implementation?

E. If I were to make the decision by myself, is it reasonably certain that it would be accepted by my subordinates?

F. Do subordinates share the organizational goals to be attained in solving this problem?

G. Is conflict among subordinates likely in preferred solutions? (This question is irrelevant to individual problems.)

H. Do subordinates have sufficient info to make a high quality decision?

methods that have a substantial likelihood of jeopardizing either of these two components of an effective decision. The interested reader should consult Vroom and Yetton (1973) for a detailed statement in both verbal and mathematical form, of these rules.

If more than one alternative remains in the feasible set, there are a number of bases for choosing among them. One of them is time. The methods are arranged in ascending order of the time in manhours which they require. Accordingly, a time minimizing model (which we have termed Model A) would select that alternative that is farthest to the left within the feasible set. An alternative to minimizing time is maximizing development of subordinates. This model (which we have termed Model B) would select that decision process which is farthest to the right within the feasible set.

While we have attempted to phrase the questions pertaining to the problem attributes in as meaningful a fashion as possible, the reader should keep in mind that they are really surrogates for more detailed specifications of the underlying variables. The reader interested in more information on the meaning of the attributes, the threshold for yes-no judgments or their rationale for inclusion in the model should consult Vroom and Yetton (1973). Illustrations of the models' application to concrete cases can be found in Vroom (1973); Vroom and Yetton (1973); and Vroom and Jago (1974).

The model shown in Figure 1 is intended to apply to a domain of managerial decision-making which Maier, Solem and Maier (1957) refer to as group problems, i.e., problems which have potential effects on all or a substantial subset of the manager's subordinates. Recently, we have become interested in extending the model to "individual problems," i.e., those affecting only one subordinate. For these decisions, the first three decision processes shown in Table 1 represent potentially reasonable alternatives but there are at least two other viable alternatives not yet represented. One of these we have called GI, which is a form of group decision involving only a single subordinate. (A GI manager shares the problem with the subordinate and together they analyze the problem and arrive at a mutually satisfactory solution.) The other, which we have designated as DI, consists of delegating the problem or decision to the subordinate.

Many of the considerations used in building the model for group problems—such as problem attributes and rules—could easily be adapted to the domain of individual problems. There remained, however, one major structural difference. For group problems, there was a tradeoff between the short-run consideration of time efficiency (which favored autocratic methods) and longer range considerations involving subordinate development (which favored participative methods). The reader will recall that Model A and Model B represented two extreme modes of resolution of that tradeoff. For individual problems, the differences in time requirements of the five processes (AI, AII, CI, GI, DI) are not nearly as large and the alternative which provides the greatest amount of subordinate influence or participation, DI, can hardly be argued to be least time efficient. This difference in the correlation between time efficiency and participation for individual and group problems required an adjustment in the location of DI in the ordering of alternatives in terms of time. Model A and Model B retain their original meaning from the earlier model, but they are no longer polar opposites.

Figure 2 contains a model also expressed as a decision tree which purports to guide choices among decision processes for both individual and group problems. The only difference lies in the specifications of two feasible sets (one for group and one for individual problems) for each problem type.

Is the model in its present form an adequate guide to practice? Would managers make fewer errors in their choices of decision processes if they were to base them on the model? We would be less than honest if we said we knew the answers to such questions. Most managers who have had sufficient training in the use of the model to be able to use it reliably report that it is a highly useful guide, although there are occasionally considerations not presently contained in the model—such as geographical dispersion of subordinates—which prevent implementation of its recommendations. Some research has been conducted in an attempt to establish the validity of the model (see Vroom and Yetton, pp. 182–184) but the results, while promising, are not conclusive. Perhaps the

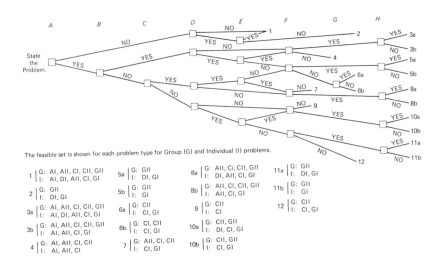

The feasible set is shown for each problem type for Group (G) and Individual (I) problems.

1 | G: AI, AII, CI, CII, GII
  | I: AI, DI, AII, CI, GI

2 | G: GII
  | I: DI, GI

3a | G: AI, AII, CI, CII, GII
   | I: AI, DI, AII, CI, GI

3b | G: AI, AII, CI, CII, GII
   | I: AI, AII, CI, GI

4 | G: AI, AII, CI, CII
  | I: AI, AII, CI

5a | G: GII
   | I: DI, GI

5b | G: GII
   | I: GI

6a | G: CII
   | I: CI, GI

6b | G: CI, CII
   | I: CI, GI

7 | G: AII, CI, CII
  | I: CI, GI

8a | G: AII, Ci, CII, GII
   | I: DI, AII, CI, GI

8b | G: AII, CI, CII, GII
   | I: AII, CI, GI

9 | G: CII
  | I: CI

10a | G: CII, GII
    | I: DI, CI, GI

10b | G: CII, GII
    | I: CI, GI

11a | G: GII
    | I: DI, GI

11b | G: GII
    | I: GI

12 | G: CII
   | I: CI, GI

Figure 2. Decision-process flow chart for both individual and group problems.

A. Is there a quality requirement such that one solution is likely to be more rational than another?

B. Do I have sufficient info to make a high quality decision?

C. Is the problem structured?

D. Is acceptance of decision by subordinates critical to effective implementation?

E. If I were to make the decision by myself, is it reasonably certain that it would be accepted by my subordinates?

F. Do subordinates share the organizational goals to be attained in solving this problem?

G. Is conflict among subordinates likely in preferred solutions? (This question is irrelevant to individual problems.)

H. Do subordinates have sufficient info to make a high quality decision?

most convincing argument for the development of models of this kind is that they can serve as a guide for research that can identify their weaknesses and that superior models can later be developed.

The reader will note that flexibility in leader behavior is one of the requirements of use of the model. To use it effectively, the leader must adapt his approach to the situation. But how flexible are leaders in the approaches they use? Do they naturally try and vary their approach with the situation? Is it possible to develop such flexibility through training? These questions were but a few of those which guided the next phase of our inquiry into how leaders do in fact behave and into the factors both within the leader himself and in the situations with which he deals which cause him to share decision-making power with his subordinates.

Two different research methods have been used in an attempt to answer questions such as these. The first investigation utilized a method that can be referred to as "recalled problems." Over 500 managers from 11 different countries representing a variety of firms were asked to provide a written description of a problem that they had recently had to solve. These varied in length from one paragraph to several pages and covered virtually every facet of managerial decision-making. For each case, the manager was asked to indicate which of the decision processes shown in Table 1 he used to solve the problem. Finally, each manager was asked to answer the questions corresponding to the problem attributes used in the normative model with his own case in mind.

These data made it possible to determine the frequency with which the managers' decision process was similar to that of the normative model and the factors in their description of the situation which were associated with the use of each decision process. This investigation provided results which were interesting but also led to the development of a second more powerful method for investigating the same questions. This method, which will be termed "standardized problems," used some of the actual cases written by the managers in the construction of a standardized set of cases each of which depicts a manager faced with a problem to solve or decision to make. In each case, a leader would be asked to assume the role of the manager faced with the situation described and to indicate which decision process he would use if faced with that situation.

Several such sets of cases have been developed. In early research, each set consisted of thirty cases, but more recently longer sets of forty-eight and fifty-four cases have been used. Composition of each set of standardized cases was in accordance with multifactorial experimental design. Cases varied in terms of each of the eight problem attributes used in the normative model and variation in each attribute was independent of each other attribute. This feature permits the assessment of the effects of each of the problem attributes on the decision processes used by a given manager.

The cases themselves spanned a wide range of managerial problems including production scheduling, quality control, portfolio management, personnel allocation and research and development project selection. To date, several thousand managers in the United States and abroad have been studied using this approach.

RESULTS AND CONCLUSIONS

To summarize everything learned in the course of this research is well beyond the scope of this chapter, but it is possible to discuss some of the highlights. Since the results obtained from the two research methods—recalled and standardized problems—are consistent, the major results can be presented independent of the method used.

Perhaps the most striking finding is the weakening of the widespread view that participativeness is a general trait that individual managers exhibit in different amounts. To be sure, there were differences among managers in their general tendencies to utilize participative methods as opposed to autocratic ones. On the standardized problems, these differences accounted for about ten percent of the total variance in the decision processes observed. Furthermore, those managers who tended to use more participative methods such as CII and GII with group problems also tended to use more participative methods like delegation for dealing with individual problems.

However, these differences in behavior between managers were small in comparison with differences within managers. On the standardized problems, no manager has indicated that he would use the same decision process on all problems or decisions, and most use all methods under some circumstances. Taking managers' reports of their behavior in concrete situations, it is clear that they are striving to be flexible in their approaches to different situations.

Some of this variance in behavior within managers can be attributed to widely shared tendencies to respond to some situations by sharing power and others by retaining it. It makes more sense to talk about participative and autocratic situations than it does to talk about participative and autocratic managers. In fact, on the standardized problems, the variance in behavior across problems or cases is from three to five times as large as the variance across managers.

What are the characteristics of an autocratic as opposed to a participative situation? An answer to this question would constitute a partial descriptive model of this aspect of the decision-making process and has been the goal of much of the research conducted. From observations of behavior on both recalled problems and on standardized problems, it is clear that the decision-making process employed by a typical manager is influenced by a large number of factors, many of which also show up in the normative model. Following are several conclusions substantiated by the results on both recalled and standardized problems:

Managers use decision processes providing less opportunity for participation (1) when they possess all the necessary information rather when they lack some of the needed information, (2) when the problem they face is well-structured rather than unstructured, (3) when their subordinates' acceptance of the decision is not critical for the effective implementation of the decision or when the prior probability of acceptance of an autocratic decision is high, and (4) when the personal goals of their subordinates are not congruent with the goals of the organization as manifested in the problem.

These findings concern relatively common or widely shared ways of dealing with organizational problems. The results also strongly suggest that managers have ways of "tailoring" their decision process to the situation that distinguish one manager from another. Theoretically, these can be thought of as differences among managers in decision rules that they employ about when to encourage participation.

Consider, for example, two managers who have identical distributions of the use of the five decision processes shown in Table 1 on a set of thirty cases. In a sense, they are equally participative (or autocratic). However, the situations in which they permit or encourage participation in decision-making on the part of their subordinates may be very different. One may restrict the participation of his subordinates to decisions without a quality requirement, whereas the other may restrict their participation to problems with a quality requirement. The former would be more inclined to use participative decision processes (like GII) on such decisions as what color the walls should be painted or when the company picnic should be held. The latter would be more likely to encourage participation in decision-making on decisions that have a clear and demonstrable impact on the organization's success in achieving its external goals.

Use of the standardized problem set permits the assessment of such differences in decision rules that govern choices among decision-making processes. Since the cases are selected in accordance with an experimental design, they can indicate differences in the behavior of managers attributable not only to the existence of a quality requirement in the problem but also in the effects of acceptance requirements, conflict, information requirements, and the like.

The research using both recalled and standardized problems has also permitted the examination of similarities and differences between the behavior of the normative model and the behavior of a typical manager. Such an analysis reveals, at the very least, what behavioral changes could be expected if managers began using the normative model as the basis for choosing their decision-making processes.

A typical manager says he would (or did) use exactly the same decision process as that shown in Figure 1 in about forty percent of the group problems. In two-thirds of the situations, his behavior is consistent with the feasible set of methods proposed in the model. However, in the remaining one-third of the situations, his behavior violates at least one of the seven rules underlying the model. Results show significantly higher agreement with the normative model for individual problems than for group problems.

The rules designed to protect the acceptance or commitment of the decision have substantially higher probabilities of being violated than do the rules designed to protect the quality or rationality of the decision. Assuming for the moment that these two sets of rules have equal validity, these findings strongly suggest that the decisions made by typical managers are more likely to prove ineffective due to deficiencies of acceptance by subordinates than due to deficiencies in decision quality.

Another striking difference between the behavior of the model and of the typical manager lies in the fact that the former shows far greater variance with the situation. If a typical manager voluntarily used the model as the basis for choosing his methods of making decisions, he would become both more autocratic and more participative. He would employ autocratic methods more frequently in situations in which his subordinates were unaffected by the decision and participative methods more frequently when his subordinates' cooperation and support were critical and/or their information and expertise were required.

It should be noted that the typical manager to whom we have been referring is merely a statistical average of the several thousand who have been studied over the last three or four years. There is a great deal of variation around that average. As evidenced by their behavior on standardized problems, some managers are already behaving in a manner that is highly consistent with the model, while others' behavior is clearly at variance with it.

The research program that has been summarized was conducted in order to shed new light on the causes and consequences of decision-making processes used by leaders in formal organizations. In the course of research, it was realized that the data collection procedures, with appropriate additions and modifications, might also serve a useful function in leadership development. From this realization evolved an important by-product of the research activities—a new approach to leadership training based on the concepts in the normative model and the empirical methods of the descriptive research.

A detailed description of this training program and of initial attempts to evaluate its effectiveness may be found in Vroom and Yetton (1973, Chapter 8). It is based on the premise that one of the critical skills required of all leaders is the ability to adapt their behavior to the demands of the situation and that a component of this skill involves selecting the appropriate decision-making process for each problem or decision they confront. The purpose of the program is not to "train" managers to use the model in their everyday decision-making activities. Instead the model serves as a device for encouraging managers to examine their leadership styles and for coming to a conscious realization of their own, often implicit, choices among decision processes, including their similarity and dissimilarity with the model. By helping managers to become aware of their present behavior and of alternatives to it, the training provides a basis for rethinking their leadership style to be more consistent with goals and objectives. Succinctly, the training is intended to transform habits into choices rather than to program a leader with a particular method of making choices.

A fundamental part of the program in its present form is the use of a set of standardized cases previously described in connection with the descriptive phase of the research. Each participant specifies the decision process he would employ if he were the leader described in the case. His responses to the entire set of cases are processed by computer, which generates a highly detailed analysis of his leadership style. The responses for all participants in a single course are typically processed simultaneously, permitting the calculation of differences between the person and others in the same program.

In its latest form, a single computer printout for a person consists of seven $15''$ by $11''$ pages, each filled with graphs and tables highlighting different features of his behavior. Understanding the results requires a detailed knowledge of the concepts underlying the model, something already developed in one of the previous phases of the training program. The printout is accompanied by a manual that aids in explaining the results and provides suggested steps to be followed in extracting the full meaning from the printout.

Following are a few of the questions that the printout answers:

1. How autocratic or participative am I in my dealings with subordinates in the program?
2. What decision processes do I use more or less frequently than the average?
3. How close does my behavior come to that of the model? How frequently does my behavior agree with the feasible set? What evidence is there that my leadership style reflects the pressure of time as opposed to a concern with the development of my subordinates? How do I compare in these respects with other participants in the program?
4. What rules do I violate most frequently and least frequently? On what cases did I violate these rules? Does my leadership style reflect more concern with getting decisions that are high in quality or with getting decisions that are accepted?

When a typical manager receives his printout, he immediately goes to work trying to understand what it tells him about himself. After most of the major results have been understood, he goes back to the set of cases to reread those on which he has violated rules. Typically, managers show an interest in discussing and comparing their results with others in the program. Gatherings of four to six people comparing their results and their interpretations of them, often for several hours at a stretch, were such a common feature that they have recently been institutionalized as part of the procedure.

It should be emphasized that this method of providing feedback on their leadership style is just one part of the total training experience which encompasses over thirty hours over a period of three successive days. To date, no long-term evaluations of its effectiveness have been undertaken, but initial results appear quite promising.

SUMMARY

How far has the understanding of leadership progressed in the 50 years since the Hawthorne Studies? The picture that has been painted in this chapter is one of false starts stemming from oversimplified conceptions of the process. An encouraging sign, however, is the increased interest in contingency theories or models incorporating both leader and situational variables. In this chapter I have spent much time describing one kind of contingency model; Professor Fiedler, who accompanies me on this panel, has developed another form of contingency model.

These two models share a number of qualities, but are different in several important aspects. I believe that Professor Fiedler sees much greater consistency and less flexibility in leader behavior than is required by the normative model or exhibited in managers' statements of how they would behave on the problem set. I suspect that we also have substantially different views on the potential for modification of leadership style through training and development. Both of these are fascinating and important questions and I for one would enjoy exploring them during our later discussion. But there is one prediction about which I feel quite confident. Fifty years from now, both contingency models will be found wanting in detail if not in substance. If either Professor Fiedler or I am remembered at that time, it will be for the same reason that we meet to commemorate the Hawthorne Studies this week—the kinds of questions we posed rather than the specific answers we provided.

REFERENCES

Bass, B. M. *Leadership, Psychology and Organizational Behavior.* New York: Harper, 1960.
Blake, R. and Mouton, J. *The Managerial Grid.* Houston: Gulf, 1964.
Gibb, C. A. Leadership, in *Handbook of Social Psychology.* Edited by G. Lindzey and E. Aronson. Vol. 4 Reading, Mass: Addison-Wesley, 1969.
Hartshorne, H. and May, M. A. *Studies in Deceit.* New York: Macmillan, 1928.
Korman, A. K. " 'Consideration,' 'initiating structure,' and organizational criteria—a review," in *Personnel Psychology.* 19: 1966.
Lewin, K. *Field Theory in Social Science.* Edited by D. Cartwright. New York: Harper, 1941.
Likert, R. *New Patterns of Management.* New York: McGraw-Hill, 1961.
Likert, R. *The Human Organization.* New York: McGraw-Hill, 1967.
Lowin, A. "Participative decision-making: a model, literature critique, and prescriptions for research," in *Organizational Behavior and Human Performance.* 3: 1968.
Mischel, W. *Personality and Assessment.* New York: Wiley, 1968.
Maier, N. R. F., Solem, A. R., and Maier, A. A. *Supervisory and Executive Development: A Manual for Role Playing.* New York: Wiley, 1954.
Sales, S. M. "Supervisory style and productivity: review and theory," in *Personnel Psychology.* 19: 1966.
Stogdill, R. M. "Personal factors associated with leadership: a survey of the literature," in *Journal of Psychology.* 25: 1948.
Vroom, V. H. *Work and Motivation.* New York: Wiley, 1964.
Vroom, V. H. A New Look at Managerial Decision-Making, in *Organizational Dynamics.* 1: 1973.
Vroom, V. H. and Jago, A. G. Decision-Making as a Social Process: Normative and Descriptive Models of Leader Behavior, in *Decision Sciences,* in press.
Vroom, V. H. and Yetton, P. W. A Normative Model of Leadership Styles, In *Readings in Managerial Psychology.* Edited by H. J. Leavitt and L. Pondy. Second Edition. Chicago: University of Chicago Press, 1973.
Wood, M. J. Power Relationships and Group Decision Making in Organizations, in *Psychological Bulletin,* in press.

PART VIII

Summary and Synthesis

Many different ideas and issues were brought out during this symposium. While some areas of agreement resulted, there were also extensive differences of opinion. In this section the following presentations make an attempt to integrate, clarify and summarize these differences. These summarizations also touch upon the question of why behavioral sciences have not made more thorough use of the information available, obstacles to its application, and ways that these barriers might be overcome or circumvented in the future. Issues touching upon generality, reliability and validity of past findings will be discussed in this context.

15

THE HAWTHORNE EFFECT: ITS SOCIETAL MEANING

Marvin D. Dunnette
University of Minnesota

DIVERSITY AND CONFUSION

Whenever I attend a conference such as this, with such startling diversity of content, I try to go home well-armed with gifts for my wife and daughters. This practice does not stem from the usual reasons such as guilt, the love of giving, or the nice feeling of warmth one feels in seeing a glow of happiness on another's face. Instead, it's typically my hope that gifts may create a tone for my homecoming that will be less inquisitive than usual, less curious about "what went on at that big conference you attended." I'm not often well-equipped to make sense to them of what goes on in a conference that has offered such a high quality of intellectual stimulation as we've experienced over these last three days. My inability to articulate all the nuances and excitement of such meetings is correctly perceived by them as a state of confusion, and the homecoming usually leads to a felt, if not openly stated, question: "Was this trip really necessary?" I presume that many of you may be faced with similarly inquisitive families or friends when you return home. This knowledge has added greatly to my level of anxiety over these days of conference attendance because I've been aware that most of you would be looking to me and Professor Lorsch to provide the succinct summary and clean integration—the "cover story," if you will—for each of you to use in your homecoming interactions.

Faced with this responsibility, I've been waiting for serendipity to strike. Some of you may have noted the look of expectancy that's been on my face these three days. I've taken note of all that's been said. Each and every phrase, all the tables, charts, slides, and figures have been examined in the hope that they might, in some hidden way, contain a masterfully brilliant and incisive unifying theme or phrase. I kept pen and paper pad near my bed these nights.

237

Twice, I've risen from fitful slumber—but for other reasons than to record any inspirations or insights. Serendipity has failed me in my hour of need. But, then, I should have known it would. Our social psychological brethren have shown that its likelihood of occurrence is least at exactly those times when it's most desired.

A FRAME OF REFERENCE

I turned finally to my strategy of last resort. When confronted with similar tasks in the past, I've usually brought along to the particular conference a suitcase load of things I've done for other purposes. The reason is twofold: First, surrounded by such tangible evidence of my so-called scholarly activities, my self-esteem is maintained at a level just slightly above that of black despair, thereby guarding against my becoming completely immobilized. More important, that stuff may itself contain a frame of reference or some obscure bit of wisdom around which to create a summarizing or integrative statement. Or, as this session was billed in the program, "issues will be integrated, clarified, and summarized."

One task that was completed during the summer of 1974 did emerge as a possibility for providing the necessary frame of reference. In effect, it is merely a set of 17 categories; or, if you like, critical dimensions, that I believe encompass quite completely the domain of effective leadership in organizations. It is my intention to cast what has been said during this conference within the framework of what it is that managers must do to get their jobs done properly. In essence, I seek to view the last three days' commentary, the prescriptions and proscriptions, the theories, practices and research results from the eyes of an operating manager in an organization, and to derive from that viewpoint some general principles about getting work done and/or improving how work gets done in organizational settings.

First, let me describe how these 17 categories were created. Over the last five years or so, various colleagues and I have had occasion to collect critical incidents descriptive of unusually effective and unusually ineffective supervisory behavior. Others also have carried out such anecdote-gathering tasks. We accumulated the raw data for all the studies we could get our hands on quickly and easily. This amounted to a total of 12 studies including thousands of critical incidents of supervisory behavior for such persons as front line production foremen, top executives in industry, office supervisors, research and development directors, Air Force officers, Naval officers, retail store department managers, and police sergeants, lieutenants, and captains.

My colleagues, David Bownas, Stephan Motowidlo, and I independently sorted behavior statements based on these incidents into categories—a sort of conceptual cluster analysis. I examined the three categorizations, noted areas of agreement—and of disagreement—and then relied on my own "executive judgment" to derive the 17 categories depicted in Figure 1, text as shown and defined more completely in Table 1.

In Figure 1, the 17 dimensions are grouped according to different aspects of an organizational leader's attributes and behaviors. Moreover, the dimensions are arranged in a circle according to the sequence of activities that must be carried out by a manager and his work group members in order to achieve the organization's goals as they seek to utilize available resources while heeding existing organizational constraints. Thus, an organizational leader, whether he is a front line supervisor or a top executive, must depend upon his own knowledge and proficiencies (know-how, responsibility, integrity, wisdom) to engage other organizational persons and units in social interactions (empathize, communicate, represent, motivate, train, coach, coordinate) toward the end of discerning accurately what the organization's goals are as well as what the nature of its resources and constraints may be. As he engages in these interpersonal exchanges, he is, of course, identifying and developing the human resources necessary for carrying out actions relevant to achieving the organization's requirements. The organizational leader then does the thinking, problem solving, and planning (innovate, plan and allocate) necessary to generate action by others and himself (delegate, accomplish, crisis action) toward achieving the desired goals. Throughout, the effective organization leader keeps track of what he and others are doing and the results they obtain (follow-up and document) so that he may maintain a continually changing picture of both accomplished and emerging organizational requirements in the context of changing environmental resources and constraints.

Figure 1. Critical dimensions of effective organizational leadership.

TABLE 1.   Detailed definitions of critical dimensions of organizational leadership portrayed in Figure 1.

1. *KNOW-HOW: Keeping Thoroughly Informed of Organizational Needs and Keeping Up-to-date Technically.* Demonstrating a thorough knowledge of technical specialty; keeping informed of the latest developments in technical specialty; keeping in touch with events happening both inside and outside the organization which may affect organizational goals, resources, and constraints.

2. *RESPONSIBILITY: Readiness and Acceptance of Personal Accountability for Actions.* Being physically and emotionally prepared to carry out assignments; accepting accountability for unit's performance; performing duties conscientiously without requiring close supervision; meeting deadlines; being punctual for meetings.

3. *INTEGRITY: Maintaining High Standards of Business, Professional and Social Ethics.* Behaving according to high standards of business, professional, and social ethics; unimpeachably correct moral and ethical conduct.

4. *WISDOM: Informed (as opposed to "blind") Commitment and Loyalty to Organizational Goals, Policies and Practices.* Accepting company goals and complying with orders and directives from above; endorsing the policies and actions of superiors; offering constructive criticism about policies and decisions formulated by higher management.

5. *EMPATHIZE: Showing Personal Concern and Understanding for Other Persons.* Maintaining harmonious social relationships with others; showing consideration for others' feelings; showing interest in personal problems; being able to size people up accurately and develop constructive working relationships with them.

6. *COMMUNICATE: Communicating Effectively, Thoroughly and Accurately.* Providing complete, concise, accurate, and prompt information to superiors; disseminating full information to subordinates about company policies and objectives; sharing information with other units as necessary; reporting truthfully job activities and progress toward objectives.

7. *REPRESENT: Promoting a Positive Organizational Image to the Public.* Promoting a positive company image to the public; participating actively in community affairs as a company representative; showing genuine concern for the community and society at large; exercising tact and sensitivity while conducting economically advantageous transactions with consumers and suppliers.

8. *MOTIVATE: Motivating both Subordinates and Other Persons Through Example and Challenge.* Setting high performance standards for subordinates and other persons; establishing challenging goals; giving increased responsibility and stimulating assignments; setting an example of dedication and conscientiousness by working diligently and by putting in long hours when necessary.

9. *TRAIN: Determining Subordinates' Training Needs and Instituting Programs to Meet those Needs.* Determining subordinates' training needs; instituting standardized training programs to meet those needs; monitoring the training and development of subordinates; guiding and assisting subordinates on technical matters.

10. *COACH: Providing Direct Performance Feedback to Subordinates and Showing Them How to Improve Performance where Necessary.* Providing performance feedback and job coaching; correcting subordinates whose job performance is not acceptable; using appropriate disciplinary techniques when necessary; rewarding subordinates suitably for superior job performance.

11. *COORDINATE: Negotiating with and Cooperating with Other Organizational Units for Optimal Use of All Resources in Meeting Organizational Goals.* Coordinating and cooperating with other organizational units to achieve company goals with maximum effi-

TABLE 1. *(Continued)*

ciency; volunteering experience and expertise to assist other units to reach their objectives; negotiating with other units for organizational resources; showing broad knowledge about the operations of other units and the company as a whole.

12. *INNOVATE: Developing and Applying Innovative Procedures to Accomplish Organizational Goals and Assignments.* Developing and applying innovative procedures to accomplish assignments; developing new ideas and unique solutions to planning and problem solving; anticipating and coping effectively with change in relation to meeting organizational goals.

13. *PLAN and ALLOCATE: Forming Goals and Allocating Resources to Meet Them.* Taking into account all available information to make timely decisions; formulating goals, policies and plans; monitoring progress toward objectives and adjusting plans and actions as necessary to meet them; anticipating obstacles and contingencies; allocating and scheduling resources to assure their availability when needed.

14. *DELEGATE: Assigning Tasks to Others and Monitoring Performance to Assure High Quality Task Accomplishment.* Delegating and assigning tasks; ensuring that assignments are clearly understood; scheduling and allocating work among subordinates and others equitably and for maximum efficiency; monitoring and evaluating others' performance.

15. *ACCOMPLISH: Persisting with Consistent High Effort in All Facets of Performance to Assure Meeting Organizational Objectives.* Working long hours when necessary to complete assignments; performing "beyond the call of duty;" seeking and willingly accepting challenging assignments and added responsibilities; persisting and overcoming difficult obstacles; sacrificing personal convenience in the pursuit of company objectives.

16. *CRISIS ACTION: Recognizing Critical Problems and Acting Promptly and Decisively to Alleviate Them.* Taking charge quickly in crisis situations; behaving deliberately and rationally under stress; deciding promptly on an alternative course of action when necessitated by unforeseen emergencies.

17. *FOLLOW-UP and DOCUMENT: Documenting Actions and Keeping Accurate Records of Results Obtained to Maintain Up-to-Date Information about Organizational Goals, Resources, and Constraints.* Processing paper work promptly, properly, accurately, and with attention to details; maintaining accurate and current records about projects, personnel, costs, schedules, and equipment; documenting important aspects of decisions and actions; documenting and recording results relevant to organizational goals.

Some may believe that this way of looking at the attributes and functions of organizational leaders is oversimplified. Perhaps it is. Nonetheless, I offer no apology for whatever degree of simplification may have been introduced, because I do not believe that it is possible for anyone to conclude from Figure 1 that the leader's job is simple or easy or lacking in complexity. In fact, I believe that the difficulty of properly and successfully carrying out the functions of leadership portrayed there mirrors very accurately the diversity of content that we have experienced over these three days in this conference. Portrayal of the critical dimensions of effective organizational leadership serves, therefore, as a heuristic model to aid in my attempt to weave a thread of continuity through the many things discussed at this conference.

INSIGHTS OF HAWTHORNE FROM THE LEADER'S VIEWPOINT

First, our view of the makeup of effective organizational leadership forces a strong reassertion of Leavitt's arguments in favor of the basic fact that an important unit of analysis is the group—not only the group looking to our particular manager as the "boss," "rule enforcer," "coordinator," or "leader" (to use Levinson's terms) but also all other groups claiming his membership. Some of these other groups may place our focal manager in subordinate roles; others will find him in coordinate roles as he pursues the interpersonal actions requisite to doing his job. Leavitt's contentions about the usefulness of groups and his ideas about applying the usual personnel administration procedures (selection, compensation, job design, etc.) to groups as units of analysis make good sense. The suggestion can be seen as a step toward formalizing the emphasis on groups as units of work and task analysis and task-oriented behavior that already constitutes important facets of an effective organizational leader's functions.

We should continue to acknowledge, however, that the use of one or more groups as units of study is in no way prejudicial to a continuing attention to individualism. In fact, as someone from the audience suggested, to a great degree, personal identity is defined by and derived from life's group memberships. Thus, we acknowledge the viability of individualism and group or social processes as crucial elements or units of study and reject, thereby, the unstated but mildly implied theme of individualism *versus* social processes which has seemed to be prevalent during these sessions. In fact, individual differences between persons in their underlying aptitudes, dispositions, and proficiencies cry out for attention as important determiners of different levels of leadership and organizational effectiveness in all the dimensions portrayed in Figure 1. Not only our focal manager but all the persons with whom he works may show striking differences in know-how and in all those other behaviors represented by labels such as empathize, communicate, coordinate, innovate, plan, delegate, etc., etc. Lawrence very elegantly pulled together many of these human proficiencies in the exposition of his twin constructs of degree of job uncertainty and capacity to handle job uncertainty. Conceptually, much can be included and understood within Lawrence's constructs, but systematic psychometric research designed to unravel some of the empirical linkages between jobs and persons still must follow the rather complicated but highly creative avenues of endeavor suggested by Guion.

Figure 1 also highlights the importance of environmental circumstances as a basis for understanding how a leader may behave and how effective he will be. As a member of an organizational entity, our focal manager will, to a degree, reflect and behave according to the cultural mores caricatured by Levinson. We can well imagine the possible differences in the relative emphasis a manager might give to the 17 behavioral dimensions depending upon the cultural orientation of his organization. In the power organization, accomplishment, often in response to crisis, and moralistic surveillance may be the most frequent behavioral orientation. In the task organization, know-how, information gathering through communication, coordination, growth of subordinates, and mastery through group efforts and sharing will be the common behaviors.

In addition to his organizational culture, our manager may be expected to appreciate the importance, to his own well-being, of membership in one or more groups. As a member, he will presumably like to have a part in helping to decide issues that are important in affecting his own life. Though he may not use the same words, he will behave in a way to suggest, in agreement with Kahn and Marrow, that "real effects for him rest on feeling a sense of real participation." It is hoped that he may be a party, at least occasionally, to such participation, for he will then begin to gain mastery, develop feelings of worth, and have a sense of trust as suggested by Menninger. Unless he himself has a personal makeup or other severe external social stressors that make him highly vulnerable, his growth and sense of increasing mastery in work will provide a safeguard against such symptomatic responses as those suggested by McLean—withdrawal, increased dependency, loss of energy, and potentially self-destructive responses such as excessive drinking or hyper-agressiveness.

If these generally good outcomes accrue to our manager as a result of being reasonably assured that he is indeed often involved in deciding his own work or career fate, will he then also be a manager who accords similar collaborative privileges to his subordinates? Here, the answer from our panel members is considerably less settled. We can, perhaps, take Schein's word for the one condition when our manager will not empasize participation. If he truly is a believer in Theory X—that "other" people are all lazy, passive, no good, rotten blobs—it is not too likely that he will entertain any great amount of interaction with others; much less, solicit their participation. What if he, however, is a believer in Theory Y? He then believes, essentially, that people are active, potentially capable of hard work and competent effort. As a manager, according to Schein, the believer in Theory Y will be a flexible, alert, analytic and diagnostic, problem-solving manager. In a very important sense, his disposition toward Theory Y may complicate his life as a manager. The Theory Y manager truly does believe in individuality. He recognizes and probably is even excited by human differences. He acknowledges other persons as being capable of adult behavior—even, perhaps most particularly, his subordinates. He will develop expertise in all the interpersonal managerial skills among the 17 dimensions you see labeled in Figure 1. He's the kind of manager who could perhaps even be expected to engage Guion in a dialogue about nomothetic trait theories and to press for some practical answers to questions about static traits, process variables, and what "typologies" among people might be useful to know about for selecting, training, coaching, and motivating people.

Most certainly, our Theory Y manager will be attuned to differences among persons in their capacities for handling and/or preferring various levels of uncertainty in their jobs. I believe he would agree with Lawrence that jobs should be "big" enough so that people will have room to grow in them.

He ought to be the kind of person too that Professors Hackman and Walton would find amenable to and able to cope with the complexities of designing a new plant from scratch, redesigning or enriching jobs and sticking it through to see to it that such efforts work. His respect for the individualities of other persons should do much to assure that he could work patiently and collaboratively within the total system to help change take place rather than merely clutching at "job enrichment" as the latest in a series of potential panaceas.

But will he engage exclusively in what has come to be called participative management? According to several of our panelists, the answer is a clearcut no. Vroom offers empirical evidence showing that intra-individual variability in managerial styles is fully four times larger than between individual variability. Fiedler's evidence, derived from a very different methodological perspective, comes to an essentially similar conclusion. The effective manager, as Schein so tellingly argued, is first of all a diagnostician and a flexible and rational human being. Vroom and Fiedler have shown that an effective manager will behave in a variety of styles depending upon whether he is task or relationship oriented, his level of control and influence, his level of experience or training, his tenure in his current superior-subordinate hierarchy, the time he has available, the completeness of his information, how important subordinate acceptance is for implementation to occur, and whether development or "growth" of subordinates is desired as a consequence of the particular task or problem which is being addressed.

Finally, there is the important leadership function called "motivate" in Figure 1. The behavioral definition for this dimension reads "Motivating both subordinates and other persons through example and challenge." It would include such activities as setting high performance standards; establishing challenging goals; assigning stimulating tasks; and, setting an example of dedication and conscientiousness. In a way, this dimension seems to encompass much of what we have been talking about during these sessions. Certainly, it incorporates, very clearly, the parsimonious explanation offered by Parsons that the Hawthorne results may be seen as reflecting the consequences of goal setting and performance feedback. It is related too to Lawler's wise counsel that pay is most likely to be an effective performance incentive if the connection between performance and pay is made very clear; and further, that that connection may be most readily pinned down and interpersonal trust most clearly developed if employees are closely involved in the design of their pay plans.

THE HAWTHORNE EFFECT: ITS SOCIETAL MEANING

Pause for a moment to consider the rather amazing impact of these early experiments on what we today, as behavioral scientists and as members of society, know and think about the world of work. Emphases on cultural and organizational environment factors, group processes, individual differences, leadership styles, job, work and plant design, individual and group motives, and interpersonal competence were all represented in some way in those classic experiments and highlighted in many ways in the reports of results by Mayo, Roethlisberger, and Dickson. It is little wonder that a first impression of these far-ranging results and their diverse implications would include some sense of disarray and confusion. However, for me, the view now seems quite different. The discipline of seeking to tease out the threads of continuity in these conference papers has left me with a sense—which I hope you may now share—of how very unified it all really is. Our understanding of the world of work does not now seem to me to be in a state of disarray or confusion. Instead, I believe it to be rising—emerging, very much in the spirit of Kenneth Niimi's sculpture of the emancipated worker which has served as our symbol throughout this commemorative conference.

I am optimistic about what we will encounter in our worlds of work of the future. I believe the research, theory, and practice spawned by these pioneering Hawthorne Studies have indeed given us a most remarkable societal Hawthorne Effect. The effect is not to be seen as merely the unplanned behavioral consequences of an experimental investigation nor even the predictably beneficial outcomes of working collaboratively with employees so that they themselves become, to a much fuller degree, masters of their own futures. No . . . the Hawthorne Effect is far more pervasive. It is the willingness, indeed the seeming eagerness on the part of an ever-increasing number of organizational officials, from both public and private sectors, to engage with behavioral scientists in large, system-wide organizational experiments and change efforts. The Hawthorne Effect, for me, means that 25 years from now the social systems of our work worlds will indeed have become experimenting societies—as envisioned and as so deeply desired by Donald Campbell. Best of all, the work groups and organizations of the future will be administered and coordinated by experimental administrators who will be constantly intent on innovation and change and who will be alert always to the evaluation of change according to how human work lives are affected and how they may be improved still further in the years ahead.

16

MANAGERS, BEHAVIORAL SCIENTISTS, AND THE TOWER OF BABEL

Jay W. Lorsch
Harvard University

INTRODUCTION

When I was originally asked to summarize this symposium I agreed to do so, to be very candid, because I had an a priori notion of the theme I wanted to develop. Simply stated, it was that on the book shelves in my office and in those of the distinguished scholars who have presented papers here in the past few days there was sufficient knowledge to solve many of the issues of worker productivity and morale which were at the center of the Hawthorne Studies fifty years ago and which continue to plague the economy today. The problem as I saw it was that because of a variety of forces, managers had been unable and/or unwilling to utilize this knowledge. My basic premise was that in spite of the studies cited in these chapters, managers have failed to use this knowledge outside of a relatively few well-defined experiments.

Among the reasons for this, which I wanted to mention are, the climate of mistrust which characterizes many union-management relationships. This makes it difficult for either side to agree to new approaches to job and organization design. The huge capital investment in existing technology also makes it unrealistic for many industrial managers to consider adopting new ideas in these areas. Similarly the ideas of Frederick J. Taylor have become so engrained in management thinking that it is difficult for many industrial managers to consider and accept the ideas flowing directly and indirectly from the Hawthorne Studies (Taylor). Further, the traditional views of Taylorism, according to our own research data, may be more consistent with the underlying personalities of most factory managers and the existing technologies they use than the prescriptions being offered by many of my behavioral science colleagues (Lorsch and Morse). Richard Hackman, in his paper, did an excellent job of summarizing many of these issues and pointing to the problems they create in implementing the knowledge we have been accumulating. I am delighted that he has made these points and would like to underscore the importance of what he said.

However, I want to focus my attention on another related issue, not because Hackman has stolen my thunder, but because as I have read and thought about the papers presented here, I have come to the realization that the failure of managers to apply behavioral science knowledge broadly in the work setting may also be attributable to a quite different and equally important set of reasons; and one which is related to the quality of what is in all those books which line our office walls. To put it simply and concisely, as we have built our knowledge about behavior in work organizations we seem to have created a babel of concepts and theories, which not only may be confusing to the practitioner, but which have caused behavioral scientists to have disagreements such as those which have characterized the various interpretations of the meaning of the Hawthorne Studies in the papers presented here. In fact I shall argue that this babel has caused us to almost miss the essential meaning of the Hawthorne Studies as the researchers themselves saw it.

THE DIALOGUE BETWEEN PETER AND PAUL

Santayana has said, "When Peter tells you about Paul, you learn more about Peter than Paul." Translated into our context, "When a behavioral scientist tells you about Hawthorne you learn more about that behavioral scientist than you do about the Hawthorne Studies."

To illustrate why I draw this parallel, let me list a sample of what my distinguished colleagues have said was the central meaning of the Hawthorne Studies. Fred Fiedler stated, "The Hawthorne Study acted as an important catalyst to . . . human relations, that is, concern for the employee and warm sympathetic understanding from his supervisor . . . The culmination and the logical limit of this management philosophy was realized by the T-Group and the sensitivity training methods which implicity promised effective leadership by understanding self and others."

Vroom, in contrast, recognizing correctly, I feel, that the Hawthorne Studies raised many questions, indicated that one was whether the changed role of the supervisor, who more frequently consulted with the workers and dealt with them informally, was related to the dramatic increases in productivity in the Relay Assembly Test Room. However, for Marrow and Kahn this is not an open question, but rather the Hawthorne Studies were the first of many studies to demonstrate that participative management does have a positive impact on productivity and satisfaction. To quote Kahn, "Real participation has real effect." Schein, however, seems to disagree. He argues that, "Such data (from the Bank Wiring Room) do not constitute negative evidence for Theory Y, *though they do constitute negative evidence for participative management,* because in all the situations described above, participative management methods might not work at all." (Italics mine.)

This is the only example of an outright conflicting interpretation of the meaning of the Hawthorne Studies, but the other authors have clearly chosen to emphasize different aspects of the studies. For example, Leavitt sees the importance of the studies in their discovery of the role of informal groups. McClean agrees that these studies led to the discovery of informal groups, but adds that they also taught about "a job's social aspects; the importance of recognition and satisfaction; and that job satisfaction and productivity are connected." Walton, too, includes on the list of the significant findings from Hawthorne the importance of informal groups, and then does an excellent job of identifying the several other factors in the Hawthorne experiments which led to the reported results.

So here we have some of the most eminent scholars in the field disagreeing about the meaning of a particular study. This is a concrete example of the babel that may be confusing those in the audience who are practitioners. If behavioral scientists are to develop knowledge which can be useful to the practicing manager, they have to be able to not only draw a coherent set of conclusions about the meaning of one study, but also to find ways to communicate more consistently with each other about the diverse studies in which they engage.

It, therefore, seems critical to understand why we find such confusion about the meaning of the Hawthorne Studies. Is it really just the problem of Peter and Paul, which most of us would agree is not uncommon in everyday discourse? Or is it that the Hawthorne Studies are so complex and wide ranging in their implications that there is something in them for everybody? In this sense the problem may only be that we are like two blind men describing an elephant from different ends by touch.

Certainly the second reason has something to do with the variations in interpretation. Each pair of presenters was asked by the symposium organizers to address a different implication of the main studies. There is no doubt these studies provided a broad range of insights and provocative questions for further research. Even recognizing this, however, I believe the Peter-Paul problem is real and important because not only have the various presenters pointed to different findings, some have also interpreted the same findings differently (i.e., the Schein, Vroom, Marrow and Kahn difference on the Hawthorne Studies' meaning with regard to participative management.) Further, not one of them has really told us what Mayo, Henderson, Roethlisberger, and Dickson, et al. thought Hawthorne was all about. This is particularly disturbing to me because like the other "Peters" who have addressed you, I have my own view of "Paul" (the Hawthorne Studies), having had the privilege of spending over ten years, first studying under and then in direct personal contact as a colleague with our last direct link to these studies, Fritz Roethlisberger. I, and my associates at Harvard, naturally feel that we are in an advantageous position to describe the meaning of the Hawthorne Studies as they were originally seen by those involved with them.

THE "CENTRAL" SIGNIFICANCE OF THE HAWTHORNE STUDIES

So I want to take a few moments to tell you what I think is the "central" meaning of these studies.   As I do so I should make it clear that I put the word "central" in quotation marks to connote that this again is one Peter's interpretation of what was central.   This may seem like a digression from my major theme, however, I do not think that it is, because one of Roethlisberger's greatest frustrations in the years I knew him was the misinterpretations of the Hawthorne results and particularly the failure of others to recognize what he saw as the central conceptual thrust.   In fact, I am sure that much of what we have heard here would have caused a considerable rise in his blood pressure.   As Ed Schein has pointed out in his paper, I suspect Doug McGregor may have felt the same way about various misinterpretations of his work.

The clue to understanding what these studies meant to the original Mayo group I think lies in a habit Fritz Roethlisberger had when he read a new book. He always read the first and particularly the last chapter first to see what the author was up to.   What was the big picture?   If we assume that he thought about his own books in the same way we should then focus our attention on Part V of *Management and the Worker*.   From numerous seminars with him, I have no doubt that to him the really significant conceptual ideas from this study were in fact contained in Chapter XXIV "An Industrial Organization as a Social System."   Building on the ideas of Radcliffe-Brown and Pareto, Roethlisberger and Dickson state "The point of view which gradually emerged from these studies is one from which an industrial organization is regarded as a social system." In this chapter Roethlisberger and Dickson develop this conceptual perspective. In the final two chapters, which follow, they applied the ideas to various management problems in general and to problems of personal practice specifically.

From this social system perspective the industrial organization was seen as having two major functions—problems of balance with the external environment and problems of internal equilibrium in maintaining the type of social organization in which members can work together and satisfy their own desires.   There are two major parts of the system: the technical organization (tools, machinery, physical environment) and the human organization.   The latter was made up of the individuals and the predispositions which they brought into the company and the social organization.   The social organization in turn was made up of the formal organization which was shaped by management and the informal organization.   These parts were seen as interrelated and interdependent.   Jointly they shaped the behavior of the members of the organization.

To the original researchers this was the "central" insight of the Hawthorne

Studies and it has been refined and elaborated by subsequent studies and writings. None of us, including Roethlisberger himself, are wed in perpetuity to the original formulations. In fact, Roethlisberger was usually more comfortable using the improved scheme developed by our colleague George Homans in the Harvard Sociology Department.

From the original Hawthorne study, Homans' work, subsequent studies by students of Roethlisberger at Harvard, a school of thought which viewed organizations as social systems developed. This group of scholars developed a commitment not only to this conceptual scheme for viewing organizations, but also to the method of clinical field research. In order to understand the complex set of situational forces which shaped behavior in organizations one had to make close-in and first-hand observations of the setting. Even though more recent work out of this school has expanded the methodological perspective (e.g. Organization and Environment) this fundamental precept has still been retained. This also meant adhering to "Occam's Razor"—as many variables as you must, as few as you dare. This concern with parsimony was consistent with the school's values which emphasized a pragmatic view of human problems from the point of view of the administrator involved in the situation. Finally this school of thought has developed assumptions about the individual which are consistent with those of Roethlisberger and Dickson. The individual is seen as having a personality which is shaped not only by "a certain native organic endowment," but also by socializations in family and wider society. The "process of socialization is never ending and continues from birth to death" (Roethlisberger and Dickson, page 554). Using these perspectives the Harvard group has not only done research and trained subsequent generations of scholars, it has also trained upward of 20,000 practitioner-oriented students in using this view of organization as a way of thinking about and dealing with human issues. Lest this begin to sound like an advertisement for the Harvard Business School, the reason for describing these outgrowths of Hawthorne, is their similarity, it seems to me, to what Thomas Kuhn in his excellent book on the development of scientific knowledge calls a paradigm. Kuhn characterizes as a scientific paradigm knowledge building achievements that share two characteristics (Kuhn, page 10).

1) "The achievement was sufficiently unprecedented to attract an enduring group of adherents away from competing models of scientific activity."

2) "Simultaneously, it was sufficiently open-ended to leave all sorts of problems for the redefined group of practitioners to resolve."

PARADIGMS AND THE TOWER OF BABEL

Kuhn's basic point, as I understand it, is that such paradigms become the dominant way of thinking in science and that knowledge building in the physical sciences progresses through revolutions; that is, a new paradigm is created which throws over the existing paradigm. When Kuhn speaks of paradigms he is speaking of broad perspectives on natural phenomena. Two examples come to mind— Einstein's view of physics and Watson's descriptions of the development of biological science in the *Double Helix*. I use these examples because they suggest how Kuhn was thinking about the impact of the revolution, the number of adherents it attracts, and the magnitude of the questions it raises for further research when he used the term paradigm.

In that perspective it may seem presumptuous to label the school of thought which developed at Harvard out of the Hawthorne research a paradigm. However, in the context of our field of organizational behavior it seems to me that is exactly what has developed. Further, it seems to me that this is only one of many paradigms which coexist in our field at the moment. Each has implicit in its own assumptions about the individual, its own rules of research, its own historical antecedents and its own values. It is beyond the scope of this paper to try to describe all of these paradigms. That would require an inquiry into the history of knowledge in organizational behavior. However, a few observations can be made. It seems to me that some of the paradigms revolve around the work of one man and his immediate students (e.g., Fred Fiedler and his interesting research on leadership). Others are broader and involve many scholars. Two examples of the latter may suffice to illustrate my point.

At Michigan, out of the work of Rensis Likert, has evolved a paradigm which places value on participation and views the individual as wanting such involvement in his work. The methodology of this group, it seems to me, has focused on large-scale surveys to gather data, as well as action research aimed at moving the behavior of organization members toward what they label "systems 4 values" (Likert). Similarly at Carnegie-Mellon around the work of March, Simon and Cyert there has evolved another paradigm which views man as more rational, puts less emphasis on systematic field data, and more on computer simulations. What I have described, of course, is my own personal view of these paradigms. Others from their perspective might cite different examples or place different emphasis on the characteristics of various paradigms. Nevertheless, I am confident that such multiple paradigms do exist and that they are at the root of the Peter-Paul problem.

The existence of multiple paradigms in organizational behavior at this point in time seems to me to be consistent with the state of social science knowledge in general. For example, in psychology the advocates of Freud coexist with those of Skinner, Maslow, Jung, etc. The reason for the existence of so many paradigms in the social sciences is due to the fact that at this stage of the development of our knowledge there simply is not sufficient believable evidence to overwhelm and discredit any one school of thought. This is compounded by several factors which Myrdal has identified as being responsible for the slower rate of development of the social sciences as compared to the natural sciences (Myrdal-Allport Lecture).

First he points to the fact that social phenomena are more complex and change more rapidly than natural phenomena. There are more contingencies. Data collected at different sites or at different points in time may not be comparable. Therefore, even when students of organization or other social scientists feel they are examining the same phenomena they may in reality not be doing so. This leads to miscommunication and misinterpretation, such as we have seen in the papers presented here, and slows progress.

Myrdal's second point is that social phenomena are much more apt to induce a value bias in the researcher. While natural scientists, because of their own personality predispositions, may feel more or less positively about certain classes of matter, it seems obvious that those of us studying social phenomena are apt to have much stronger values about the people we are studying: what they should be like; what they should believe; how they should behave. It is difficult to separate out these values to develop an objective view of one's own data or the interpretation of others' work. Again the net result can be miscommunication and misunderstanding and painfully slow progress in developing knowledge.

Finally, Myrdal points to the fact that there are more problems of applying knowledge in the social sciences than in the natural sciences. Feedback from applying knowledge in the natural sciences provides insights which accelerates the development of knowledge. Myrdal, I believe, is correct that this is a general problem in the social sciences. However, I believe organizational behavior is fortunate in that we do have a practitioner audience, some of whom are represented here today, who might be willing to more actively apply our knowledge, if we could overcome the sorts of problems which I have been discussing.

If you accept Myrdal's three points, the complexity and changing nature of the social sciences, the value bias and the lack of application, they go a long way toward explaining the existence of multiple paradigms and the retardation of social science knowledge building. However, there is still one other aspect of the present situation we need to understand well; why these multiple paradigms lead to such problems of miscommunication and misunderstanding.

One obvious reason, as I suggested implicitly above, is the fact that the various paradigms each have their own assumptions, value codes and language, which make it difficult for persons associated with one paradigm to hear those associated with another. This also helps explain why so often we find that Peter tells us more about himself than he does about Paul. Not really understanding the other paradigm, each behavioral scientist naturally tells us more about what he knows than what he doesn't. As Kuhn points out, a similar situation exists in the natural sciences (Kuhn pages 200–204). Kuhn also indicates that in the natural sciences even when the translation process is completed successfully, i.e., when a scientist in one group is able to understand the language of a new paradigm and is persuaded by the evidence that it is superior to his own, he has great trouble internalizing it. In a sense he is a bit like a person of one country going to live in another country. He accepts the mores of his adopted country and maybe a part of it, but it is never really a part of him. Again, I believe this is precisely parallel to our own field. We are socialized by our education into one paradigm and become so committed to it that we find it difficult to fully accept and internalize new and contradictory evidence.

All of this I believe is accentuated by the institutional arrangements within which we do our work. The reward and promotion practices at both the doctoral and postdoctoral level encourage us to work within the existing paradigms at our institution. Since, as Watson so aptly demonstrated, even scientists have certain competitive tendencies, we encourage younger scholars to attack other paradigms and do so ourselves. Besides, there is nothing a professional journal editor likes more than a good argument. It is certain to stimulate reader interest.

In a nutshell then, my argument is that our field, like other scientific disciplines, advances through the emergence of new competing and conflicting paradigms. Because of the state of our knowledge and the nature of the phenomena we study, we find ourselves fifty years after Hawthorne confronted with multiple paradigms none of which is dominant. Because those of us in the field are human and work in institutions which induce a certain amount of competition, we find ourselves as scientists, and our practitioner audience finds itself with a babel of concepts, interpretations, and prescriptions.

A MODEST PROPOSAL

I am not naive enough to assume that anything I say will make these difficulties disappear. As I suggested above, these problems exist because scientists—natural and behavioral—are human. Another one of those many ramifications of the Hawthorne Studies highlighted the difficulty of human communication. Further, even if we could make the competitive spirit disappear, I'm not convinced that it would be useful. Since we are human, the competitive opportunity may be an important impetus to our creativity as behavioral scientists. What I would like to do is outline a set of modest proposals for how behavioral scientists and their managerial audience might, from their perspectives, manage this problem so that we can accelerate the rate at which we accumulate and apply knowledge about human behavior in organizations.

First, I believe we all, managers and academicians alike, must take greater care in reading and interpreting the work of others. In my judgement Ed Schein in his paper has tried to give us a concrete lesson in the importance of this. As Schein suggests, McGregor's work has been misinterpreted as much, if not more, than anybody's. And candidly, I would have to admit that I, myself, have contributed to this (Morse and Lorsch). In reading books in this field, we have to learn to read critically, in the best sense of that word. What is the author trying to accomplish? What are his/her values? What is his/her intellectual heritage? What concepts and variables does the author use? Are they clearly defined? What data does the study provide? What are the limits of generalizing from that data to other situations? If the author makes prescriptions, to what extent are they consistent with the author's personal values? These are obviously tough questions to answer. Probably it is impossible to answer any of them fully. Yet, if we learn to read with care, we may be able to break through the armor of our own values and paradigms and more objectively judge the work of others.

Consistent with these suggestions to the readers in the audience, I believe there are complementary steps which those of us who do research and write should follow:

1. First we need to be more explicit in our writing about where we come from. Let us state our intellectual heritage and our values clearly and frankly so that our work can be judged in those terms.

2. We also should be more explicit about our assumptions about the nature of individuals. What is our view of human motivation; to what extent and how do we believe the individual can grow, develop, and alter his/her behavior? As Harry Levinson has pointed out to me in several conversations, one cannot assess a theory about organization unless one first understands the author's beliefs about the make-up of the individual actors in that organization. One of the pleasant surprises for me in renewing my acquaintance with *Management and the Worker* was that Roethlisberger and Dickson had followed this prescription forty years ago (Roethlisberger and Dickson, page 554).

3. It is also important to be explicit about the situational conditions which were present in the locations where data are gathered. What is the nature of the work? What is the ethnic, sex, age, educational level, and composition of the workforce involved? Are they union or nonunion; from small town, country or city? What is the history of the organization(s)? How large is the organization(s)? Are there aspects of the organization's culture not reflected in the data, which are helpful in understanding it and/or the author's interpretation of it?

4. Finally, we need to be much more precise and explicit in defining our concepts and variables. Connected to this wherever possible, let us try to use the concepts and/or variables and methods developed by others. That is, let's not reinvent the wheel, but rather try to use common instruments, scales, etc., when this can be done.

I have used the word "modest" to describe these ideas to emphasize that I see them as avenues for controlling our dialogue across paradigms and reducing miscommunication. If the view of knowledge building and the state of our field which I have described is at all accurate, I suspect we and our successors shall spend the next fifty years sorting our many of these issues. This does not mean that the practitioners in the room should close their briefcases in despair. For I am firmly convinced that our book shelves already contain useful knowledge you can put to work. If we, as behavioral scientists, can reduce the level of our babel by trying as Peter to understand ourselves, as well as the Pauls about whom we are writing, we can help the practitioner understand which of these existing ideas are relevant to his/her problems, as well as build new knowledge more rapidly.

If in conclusion, I may allow my own paradigm to show, my own bet is that if we follow the prescriptions I have spelled out above, we shall find that many of the arguments in which we are now engaged will be resolved by understanding more fully, from a social systems perspective, the situational factors which shape behavior in the various places we gather research data and apply our ideas. We will then be building the contingency theory mentioned several times during this symposium. But then I promised myself I would not contribute to the babel . . .

REFERENCES

Homans, George. *The Human Group.* Harcourt Brace, New York, 1950.
Kuhn, Thomas S. *The Structure of Scientific Revolutions.* Second Edition, Volume 11, No. 2, The University of Chicago Press, 1970.
Lorsch, Jay W. and Morse, John J. *Individuals and Their Members.* Harper & Row, New York, 1974.
Myrdal, G. Gordon Alport Memorial Lecture. Harvard University, November 4, 1971.

APPENDICES

THE LEARNING OF DOING: HAWTHORNE IN HISTORICAL PERSPECTIVE

Henry M. Boettinger
Director of Corporate Planning
American Telephone and Telegraph Company

(Keynote Address for the Symposium, *Man and Work in Society*, on the occasion of the 50th Anniversary of the Hawthorne Studies, November 11, 1974.)

INTRODUCTION

Since the birth of the Hawthorne Studies occurred simultaneously with mine, any knowledge I have of their conduct is necessarily hearsay. Yet my life—and the lives of countless others—has been subtly altered by what began in the most unlikely locale for the genesis of a quiet social revolution, a factory room near Chicago where young women assembled electrical relays.

We are right to commemorate those pragmatic pioneers, not in idolatrous awe or maudlin nostalgia, but as a landmark in man's quest for bettering the condition and quality of his working hours. Like most explorers, they did not find what they sought, but, instead, like the great ones, they were sharp-witted and open-minded enough to recognize a genuine discovery beyond their original intent. Yet, the listing of their findings and recommendations for application strike modern managers as banal and obvious. (Much as the ideas of Einstein appear to today's young physicists who studied their relativity in high school.)

Why, then, look back? I submit two reasons. First, the concepts and approach display an awareness of possibilities—perhaps inarticulate—for improvement of complex human-technical systems, and we could sorely use that confident outlook today. Second, we can acquire, from our own vantage point, a perspective of ourselves, the Hawthorne experimenters, and their progressive predecessors. A good antidote to the cynical and pessimistic malaise which afflicts and sours our own age's *Weltanschauung* may be found in perceiving our place in a historical continuum reaching back to those ancient river civilizations when men built great cultures for the first time by organized social effort.

THE FACTORY AS A SOCIAL SYSTEM

The rise of the factory is linked to the early phases of the Industrial Revolution, and the social history of America, Britain, and Western Europe shows it to be both a major cause and effect in every nation's development. The well-run factory was at once the microcosm of many nineteenth-century rationalists' ordering of the good society, and of many humanists' horror as to how civilization was tending toward a world of insects. Owners called their employees "hands," and appeared interested only in paying for what that part of human beings could do for them.

My own introduction to factory life occurred when I was thirteen. (Though the requirements for drama call for an experience of Dickensian misery, I must confess enjoyment of every minute during those three summer months.) The factory at Baltimore employed about 600 persons, most of whom lived nearby. Its products were brushes, ranging from extremely expensive tools for master painters to items sold over five-and-ten-cent store brand names, and monster industrial roll-brushes with "wire" bristles. Several generations of families came there as youngsters and retired in their seventies. My own family was one of those, and I was given the job of office boy as a social benevolence on the death of my father, who had been a popular foreman. Almost none of the personnel had ever been to a college—including the executives. No more exciting job for a youngster could be imagined, and I see it now as an unparalleled preparation for appreciating the events at Hawthorne.

That world has vanished—and so have such jobs as mine since the Child Labor Laws—but consider what wonders I saw with eyes fresh from grammar school. Each morning at 7:00 A.M., I picked up two canvas sacks of mail from the post office across the road (once trod by General Braddock's troops on their march to Pittsburgh). The main line of the Pennsylvania Railroad ran perpendicular to that old road, and the morning freight train rattled by as I entered the fan-lighted, columned doors of the office. (I learned later that the road and railroad had dictated the plant's location.)

I reported to the General Manager's secretary and had to sort out all the mail, time-stamp it, and get it ready for my rounds by the time the steam whistle blew at 8:00. There were two great stimuli to the imagination: the mail itself and the four walks around the entire plant each day. In those bags were orders from all over the country and the world, bills of lading for bristles from China carried on romantically named ships, checks on banks in foreign countries, letters from salesmen, bills for machine tool parts, complaints, employment applications, and advertisements for every kind of new machinery. Those bags were the links to the outside world of that entire economic community, and I saw how those flimsy sheets could cause alarm, despondency, or joyous celebrations as I blithely deposited them on the desks of my clients in that depression year.

I discovered early the two "cultures" of the little world—the clean, Georgian office (where I worked in an alcove), and the five-story brick factory which could have been transported from Manchester at the time of Napoleon. They were separate, socially and physically, with yards and bridges between. I see now that my job was the information system of its day. The world of "the office" was one of salesmen, advertising, secretaries, accountants, visitors, and bosses. The "factory" was the domain of seven feudal chieftains, called foremen, who dressed in the same rough clothes as their people, but wore neckties as their badge of office! Each "department" had its own character and mystique, a distinct code of social behavior evolved over decades, and there was little personnel movement between them. Men bare to the waist worked like stokers before the boilers where bristles gathered by Chinese peasants from wild hogs were cleaned; others in the power house attended huge steam engines which drove the factory's belt and shafting; overalled mechanics worked at lathes and drills; ink-stained printers fed their presses; venerable master-brush makers—in a graded society all their own—worked at benches with chemists' balances for weighing bristle, and helped apprentices learn their trade; young women packed and labeled boxes made by a group of young men nearby; dark, shelved halls held the inventory stock; black men led by a German-speaking foreman held the shipping docks; and on one noisy floor, men turned oak, maple and pine planks into handles, distinctively lacquered and colored for every grade and model; and the boiling vats and heat of the vulcanizers still rises in my nostrils.

Every variety of industrial noise and rhythm abounded; a wild assortment of odors could tell a blind man where he was, and the hum, buzz, shouts and laughter of human beings at work made its own peculiar harmony. I see now that I was a strange link between office and factory, carrying colored coupons on which pay envelopes for piece work were based, production reports compiled, and alterations in management determined. Just before I left I even saw technological change when a raffish type called a "chemist" reported for duty after the supply of bristles from China was stopped. He was joined later by an "engineer." Both were considered exotic imports for years, I'm told, though their efforts eventually saved the plant's life. (These scientific commandos found chemical substitutes for a basic material cut off by war. May we be as lucky today in coping with our own shortages.)

Why detain you with such an autobiographical snippet? Later knowledge showed me that tens of millions of our fellow citizens spent their working lives in places very similar to that factory-office. Also, nearly every economic and social dimension of our national evolution was there to see, manifested in the stark reality of living, breathing human beings, each interdependent on the other—even if unaware of it—and whose lives were affected by forces and events far beyond their control. That little production module—together with thousands of others—added its contribution to that intellectual abstraction we call "the national economy," but its nature was assimilable by a child. It existed because of evolutionary forces unknown to all of its members, and yet had its unique place in the continuum of history.

I believe everyone working there still possessed a naive faith in the idea of progress, which now, of course, is unfashionable. They felt life for their children would somehow be better than theirs, even if they had no notion of how that would be done, or who or what would be the driving force for expected improvement. In this, they were legatees of an immense inheritance from thinkers past, of whom they had never heard. Their attitudes, I saw later, were derived osmotically from three sources, nearly all contemporary with one another. Saint-Simon (1760-1825); Fourier (1772-1837); and Owen (1771-1858), each an almost fanatical rationalist for the improvement of the condition of man, and whose detailed programs and polemics embraced the social, moral, economic, and scientific dimensions of life.

How could we make improvements in that factory process of benefit to all? Taylor, of course, made great strides through analysis of work processes, and then, by resynthesizing the analyzed parts according to the principles of his Scientific Management, produced increased efficiencies and lowered costs. Yet, there was a whiff of exploitation about it that has never been completely eliminated, and few "stop-watch men" have ever won awards for popularity. (Lenin's enthusiasm for the method should have suggested that we be wary of secondary consequences.)

That great pioneer in workmen's welfare, Josiah Wedgwood (1730-1795), benevolent to his core, described his intended method for producing pottery of the highest quality as: "I wish to make such machines of my men as cannot err." By this, Wedgwood, who began work as a potter at eleven years of age, meant to eliminate the evils of drunkenness, sporadic employment, unsanitary housing, and absenteeism, but lesser men truly saw their employees as a form of abundant and low-priced machinery. Under their ascendancy, the social glue of a community gradually dissolved, and their dour, harsh attitudes laid the foundation for hostility between "Capital" and "Labor," between "Us" and "Them," which still plagues both industrial relations and politics in Europe. Thus, the factory as a community declined. But while its basic nature as a social aggregation did not die, it did become comatose, awaiting some unknown agent to waken it from decades of slumber.

THE SMEATONIAN TRADITION

Another contemporary of those social reformers above was the Englishman, John Smeaton (1724-1792). The greatest civil engineer of his age (he built the Eddystone Light), Smeaton turned his fertile, quantitative imagination on nearly every facet of the Industrial Revolution. Although his life is filled with significant innovative achievements, his greatest invention was conceptual: the method of making incremental improvements in existing technological systems. Thousands of our contemporary engineers who have never heard of him apply his approach in the daily practice of their profession. Smeaton set himself the task of improving the efficiency of water wheels, steam engines, and mill machinery. He devised ingenious ways of precisely measuring input energy and output, and then, by varying one parameter of the system at a time in experimental set-ups, determined the design criteria, or settings, which produced an optimum relationship between input and output. He achieved fantastic multiples of improvement in devices, many of which had been subject to years of groping, intuitive ingenuity from master mechanics.

Smeaton's method does not lead to breakthroughs, but does produce the kind of gradual progress most managers and employees prefer. It also assumes that all other factors can be held constant while one is varied, and that the ensemble of optimized variables will add to an optimized totality or system. The method also assumes the common sense notion that every variable has one best point, i.e., that the output-input function is concave with a peak. He undertook to find that point by successive, stepped iterations of an incremental measure. The Hawthorne engineers were direct descendants of this tradition, and a great deal of the world's technological progress follows from its application.

Consider the origin of the Hawthorne Studies. The research question to be answered was: "How does the output production of telephone relays vary with the light intensity at the bench where they are assembled?" This appears to be a classic Smeatonian experiment, and the question assumes that an optimum light intensity should exist. Common sense says that it is hard to do the work in total darkness or under the glare of an arc light, therefore the best level of light for the job is somewhere in between. Presumably, after solving the "light" problem, one would go on the solve the "chair height" problem, the "pliers" problem, the "reach" problem, the "pace" problem, etc., until the entire ensemble of factors involved were all "solved" for their optima. Anything more straightforward or mundane is hard to imagine. Yet we are here today to celebrate their effort. Why? Simply because Smeaton's method, so powerful with machines, did not work with human beings. Seldom has a negative result or counter-instance to a theory's prediction had such profound reverberations on managerial thought.

"THE HAWTHORNE EFFECT"

Oversimplified, the result which baffled the engineers was that production increased no matter what changes they made in any direction, even return to the original conditions! The experiment later blossomed into studies of almost everything which might have a bearing, and methods extended to in-depth interviews, physical examinations, and sociological group analysis. What has been called "the Hawthorne Effect" is the "discovery" that "other factors cannot be held constant" in dealing with conscious persons who are part of a production process. The mere observation of human beings, the showing of management concern, the processes of experiment, and the interaction of the people with those conducting the experiment—all these themselves were a stimulus to progress (measured in production efficiency) which swamped the purity of classic hypothesis testing. Notice that the phrase itself—Hawthorne Effect—seems drawn from the vocabulary of physics where such labels are applied to anomalous phenomena requiring "new theory." So did these phenomena. Alfred North Whitehead's insight that "every human being is a more complex system than any other system to which he belongs" here finds profound affirmation.

The experimenters had rediscovered the social nature of the production process, and the tripartite collaboration of workers, management and academic investigators from several disciplines was forged. Where natural science had made its incursions to production a century before, here was the penetration for contribution by the social and behavioral scientists. The Germans distinguish between *Naturwissenshaft* and *Geisteswissenshaft*, i.e., the natural and the moral sciences. That adjective of "moral" somehow strikes me as more appropriate in this context. All work of this kind seems based on improving the condition of man-at-work, and the implicit teleological attitude of a normative "human goal aimed at" more in line with the reality than the descriptive "behavior," with its pejorative—if unfair—association of manipulation. It is a quest, with many roads and vehicles now available to us for the journey toward "progress"—however defined.

SOME OBSERVATIONS

The possibilities for improvement, whether in that factory I described earlier, or in the most modern facilities, are legion. Brilliant men of intellect and passionate men of action can complement each others' contribution. (Especially when the men of action conduct themselves as men of thought, and the men of thought as men of action.) Since Hawthorne, a new system, theory, or program comes to prominence about every five years. Whether human relations, organization development, management by objectives, appraisal systems, psychological testing, job enrichment, the "Work Itself," participatory management, X and Y motivation styles, freeform and matrix organization, sensitivity training, or whatever, each has its momentum to contribute to the dynamics of work, and as new schools of thought emerge and are applied, its hard kernel of truth is stripped of the irrelevant or obsolete and becomes a permanent addition to our culture. Excessive skepticism or dismissal of an innovation because it is not a panacea is foolish. Our advances here are more like the accretions of a coral reef than a philosopher's stone which solves all problems of a class at one stroke. We also know "Forrester's Law" states that intuitive interventions—however well-intentioned—in a complex system will almost always cause it to become worse.

History is replete with breakthroughs made by "marginal men" who have forged, sharpened and honed their skills in one field but take them to another in the spirit of adventure. So was it in Hawthorne, and it can be so again. We have our chance in that both men trained in academic disciplines and those with a passion for humane leadership are beginning to pursue the common quest in tandem. There is a long road ahead, and some measure of mutual suspicion of each other will never be eliminated, but their efforts can be more than the sum of its parts—in fact, must be.

All of us are in a learning mode, with more questions than answers, with more problems than solutions, and in coping with the uncertainties and instabilities of our time might be guided by the maxim of Michael Faraday: "That man only is to be condemned and despised who is not in a stage of transition."

The scholars who will present here the results and inferences of their current research are in Faraday's tradition. Hawthorne was a milestone on a road which began centuries before and whose end we cannot see. Perhaps we honor it best by taking measure of our progress since that brilliant marker was placed on man's journey toward a better world.

A PERSONAL REPORT FROM HAWTHORNE

Wyllys Rheingrover
General Manager, Hawthorne Works

(Editor's Note: The Hawthorne Works today is a seventy-year-old plant spread over 140 acres with nearly five million square feet of floor space under roof. It is the oldest and largest of Western Electric's 22 manufacturing plants, employing approximately 10,000 people, many of whom have service dates going back to the period of the Hawthorne Studies. The physical layout of the plant remains essentially what it was in 1924, although much of the interior has been modernized to accommodate newer, more sophisticated manufacturing techniques.

Its major product lines, once ranging across the spectrum of electrical equipment, today are limited to telephone cable, electromechanical switching equipment and electronic components. Still, it prides itself on remaining competitive with the company's more modern plants, and great effort is made by its management and workers to maintain the tradition of pride in workmanship which has sustained the huge factory for nearly three-quarters of a century.

Wyllys Rheingrover, the Hawthorne Works' general manager, provides some of the flavor that continues to permeate the historic factory in his welcoming address during the 50th anniversary symposium's visit to Hawthorne.)

In trying to decide what I could say to you today—something that might be meaningful to an august group such as this—I decided to tell you a little about how we run the business today. That could possibly do two things: 1) help you a little bit to understand where we are—how far we have come—and how far we still have to go; and 2) provide some kind of response to the question of the practical value of the Hawthorne Studies. In the light of how we operate, you can decide for yourself whether there is a relationship.

At the outset, I can tell you one thing for certain—we do not manage as well as we know how. That may surprise you, but it is true. Remember the old farmer who was visited for the first time by the young county agent—fresh out of college and eager to show the way to bright new worlds? "Mr. Brown," the young man exuded, "we can show you ways to improve your production beyond anything you ever dreamed. Doesn't that excite you?"

"No, I guess not," the old farmer replied. "I already know a lot more than I'm using." If you will let me develop that point a little more, I would like to relate some experiences we have gone through here at Hawthorne during the past two or three years.

A few years ago we started a supervisory newsletter to keep our first and second level supervisors up-to-date with changes in the business. From our point of view at the time, we could not have started at a worse time. Business was bad, we were laying off people, we were demoting supervisors—and things were getting worse. Of course we recognized that a newsletter for our supervisors had to be accurate and honest—but we were actually fearful of putting bad information in print. We did it, however, and then quickly turned our backs to deaden the noise of the explosion we thought would follow.

But do you know what happened? The feedback was terrific! Supervisors called us up to tell us what a great idea the newsletter was. Now they could get up-to-date and accurate information on the state of the business. Nobody blew up and no one collapsed in a state of shock because we admitted that business was bad. They already knew it was bad but they didn't know the full effect. That put them at a disadvantage in dealing with their own workers. People want the truth, even when it's bad. We know that, but we often act as though we don't. We are unwilling to accept the evidence, even when we witness it ourselves. So we do not manage as well as we know how—frequently because we do not have the courage to act on our own convictions.

It is not easy to bridge the information gap between management and the worker. A lot of managers I have known—including some right here in this factory—rarely get out and talk to their people because they don't have the time. A manager who has time on his hands is not managing. He is occupying a position. But in my opinion, the manager who waits for some free time to get out and talk to people will never make it.

We talk about communication gaps! The best way to bridge a communication gap is to talk to each other. It is better than documents, letters, memos, and a lot better than house organs. I would like to know how many companies put out a monthly house organ and think they are giving their employees adequate information! I don't want to take anything away from house organs, but did you ever try to talk back to one?

Talking to each other is better, I think. We are spending more and more time talking to each other here at Hawthorne, and I think it pays off. We have a program that we call, "breakfast break," which we think encourages us to talk more comfortably with each other. Two or three times a month, the manager sits down with a group of people—selected at random—and has some coffee and cake with them. They talk about the business—anything the group wants to bring up. There are no taboos. The talks often last three or four hours. The people involved come from every part of the plant. They are punch press operators, cable formers, tool makers, engineers, accountants, supervisors. This program has been going on for a couple of years. We think it pays dividends. People ask tough questions and we can't fake the answers in this kind of a session. Many of these people have 30, 35 and 40 years of service and they aren't afraid to challenge the boss.

But not every manager in the plant holds these breakfast meetings. That is not the way we operate. But it is a program available to everyone who wants to use it—always with the condition that there are no free rides. We do not give any free rides here. We do not say to anybody, "Okay, we think you ought to talk to your people once a week, so we'll let you subtract that from your results bogie!" Who wouldn't sit around and talk for an hour or two every day under those conditions! We encourage people to talk to each other, and we thing it will help their results if they do it with honesty and respect for each other. I think that is the reason and the way to do it.

Perhaps you are asking why, if we think it is so effective, we do not require all managers to get involved in a similar program. Well, that word "require" has always bothered me. The concept of "requiring" someone to communicate seems rather ludicrous to me. It is like "requiring" a professor to publish a book—which I understand some universities do. At the same time, I have to admit that we have not yet invented the perfect mold for a manager—through which we can pass all of our candidates and get neat little rows of soldiers who do everything the right way. What we are trying to create is an atmosphere in which every manager feels free to relate to people in his organization in whatever way he thinks is most effective.

The word "atmosphere" is important. We are trying to generate an atmosphere in this old plant in which everyone feels at liberty to express himself. We want to make certain that when a person wants an audience, he can find one. So we provide a variety of avenues. The "breakfast break" is only one of them. Another is an answer-back program which we call "Open-line."

I am sure you are familiar with this device. A number of companies are beginning to use it. It is similar to the action line columns in daily newspapers. People with problems or questions can send them to the editor, who forwards them to the appropriate manager. The manager is expected to answer within about two weeks. If the program is to be useful, the answers must be accurate and honest. We try to make them so.

We had several letters, for example, wanting to know why factory people were not eligible for a special investment fund which the company makes available to management people. The answer was difficult to couch in flattering terms. It boiled down to the fact that management people are in a more competitive market than are factory workers. We offered the investment opportunity as a lure to certain kinds of people. We did not feel we needed it to attract shop workers. To the shop worker, the program seems discriminatory. To us, it was simply a business decision.

Whether our reasoning was good or bad—and that would depend on your own particular value system—we had to explain in very candid terms why certain people were excluded from the investment opportunity. We are fairly certain from our freedback channels that they did not like the answer. But we are just as certain that they respect the program for giving an honest· answer. Based on surveys we took, the level of trust for Open-line replies runs above 80 percent. I would like it to be 100 percent, but I think 80 is pretty good.

People respond more positively to candor and honesty. We know that. None of us likes to be manipulated, and if we begin to feel that we are, we resist. We lose our incentive. Yet, how many organizations—business, government, educational—operate on the premise of "Tell them no more than you have to. They won't understand." That is the very acme of conceit. They are not as smart as we are, so they would not understand! Therefore, we won't tell them anything to get them upset. We all know this is not good management, but we do it anyway! We do not manage as well as we know how.

For the past two years, we have had a "communications experiment" going on here in this factory. We decided to see if we could test the value of communications. The idea was to isolate a few organizations, open up the flow of information in all directions and see if there were any visible bottom-line results.

At the outset, we made some assumptions which almost dumped us in the creek. For one thing, we assumed that everybody would want to improve communications. We learned quickly, however, that when you say to someone: "Let us help you improve your communication," there is a good chance his reply will be: "Thanks, but no thanks. I'd rather do it myself." It took a lot of persuasion to convince some people that our study was not intended as an affront to their own management skills.

Another mistake we made was a failure to communicate our plans quite adequately to our unions. In the beginning, when we started to pass out questionnaires to test employee attitudes, union stewards went around advising members not to fill them out because they didn't know what it was all about. It took us a few days to clear that up.

The biggest error we made, however, was the assumption that supervisors would see the program as a potential aid to their own bottom-line results. Instead, many saw it as a threat. Since it was a voluntary program, they were not willing to support something that might damage those results. I cannot blame them for that. They know, as I do, that when all the pretty words have blown over the fence, the stalk that is left behind for all to see is called in industry—bottom-line!

Yet, not a single one of those supervisors would tell you that he does not believe in communicating with his people. It is all a matter of priorities. If I am a supervisor on the line and I have to deliver a million relays this Friday, I have to consider which is more important—taking my people off the line for 30 minutes of communications—or having a million relays on the dock when the truck arrives.

We did get our experiment off the ground, however, with varying degrees of participation and enthusiasm. We proved to ourselves once again what we knew at the outset that people respond in a positive way when shown attention. In every area but one where we tried some new communications techniques, there was improvement in bottom-line results. There was improvement in attitudes, too. So why don't we do it all the time? Priorities! There is nothing more effective in slowing down a good flow of information than a higher priority, and priorities in business change about every minute and a half! The point is, of course, that we know the value of good communications and we still don't use it to our best advantage. Other things get in the way. So we do not manage as well as we know how to manage.

At the same time, running a business the size of this plant requires an immense amount of time, effort and money in the area of human relations. We are told—and I suppose it is true—that people used to go to work expecting the boss to tell them what they needed to know and they did not ask too many questions about the other stuff. It isn't that way anymore—at least not in this factory. People want to know what's happening, what plans are being made, and how they are going to be affected. More important, they want a voice in shaping the future of the company they have decided to settle down with. That is the way it should be. If we expect people to invest their lives in industry, then they have a right to be heard. Management in the business world is beginning to listen. Actually, we have no alternative. The result, I think, is that everyone benefits.

About eight months ago we had 125 people in our cable plant walk off the job. We had just introduced some new wage incentive rates in their work area because of engineering improvements in the equipment. The change allowed one man to handle more wire than he could before.

The workers walked out because they said they did not like the new rates. But when we sat down and talked to them, we learned that the new rate was only one of several problems which had been building up over a period of time. Some of their complaints were legitimate. When we corrected them, the strikers dropped their pickets and went back to work at the new rates. The company benefited and so did the workers because we sat down and talked to each other.

But I do not want to imply that our concern for people is limited to the art of conversation. Talking to each other is important but it is not everything. There is that most important thing—the job itself. If people are not interested in the work they are doing, no amount of talk is going to change that.

Unfortunately, industry has a lot of dull, routine jobs which it does not know how to improve. It just so happens that an assembly line operation is the most efficient way to get a lot of things done. Yet, we recognize that, as people become better educated, a smaller percentage of them will be satisfied to spend their lives on jobs that provide little or no challenge or that require very little skill. We have experimented with some job enrichment projects. Most of them have not worked out because they are too expensive. We have to be concerned about the cost of our product or we will not be in business.

Several months ago we invested a few thousand dollars trying to find a more challenging way to build telephone switches. We took some people off a traditional assembly line and trained them to make the entire switch. They liked the work but they could not make it pay off. On the old assembly line, they produced about 120 switches a day, per worker. After six months on the new system, they were still averaging only 100 switches a day.

A lot of job enrichment ideas certainly work. But we are a long way from solving the problem of the dull, routine job in industry. I think the concept of job enrichment can help, but it seems to me we have to look in other directions as well. Automation has not quite fulfilled its promise in that respect. Every time the computer replaces a routine job, it seems to create two. We have to keep in mind, of course, that there are great numbers of people who seek the routine job. For them, the assembly line is not an insult. They want a job that will not tax the intellect, that lets them plan the Friday night party or the weekend picnic. That is what we are told, anyway. I do not know how to provide stimulating work for everyone who wants it. It seems to me there is a fertile field for exploration.

What I have tried to give you here today is a very abbreviated version of how we operate here at Hawthorne. I hope you can relate it in some way to the significance of this symposium. There has been a lot of disagreement over the value of the Hawthorne Studies, but there are a couple of things that we have to accept as fact: 1) They represent the first serious effort to measure the effect of human attitudes on the job; and 2) Management concern for people and their attitudes is apparently different today than it was in 1924. I do not know myself what all the facts are in the chain of events which connects that experience with the present, but except for the symbolism, I would say it is not really very important. I say that because I don't see this symposium as a commemoration of the Hawthorne Studies. I see it as an opportunity to re-evaluate what we know, where we are going, and how we can get there. We have brought together some of the finest minds in the world to examine one of industry's most persistent problems—how to make jobs meaningful to the shop worker. That is a noble challenge for all of us. The real measure of our success, of course, will not be in what we say and do here this week, but in what we do afterward. There is a lot to be done, and if we in this room today do not do it who will?

In conclusion, I would like to make an announcement which I hope will be significant in future relationships between management and workers. Those of you who are familiar with the Hawthorne Studies know that 20,000 interviews were conducted with our employees in the 1928-1930 period. We have narrative reports in our files of every one of these—all anonymous, of course. So we know how the worker felt about his job, his boss, his peers. We have a record of the concerns expressed over family and financial troubles. We know what fears developed for the security of himself and his loved ones as America sank into the Great Depression.

Today, as inflation eats away at savings and buying power, some of the same concerns are evident in our society. People also worry about change in values and morality. They fear for their safety on the streets. In the next several months we will try to measure 'some of these attitudes among Hawthorne's present employee group. We will compare them with those of the 1928-1930 period. We will remake, as well as we can, the conditions under which the earliest interviews were taken, to preserve a valid base for comparison. Our plans are to summarize the findings in published form, and we hope to be able to provide each of you with a copy of the report. We hope this will add something of historical value and further the understanding of man in his work place.

Presented 11/11/74

THE HAWTHORNE STUDIES: THE LEGEND AND THE LEGACY

Howard W. Johnson
Chairman of the Corporation, Massachusetts Institute of Technology

(Banquet Address for the Symposium, *Man and Work in Society*, on the occasion of the 50th Anniversary of the Hawthorne Studies, November 12, 1974.)

It is a pleasure for me to be back in Chicago and an honor to be part of the celebration honoring the fiftieth anniversary of the beginning of the Hawthorne experiments.

Others have dealt with the significance of the Hawthorne Studies and their relevance to the work of today. I would like to address questions that are closer to my own experiences, two in particular: How did the work happen to get done—the work that made the book *Management and The Worker* (published in 1939) and the sequel to it, *Counselling in an Organization* (published in 1966)—and what can we learn about organizations from that process. Second, what are the implications for doing work of this kind today?

On the first question I have turned to two friends from the Bell System who were involved with this work from the early 1930's up to the publication of the second book in 1966. I have sought to draw some conclusions concerning organization on the basis of their careful observations. On the second question, the implications for today, I draw upon my own experiences. As I have been able to piece together the history of this work, seven remarkable men needed to be in the right strategic places for this to happen. Three of them were in Harvard University, four in the Western Electric Company.

At Harvard, the chain begins with A. Lawrence Lowell, who was President in 1919, when he was faced with the choice of the second dean for the Harvard Business School. Lowell had been president of Harvard since 1909 and perhaps could have been expected to make a routine appointment. Instead, he did a rather unusual thing and chose a Boston lawyer (a man with some administrative experience) whom he, Lowell, remembered as his student twenty years before and with whom he had kept in touch. The new dean was Wallace B. Donham who presided over the School for the next twenty-three years and is often regarded as the chief builder of the present institution. A student (both master's and doctoral) during his period as dean says of him, "Donham was a rare combination of experience and talents which gave him a large amount of administrative skill, but much more. His administrative skill was supported not only by a capacity to be pragmatic, but also by a sensitivity to the human values at stake in situations of the moment, as well as in the long run. These capacities were crowned by an outlook that focused on the relation between the educational institution and the community and national life."

The next link in the chain was forged when Donham brought Elton Mayo to the faculty. It was a significant act and was typical of his ability to attract and hold together a faculty of several like Mayo.

Mayo was an Australian with training in psychology and philosophy who taught in Australia for eight years before he came to the University of Pennsylvania as a research associate in 1923 on a study of labor turnover problems in a textile mill. Mayo came to Harvard Business School in 1926, two years after the illumination experiments had started in the Hawthorne plant as a cooperative venture between Western Electric, the National Research Council, and the National Academy of Sciences. Mayo soon became involved in his work, and I am told that it was his leadership and persuasive skills that expanded it into a series of experiments over the next several years. The result was the landmark publication of *Management and the Worker* in 1939 and in the counseling program that grew out of this work.

Let us turn now to the four men in Western Electric. First, there was Clarence G. Stoll, who was works manager at Hawthorne in 1924 when the research started, and who, in 1939, as president of Western Electric, wrote the foreward to *Management and the Worker*. Next was C. L. Rice, assistant works manager at Hawthorne under Stoll in 1924 and his successor as works manager in 1926, when Stoll became vice-president for manufacturing in New York. David Levinger, whom I remember well, was superintendent under Rice and became works manager when Rice retired in 1939. Finally, there was G. A. Pennock who was superintendent under whom the experimental work was done from 1924 to 1933. I am told that these four men were all deeply interested in the research and its fruits and, lacking this attitude by any one of the four, would have made the whole project very difficult if not impossible. The solidity of the Stoll, Rice, Levinger relationship from 1924 to 1939 (when Rice retired) carried the work through its most critical years. The influence of Stoll was to continue until 1947 when he retired. The retirement of Levinger in 1952 marked the start of the sharp decline in the counseling program that grew out of the original studies. Mayo's influence, which began in 1926, when the focus of the research shifted from illumination to the human factors in production, was substantial in keeping the course of this work steady through some of the depression years when this was not easy.

I have given only the briefest highlights of a significant bit of history to stress the importance of the institutional solidity and creativity in both Harvard University and the Western Electric Company of that period that was the absolutely basic condition for work of that kind to be done, then or now. There is, however, a chapter beyond the research work that terminated in about 1933. That was the counseling program that grew out of the work and continued in the Hawthorne plant and elsewhere in the Bell System for the next twenty years and is reported in Roethlisberger's and Dickson's book, *Counseling in an Organization—A Sequel to the Hawthorne Researches*, published in 1966.

This report counts five employee counselors on the staff in 1936. The number of counselors in the Hawthorne plant rose to fifty-five in 1948 and by 1955 it was down to eight. This was, at its peak in 1948, probably the most ambitious single effort to serve an industry and its people in this way that has ever been undertaken. It began because the researches showed that employee preoccupation with their personal problems was a significant element in satisfaction with work and productivity in jobs. Why was it discontinued at the Hawthorne plant and why did the effort fail when counseling on the Hawthorne model was introduced in other Western Electric plants and in several of the operating companies?

Roethlisberger and Dickson are inconclusive, although they discuss the question. They do, however, note that there came a time when new management (after David Levinger's retirement) began to ask questions about justifying the cost of it. Under the impact of this questioning, the program declined.

The two men I consulted, one of whom participated in the program as a counselor at the Hawthorne plant and the other who watched it with some detachment from a spot on the AT&T staff over the entire period, join in the following conclusion. Their answer goes back to the four men in line at Western Electric mentioned earlier, one of whom continued as works manager at Hawthorne into 1952. They were men of unusual interest in the human side of enterprise. The Hawthorne plant was very large and a notably sound operation, judged by the usual productivity and cost standards. It was also a very human place because that was the way the people in charge wanted it. They had been in charge for a long enough time when the counseling program started to have given the culture of that factory a stamp of unusual quality. The counseling program was justified during its peak years because it was congenial to the culture; the justification was philosophical rather than statistical. It was one of the appropriate things to do in a factory that was being managed the way that one was (which was probably why the research that was started there in 1924 was done at that location).

The counseling program disappeared at Hawthorne probably because a new management with a different philosophy came and, ultimately, the culture changed. The counseling program might be viewed, not so much as the means whereby some tangible results were accomplished, as it was just a part of the right way to run a factory. It was implicit in the character of people in charge. "It worked" because it fit into a total philosophy of how to run a successful factory.

When the effort was made to introduce counseling into other locations, even though it was done with great care, it usually was rejected, sooner or later—not because it was either a right or a wrong thing to do, but simply because it was not congenial with the whole culture. The management philosophy that prevailed was different and it did not fit.

It is not a new observation that the human side of an enterprise with some stability in it is a subculture with its own character. Some technologies are acultural and can be moved in or out of an organization with little difficulty. But anything relating to people, as were the original researches at Hawthorne and the counseling program that grew out of it, if it is to prosper and serve as an activity, must be congenial and consistent with the culture. Compatibility of method and culture is as important as understanding organic compatibility of human tissue. There may be some places that are so unstable and chaotic that they have no discernable culture, but these would probably not be the concern of many of us here.

The important conclusion of all this, as I see it, is that the guiding philosophy—the way a business is managed—is determining. If a business, or a part of one, is not performing as desired, the first step is to get a workable concept and an able leadership that believes in that concept and is resolved to operate by it. They will then do the things that are appropriate to the culture they have built. They need time to establish this culture but once established it sets deep roots. There may be short-run strategies that produce short-run results, but the culture that prevailed in the Hawthorne plant under the long tenure represented by Stoll, Rice, and Levinger as works managers, and supported early in the course of the work in New York by a man as strategically placed as Stoll, was a solid, durable thing. It was solid over a period of nearly thirty years, from the start of the illumination studies in 1924 to the decline of the ensuing counseling program in the mid 1950's. But this solid, people-oriented culture (and a very effective production organization as well) seems now in retrospect to have been a matter of chance.

The valiant, but unsuccessful, effort to transplant the counseling program to other parts of the Bell System, as a means whereby a more benign situation than was recognized at Hawthorne might be generated elsewhere, suggests that the personnel administration at AT&T at that time did not recognize that, valuable as this work was at Hawthorne, it would be rejected elsewhere like an inappropriate skin graft. By no means do I make here a negative judgment regarding the leaders of that day for that attitude. It is still the prevalent attitude in most large organizations today. Of course, there is still a widespread belief in the magic of "gimmicks", that is, that if one installs enough of the right procedures—

even in the human area—a superior institution will result, or, at least, some of the pain will be allayed. There may be, of course, a short-lived aspirin effect; by taking successive aspirins, something resembling health may be maintained. But the climate of an exceptional factory that prevailed over that long period from 1924 to 1952 was not built that way, it was not the product of the research or the programs that emerged as the fruits of the research. It was basic in the philosophy of a group of very able and very human men. We do not know how they got that way.

All that we know is that the research and the ensuing counseling program, both of which were landmark ventures, were a natural thing to be done in that kind of a factory and that the skill and insight and unflagging interest of an extraordinary academic like Elton Mayo had a good deal to do with keeping the work there on a steady course.

We have moved a long way in research sophistication in the intervening fifty years. Our knowledge about institutions, both universities and businesses, is vastly greater than it was then. With the perspective of those two thoughtful men who have been eyewitnesses to the events, I have briefly related both the situation in Harvard University that produced an Elton Mayo, and the situation in Western Electric that produced, in one major plant at least, a long-sustained and exceedingly able and human management. Both of these situations were accidents, and their collaboration in a joint venture was an even greater accident.

The question that now haunts me is: Do we now know enough, are our research skills sharp enough, is our will to build institutions of quality great enough so that what we have learned from the event we are here to commemorate might serve as a guide for the future; so that fifty to seventy-five years from now those who are meeting to review our work in the last quarter of this century will not have grounds to say, "What happened there was an accident that we cannot explain." Rather, do we have realistic grounds for hope that they will say, "Those people learned something from the experience they reviewed. They learned how to build and sustain great institutions: great universities that are great because they nurture and release scholars who wield a profound influence on the shape of society; and great businesses that are great because they produce major productive results in deeply human ways; and that the society is strong partly because the university and the business worlds interact in a way that sustains them both." This is the kind of framework we need.

Finally, can the judges of the next twenty-five years say, "This was no accident; far-seeing men and women conceptualized it and caused it to happen." I, for one, hope and believe that we are now at the stage where anticipating this retrospective view on the years ahead is a realistic expectation. I like to think that the convening of this commemorative gathering will have something to do with it.

Presented 11/12/74

THE HAWTHORNE STUDIES: A SYNOPSIS

INTRODUCTION

From 1924 to 1933, the Western Electric Company conducted at its Hawthorne Works, a research program, or series of experiments, on the factors in the work situation which affect the morale and productive efficiency of workers. The first of these, the so-called "Illumination Experiments", were studied in cooperation with the National Research Council of the National Academy of Sciences. In the remainder of the studies, the company was aided and guided by the suggestions of Professor Elton Mayo and several of his associates from Harvard University. Because of the large part that Harvard played in the project, it is often referred to as the Hawthorne-Harvard Experiments or Studies.

The following description of the experiments is drawn from the official report, *Management and The Worker*, by F. J. Roethlisberger of Harvard, and the late W. J. Dickson of Western Electric. The other primary source of information is *The Industrial Worker*, by T. N. Whitehead, dealing with the Relay Assembly Test Room. Other discussions of the subject by persons having direct or indirect connections with the studies are to be found in *The Human Problems of an Industrial Civilization* by Elton Mayo, *Leadership in a Free Society* by T. N. Whitehead, and *Fatigue of Workers*, a report by George C. Homans, Secretary of the Committee on Work in industry of the National Research Council. A portion of this report is reprinted in *Human Factors in Management*, edited by S. D. Hoslett.

ILLUMINATION EXPERIMENTS (1924–1927)

In 1924, the Hawthorne Works of Western Electric, in cooperation with the National Research Council of the National Academy of Sciences, embarked on an experiment to determine the "relation of quality and quantity of illumination to efficiency in industry."

Three formal experiments were conducted with various groups of workers. In these experiments the intensity of illumination was increased and decreased and the effect on output was observed. The effect was puzzling. Output bobbed up and down in some groups or increased continually in others, or increased and stayed level in still others. But in no case was the increase or decrease in proportion to the increase or decrease in illumination. Where a parallel "control" group was set up for comparison with the test group undergoing changes in lighting, the production of the control group increased about the same as that of the test group.

On the basis that they had not had sufficient control of the illumination in some of the areas where they had been testing, the investigators set up two groups to work by artificial light only. They kept one group, for control, at a steady level of 10 foot-candles. In the test group they decreased the light one foot-candle at a time. The efficiency of *both* groups increased slowly but steadily, until the test group was down to 3 foot-candles, at which point they complained that they couldn't see what they were doing, and production decreased.

The formal investigation having proved so inconclusive, one of the investigators tried some informal experimentation. He put two coil winders in a locker room and reduced the light until it was about equal to that of a moonlight night. The girls maintained their efficiency throughout, and in fact said they became less tired than when working under bright lights.

On the theory that the workers were perhaps responding to something other than their physical environment, the investigators tried another experiment with a coil-winding group. This time they asked the girls how they felt about the changes in illumination. When they increased the light, the girls said they liked it, could work better under the bright light. Then they *pretended* to increase the light, and the girls said they liked it even better. When they decreased the light, and then told the girls, the latter commented unfavorably. Then they only *pretended* to decrease the light, and the girls said the dimmer light was not so pleasant to work under. Throughout this experiment, production did not materially change.

CONCLUSIONS ON THE ILLUMINATION EXPERIMENTS

To the Western Electric people involved, it appeared that:
1. Light was only one factor (and apparently minor) among many which affect employee output.
2. The attempt to measure the effect of the light factor had failed because:
    a. The other factors had not been controlled.

b. Studies in regular shop departments or large groups involved so many factors that it was hopeless to expect to isolate any one of them.

At this point, the National Research Council withdrew from the studies, but Western Electric continued them, and soon thereafter had the collaboration of people from Harvard University.

RELAY ASSEMBLY TEST ROOM (1927–1932)

Inasmuch as it had appeared that some of the odd effects of the illuminating experiments resulted from the way workers felt about what they were doing (i.e., speeded up because they thought increased production was expected, or slowed down because they were suspicious of the investigator's motives), the investigators tried to set up a situation in which the employees' attitudes would remain constant and unaffected, and other variables might be eliminated.

The factors which were expected to decrease the variables were:

1. Small group
2. Separate group
3. Limited effect of changes in personnel, type of work and introduction of inexperienced operators.
4. Mutual confidence to be established between investigators and operators.

SELECTION OF RELAY ASSEMBLY JOB

The job of assembling relays was selected for this test because:

1. It was a repetitive job.
2. All employees were engaged in the same operation. (This was made even more uniform by reducing the number of relay types assembled in the test room).
3. A complete operation could be performed in a short time—no more than a minute. This would provide a large body of statistical data.
4. No machine work was involved.

SELECTION OF OPERATORS

Operators for the test room were selected on the following basis:

1. All experienced operators so that there would be no effect of "learning" on the results.
2. Operators who were willing and cooperative. (The investigators wanted normal and genuine reactions—no restricting of output as a result of suspicious attitude, no "spurting" because of over-anxiety to cooperate).
3. Two experienced operators—good friends—were asked to choose the remainder of the group.

4. The group consisted of five assemblers, and one layout operator to assign work and obtain parts.

TEST ROOM OBSERVER

An observer was stationed in the test room throughout the experiments. His job was to keep accurate records of all that happened, to create and maintain a friendly atmosphere, and to exercise a partial supervisory function. (The foreman remained responsible for rate revision, promotion, etc.).

TEST ROOM SET-UP

The test room was small, containing one workbench, benches for the recording apparatus, a desk for the observer, clothes lockers and space for storing parts.

The workbench contained holes and chutes at the right of each girl's workplace, into which she would drop each completed relay. Otherwise the equipment was the same as in the regular department.

RECORDING OF OUTPUT

1. Units
    The number of relay types to be assembled in the test room had been reduced so that the only difference would be in the number of parts to be assembled. It was now necessary to develop a unit of measurement that would enable the investigators to have comparable output figures regardless of the type assembled. It was decided to take the E-901 relay as the unit of measurement; conversion factors based on the piece rates were established for the other types assembled, so that all output figures could be shown in terms of E-901 relays.

2. Recorder
    An old printing telegraph was set up to punch a hole in a tape for each completed relay. The tape had five rows of holes, one for each operator. The tape moved at a speed of $\frac{1}{4}''$ per minute. One hole was punched for each complete relay. When the relay was dropped down the chute, it hit a flapper gate. One day's output was recorded on $120''$ of tape.

3. Numerical Register
    A numerical register was included in the circuit for each row of tape. The registers were read each half hour by the test room observer. Daily totals were checked against the operators' performance records.

4. Operator's Performance Record
The layout operator maintained the operator's performance record. The regular departmental record was used for payroll and other purposes. This showed the type of relay assembled, number completed each day, time required for 50 relays, time out for repairs, etc. This provided a record independent of the recording device or log chart.

OTHER RECORDS

1. The Log Sheet
The observer kept a log sheet which was a daily chronological record of each operator's activities, type of relay worked on, time she started on it, intervals of non-productive time, and so on.

2. Daily History Record
The observer kept a record of everything that happened, the changes introduced, remarks made by the investigators. The kinds of questions the investigators were asking themselves at various stages of the experiment were recorded here.

PHYSICAL EXAMINATIONS OF OPERATORS

The operators were examined in the company hospital before the experiments began, and thereafter at intervals of about six weeks. It would be desirable to know whether increased output, if it occurred, would be accomplished at the expense of the operators' health. Or, if rest periods did not increase output, would they serve to improve the operators' health? The investigators recognized the difficulty of measuring "health" on any quantitive basis; however, it was expected that marked changes, particularly if detrimental, could be recognized.

DIVISION OF THE STUDIES INTO PERIODS

The entire course of the studies was not mapped out in advance, but developed as the studies progressed. In the beginning the investigators were interested in the effect of a shorter working day and week. Periods I-III were introductory, to get the girls used to the test room. Periods IV-VII (24 weeks) were devoted to rest period studies. Periods VII-XIII (75 weeks) were experiments with shorter working days and weeks, interspersed with "check" periods of normal working hours.

Period I (2 weeks)

During Period I the girls remained in the regular department. Their output under normal conditions was recorded; and they had their first physical examinations, which showed that they were all normal and in generally good health.

Period II (5 weeks)

During Period II the girls were getting used to working by themselves in the test room, and the investigators were working out plans for keeping records of all that happened during the tests.

Period III (8 weeks)

At the beginning of Period III, the six test room girls became a separate wage incentive payment group. In the regular department they had been part of a large group, which would be comparatively little affected by one person's effort. In the small group, their earnings would be much more directly affected by their output.

Period IV (5 weeks)

At the beginning of Period IV the girls were called to the superintendent's office to talk over plans for two five-minute rest periods during the day. They voted to have the rests at 10:00 o'clock in the morning and 2:00 o'clock in the afternoon. These times were very close to what the records showed to be their lowest output points.

The girls liked the rest periods very much, but still complained of drowsiness in the early afternoon. They thought longer rest periods would be better, but were afraid they would not be able to "make their rate" (a reference to the "bogey" on which their performance was measured in the department, but which was not used in the test room). During this period there was evidence that some of the girls were developing a rather free and easy relationship with the test room observers. After five weeks of two five-minute rest periods showed a slight increase in output, it was decided to try two ten-minute rest periods. The girls were again consulted and were in favor, apparently having lost their fear of not making the bogey.

Period V

Accordingly, for the four weeks of Period V the girls had a ten-minute rest period at 10:00 o'clock in the morning and 2:00 o'clock in the afternoon. Immediately there was a definite rise in output, both in the hourly average and the total. The first day's earnings were 80.6%, and the girls and investigators alike were highly interested and enthusiastic. The observers thought the girls were speeding up to compensate for the shortened working time, but the girls themselves had varied opinions, though they all agreed that they liked the longer rest periods.

During this period an incident occurred which illustrates the girls' attitude toward authority and also the method of supervision in the test room. The investigators thought that the girls' increased earnings would be very dramatically demonstrated if they paid the girls each week the percentage earned in the regular department, but also paid the girls, once a month, the difference between their earnings and the department earnings as a rather large bonus. Two of the girls immediately objected, indicating they thought it was an attempt to confuse them, so that they could not figure their own earnings. There had been some previous comments to the effect that "we earn 80%, but we'll only get 60%" and we'll never get all that money." Accordingly, the investigators dropped the idea, and the girls were greatly relieved.

The incident indicates that the girls had a latent suspicion of authority, a fear that in some way they would be cheated of their higher earnings. It indicates, too, that they felt free to comment about changes in procedure to the test room authorities, and that the test room authorities paid attention to their comments. In this case, the observers discarded a plan which they thought should have seemed perfectly logical to the girls, and re-established the procedure the girls preferred.

The observers were addressing themselves to the girls' fears rather than to the logic of the situation. This was typical of the supervisory technique employed in the test room.

Period VI

It was decided to try six five-minute rest periods. The girls were again consulted. They were opposed to the short periods, but agreed to try them. For four weeks they followed this schedule. They consistently expressed their disapproval both by critical remarks and by excessive laughing and talking and returning late from rest periods. Output during this period, however, did not particularly reflect this feeling. Two girls increased their output slightly as compared to the previous period; two decreased slightly, and one showed no change.

Period VII

During 11 weeks the girls had a 15-minute rest in the morning, during which a lunch was provided by the company restaurant, and a 10-minute break in the afternoon. The lunches were varied, but generally consisted of a sandwich, beverage, and fruit or pudding.

The investigators had had some feeling that the girls' sleepiness in the early afternoon resulted from having had too large a lunch because they had had too little breakfast. However, it did not appear that they ate appreciably smaller lunches during this period; nor was the early afternoon slump in output at all affected.

The girls were enthusiastic about the rest periods and the lunch "on the company." Two of them further increased their hourly output and one maintained the same average as for the previous period. Two girls, however, produced less and in this period they demonstrated an uncooperative and hostile attitude of which there had been occasional evidence in the earlier periods. It was decided, therefore, to transfer these two operators back to the department and to replace them with others who would like to join the test group and had output records comparable with those of the girls who were leaving.

Period VIII

With Period VIII there began a series of experiments with a shorter working day and week. The 15 and 10 minute rest periods continued except in Period XII.

In Period VIII, with new operators taking the place of those who had developed hostile attitudes, the girls were offered the choice of starting $\frac{1}{2}$ hour later than usual or stopping $\frac{1}{2}$ hour earlier. The girls chose the latter, and were very happy about it except for one girl who was breaking up with her boy friend and didn't like the long evenings at home. Despite the fact that working time was now 10% less than standard, the total production increased, and hourly output increased sharply.

This continued for 7 weeks, and the investigators, who had been planning to go back to the original working conditions of 48 hours and no rest periods, decided instead to try a further reduction in hours, to see where the total weekly output would begin to fall off.

Period IX

During Period IX, the girls again chose to stop early—one hour earlier than usual. Although encouraged to work at a natural pace, the girls seemed to feel the need to hurry. Operator 2 began to admonish the other girls to stop talking and to work faster. A contest for leadership developed between her and Operators 3 and 4, who had formerly been the fastest operators and had exercised some leadership.

Although the girls increased their hourly output, the cut in working time proved to be too drastic, and weekly production was somewhat lowered, reducing the girls' earnings. This schedule was, therefore, continued for only four weeks.

Period X

The investigators decided now to go back to standard working hours after an extended period of shorter hours. However, it was felt that the rest periods should be retained for a while.

The girls at first felt very tired working longer hours. In the first weeks, comments on tiredness were very frequent, but diminished as time went on. Hourly production decreased slightly, but weekly production reached a new high for all the operators.

Thinking about this high production, which did not seem to show the effect of fatigue resulting from longer hours of work, the investigators wondered if perhaps the frequent physical examinations had caused the girls to be more conscious of health and to improve their health practices. So they made up a questionnaire, asking the girls about changes in their diet, hours of sleep and so on. No particular change was evident in the answers, but the girls suggested that their increased output was caused by "greater freedom," "absence of bosses," "opportunity to set one's own pace and to earn what one makes without being held back by a big group."

A second questionnaire concentrating on conditions in the test room brought out very similar answers with respect to the relaxed supervision, "more freedom," the "smaller group," "the way we are treated." Only one girl mentioned their increased earnings as an important factor. The comments on "less supervision" are on the surface rather paradoxical, since the test room observer acted as their supervisor and was present all day. During this period there was an increasing amount of social activity among the girls, both inside and outside the plant. They began to have parties at home and sometimes went to the theatre together. This seemed also to affect their relationships at work. A friendly spirit, a willingness to help each other, and other signs of solidarity appeared. When one operator had to be absent, two others assigned themselves the job of keeping up the group earnings while she was away. Conversation and joking became more general, while private conversations diminished. The joking and banter was extended to include the test room investigators and other authorities with whom they had contact.

Period XI

The obvious next step would have been to cut out the rest periods, reverting to standard working conditions. But it was the end of June, and the investigators had promised the girls an experiment with a five-day week during the summer. The five-day schedule was maintained for 9 weeks, two of which were vacation weeks for the whole group.

The girls liked this arrangement very much and their hourly output increased slightly. Weekly output, however, fell off to about the level of Period IX, when they were quitting an hour early. (This, of course, was still far above their output at the beginning of the experiments.) Since they received their base rate for the Saturday mornings they did not work, there was no appreciable loss of earnings.

Period XII

In Period XII the girls reverted to standard conditions, 48 hours per week and no rest periods. The operators were much opposed to the change, though they understood that it was temporary and that there would be other experimental conditions after it. They felt tired, became very hungry and seemed generally restless. Eventually, they developed their own ways of adjusting to the conditions. They had something to eat at about 9:30 in the morning and after lunch it became customary to slack off work, talk and joke, at times quite boisterously.

Attempts of the test room observer to stop the excessive talking were not very effective, and it was interesting to note that the girls did not worry about his threats, since they did not think of him as a "boss." At one point he observed that they were limiting their output, in order to make sure that rest periods would be reinstated. When the observer told them that regardless of output the rest periods would be included in the next period, this practice stopped. During this period hourly output dropped somewhat for all but one of the girls. Operator 3, in particular, showed a marked decrease, apparently, because she was having trouble at home.

After 12 weeks under standard conditions, the rest periods were reinstated in Period XIII.

Period XIII

During Period XIII the girls worked standard hours except for the 15 and 10 minute rest periods. The girls supplied their own morning lunch, except that the company provided hot tea.

The operators welcomed the return of the rest periods. Morale reached its highest peak. They took pride in their work, tried to beat their former output records, and helped each other to maintain the group earnings. There was no attempt to speed up all along the line; when some girls felt like working fast, others slowed down a little. It was a cooperative aim toward a common goal rather than competition between individuals. Operator 2 had acquired an unofficial position of leadership and exerted pressure on slower girls. This sometimes resulted in friction, but eventually the girls achieved a kind of equilibrium so that some could speed up and others slow down without antagonism.

Period XIII lasted for seven months, during which both hourly output and total output exceeded all previous records.

SUMMATION OF PERIODS I-XIII IN THE RELAY ASSEMBLY TEST ROOM

In the two and one-half years of experimentation a number of changes in working conditions had been tried. What were their effects in terms of output, and the girls' health and mental attitude?

1. Except for Periods X, XI, and XII, the output rose steadily for all but operators 1A and 2A. In Period XIII Operator 4 reached an increase of about 40% over the base period.
2. In periods VII, X and XIII identical conditions existed,—48 hours per week, a 15-minute rest in the morning, with lunch, and a 10-minute rest in the afternoon. But hourly output was higher in Period X than in Period VII, and in Period XIII it was considerably higher.

3. Periods X, XI and XII varied widely in conditions of work, from a 5-day week with rest periods to a $5\frac{1}{2}$ day week without rest periods. Yet there was comparatively little change in output.
4. In only one case did the hourly rate behave as one might have expected. In Period XII, it did go down when the girls resumed the 48-hour schedule, with no rest periods. Even so, the output was considerably higher than it was under the same conditions in Period III.

It appears then that there is no simple correlation between working conditions and hourly output.

Now let's look at the total output per week. What happened when rest periods were introduced?

1. It is evident that weekly output did not decline; it increased. There was a decline in Period VII, but this resulted partly from the Christmas and New Year's holidays.
2. The increase in hourly rate compensated for the time lost in shorter working hours in every period except IX and XI, where working time was reduced by 15.3% and 13.2% respectively.
3. In Period XII weekly output reached a new high level for every operator in spite of the fact that hourly rate of output decreased in this period.

To sum up, output had increased steadily for nearly $2\frac{1}{2}$ years in spite of numerous changes in hours of work. Morale in the test room had steadily improved. The girls had averaged only $3\frac{1}{2}$ attendance irregularities a year (sickness and personal absences plus times late) compared with 15 a year before coming into the test room. Meanwhile, 33 girls in the regular department had averaged $3\frac{1}{2}$ times as many sickness absences, nearly three times as many personal absences, and about 3 times as many failures to register as the girls in the test room.

The investigators formulated four hypotheses to explain the greatly improved performance of the operators in the test room:

1. Relief from fatigue—the rest periods
2. Relief from monotony

Detailed study of the half-hourly output records and other data, compared with the literature on fatigue and monotony, led to the conclusion that relief from fatigue was not the answer, and that the evidence as to relief from monotony was very inconclusive.

3. Increased Wage incentive—the fact that in a small payment group their earnings more closely reflected the amount of their output.
4. Change in method of supervision—the more informal relationship with the test room supervisors diminished the girls' suspicion of management, and allowed them more freedom in their relationships with each other.

To test the possibility that the change to a small wage incentive group was responsible for the improved performance, the investigators decided to try two more experiments—one in which the *only* change in the operators' work would be a change to a small payment group; and one in which the test room situation would be duplicated without a change in wage incentives.

SECOND RELAY ASSEMBLY GROUP

Another group of five relay assemblers was formed into a separate payment group within the regular department. Almost immediately their production increased by 12% and remained at that level for nine weeks, when the group was discontinued because of the complaints of the girls in the regular department. This would seem to indicate that the small wage incentive group did have some effect. However, there were two important points to note: First, the output in this group increased immediately but then leveled off; second, the increase amounted to only 12% compared with the test group's 30%. A complicating factor, also, was that the Second Relay Assembly Group were consciously trying to show they were as fast as the test group.

MICA SPLITTING TEST ROOM

The second experiment on the effect of wage incentives was to set up the Mica Splitting Test Room, in which changes in working conditions could be introduced without a change in wage incentives. This was accomplished by segregating in a special room a group of five operators who were on individual piece rates. The first change was the introduction of rest periods, which resulted in a moderate but steady rise in output. The next change was the elimination of overtime work. Production continued to increase for awhile, then began to decline slowly but steadily. The third change was a further reduction to a 40-hour week.

Output dropped to a lower level, where it remained steady until the Depression caused such a reduction in work that the test had to be discontinued. The reaction of the girls to the test room situation was as favorable as in the Relay Assembly Test Room. Their reaction to rest periods and shorter working hours resulted in an increase in production, though there was a wide variation among the girls and only two of them had increases at all comparable with the increases of all the relay assemblers. There were good reasons for the decreasing production in the later periods, since there was a good deal of worry about the mica-splitting job being transferred to the company's plant in Kearny, New Jersey, and finally about the increasing effects of the Depression.

However, even where conditions were similar the average increase in production was only 15% as compared to 30% in the Relay Assembly Test Room.

(And the Second Relay Assembly Group, theoretically influenced by wage incentives only, increased production only 12%.)

On the original premises of the experiments, one might conclude that the 30% increase in the Relay Assembly Test Room, minus the 15% increase in the Mica-Splitting Test Room, would show 15% as the increase accounted for by the change in wage incentives. However, this conclusion depends on so many things which might or might not be true, that it cannot be taken too seriously.

The two conclusions which the investigators did feel justified in drawing were these:

1. The steady increase in the Relay Assembly Test Room was not due to the change in wage incentive only.
2. The effect of this change in wage incentive was so much tied up with the effects of so many other factors that it was impossible to tell how much influence it had.

The underlying premises of both the illumination and the test room experiments had been that a change in working conditions would result in a change in production. Let's represent this idea with a simple diagram:

C—————R   Change produces Result

A "good" change produces a good result (i.e., an increase in production); A "bad" change produces a bad result (i.e., a decrease in production).

When the illumination failed to substantiate this premise, it was assumed that extraneous factors had interfered, primarily the feelings and attitudes of the operators. Therefore the test room setup was devised with the idea of keeping the operators' attitudes constant while making other changes; there, presumably, the only reactions would be automatic physical reactions—the operators would work faster or slower.

But in their attempts to keep constant the attitudes of the girls in the test room, the investigators made many changes in the treatment of the girls which made their situation very untypical of workers in general. In the very attempt to prevent change, they introduced change.

More and more the investigators came to realize that the significant information they were acquiring had to do with the way people thought and felt—their attitudes. At this stage they began to think of the effect of change somewhat in the manner of the following diagram:

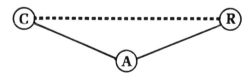

Figure 1. Change affects attitude which, in turn, affects result.

That is, that change does not lead to a direct and automatic result; change affects the employee's attitude, which in turn affects the result.

So the chief result of the two years of the Relay Assembly Test Room had been to demonstrate the importance of employee attitudes and preoccupations. All attempts to eliminate such considerations had been unsuccessful. The importance of employee attitudes had been evident in the "apprehension of authority" which had been common to all the operators, although in different degrees, and could be aroused by the slightest provocation. It had been evident in the effects of the experimentally introduced changes in working conditions, which had operated as changes in the meaning of the situation or the operations, rather than as changes in physical circumstances. It had shown itself in the output variations of certain operators, which could be related to their personal preoccupations, and which continued as long as the preoccupations existed.

What practical consequences did these results have for management?

Management regarded these experiments as an attempt to compile a sound body of knowledge upon which to base executive policy and action. And although it was recognized that such research is a long-term proposition, management was ready to make use of any findings which seemed to have been sufficiently tested.

The most important of such findings was that of the usefulness of rest periods. Although the effects of rest periods had not been exactly measured, all the evidence pointed to their desirability. Beginning in 1928, therefore, rest periods were gradually introduced throughout the plant wherever repetitive work was going on, and wherever the results were studied, production at least did not decrease.

The most important result of the research was management's improved understanding of many of its problems. For example, management had formerly tended to make many assumptions as to what would happen if changes were made in, for instance, wage incentives or hours of work.

They now began to question these assumptions and to see that such factors as hours of work and wage incentives are only part of a total situation and that their effects cannot be predicted apart from that total situation.

What impressed management most, however, were the stores of latent energy and productive cooperation which could be obtained from its working force under the right conditions. Among the factors making for these conditions the attitudes of the employees stood out as being of predominant importance.

INTERVIEWING PROGRAM (1928-1930)

The logical next step was to find out about the attitudes of employees in general about their jobs, their supervision, their working conditions, and so on.

This tied in with a current problem which had arisen in the training of supervisors. A series of supervisory conferences on "morale" had bogged down for lack of factual information. There were conflicting opinions on the factors involved in cooperation between employees and supervisors. There was no generally acceptable body of information about how employees felt about their jobs and their supervisors. The simple suggestion was made that the way to find out how employees felt was to ask them. Information gained could be used in two ways: Complaints on physical conditions would be referred to the organization responsible; comments on supervision would be used in supervisory training conferences.

In 1928 the interviewing program began, first with 1600 people in the Inspection Branch. By the end of 1930, 21,000 employees had been interviewed. As the interviews progressed, the interviewers' methods changed. At first they asked about the employee's likes and dislikes, about his working conditions, his job and his supervision. If the employee did not talk freely, the interviewer asked specific questions about these things. The interviewers began to notice, however, that it was difficult to hold employees to the subjects. The employees tended to go off on other subjects, which seemed to be so much on their minds that they kept going back to them in spite of the interviewers' efforts to get back to the assigned subjects.

This experience was so widespread that it began to appear very significant, and the decision was made to change the interviewing method completely.

In the future, the interviewer would state the purpose of the interview, which was still the same. But from that point on he was merely to listen to what the employee said, without interrupting or changing the subject, as long as the employee continued to talk spontaneously. He would follow the employee's ideas with interest, taking only enough notes to enable him to recall what the employee had said. His report would be, as nearly as possible, a verbatim account of what the employee had said.

The verbatim accounts were then studied by a group of analysts who broke the comments down to specific complaints and classified them (washrooms, lighting, ventilation, etc.). When a number of complaints about a certain subject (dirty washrooms, for instance) had been collected, they would be forwarded to the organization responsible (responsible for cleaning the washrooms, for example).

Benefits of the Interviewing Program

What was accomplished by the interviewing program?

First, a number of unsatisfactory working conditions were improved. Often enough, the conditions had been known before, and there were some plans to correct them. However, the fact that so many employees complained of them undoubtedly speeded up the corrective action.

Second, the interviews provided material for a supervisory training program,

in which supervisors read sample interviews, from which all identifying information had been removed, and discussed them in conference. The conference had
some effect in making supervisors conscious of the feelings employees had
toward their treatment by supervisors.

These benefits had been more or less assumed before the interviews began.
There were, however, some additional, unexpected benefits. One unexpected
benefit was that the very fact that the interviews were going on made supervisors
more conscious of their own behavior, more careful in their dealings with
employees. A certain amount of automatic improvement in supervision took
place. Also unexpected was the enthusiasm of the employees. Over and over
they stated how much better they felt now that they had "got something off
their chest." In addition, there was a considerable feeling of gratification that
"management" was paying some attention to them, was interested in what they
thought.

The interviewers learned a great deal from the interviews obtained from this
new method, and what they learned tied in with a difficulty the analysts were
having in classifying the complaints in the interviews. You will recall that there
was a group whose job was to break down the interviews into individual complaints, which could be classified so that all complaints on the same subject
could be counted and investigated. However, the analysts very often found it
impossible to understand what the complaints were about, when they were
taken out of the context of the complete interview. To the interviewers, too, it
was becoming apparent that many of the complaints could not be taken at their
face value.

For example, an interviewer talked with Joe Brown, who complained about
conditions in the shop, the drafts, smoke and fumes. As he continued to talk,
his conversation was almost entirely about health, diet, disease, about how
deceiving a healthy appearance may be. (Brown was very healthy looking.)
Then he talked about his brother, who had recently died of pneumonia. He
compared himself to his brother. "Here I am, healthy, just like my brother; yet
tomorrow I may be gone." Brown's complaints about drafts, smoke and fumes
took on quite a different meaning in the context of the whole interview; the
complaints were really an indication of his preoccupations about his health.

Another employee complained that his piece rates were too low. As he
continued to talk, he related that his wife was in the hospital, and that he was
worried about his doctor bills. In effect the complaint about piece rate is an
expression of his concern about his ability to pay his bills.

Another employee complained of his boss being a bully. If the boss gave him
an order, he felt the boss was abusing his authority. If the boss said nothing to
him, he felt he was being slighted and ignored. As the talk turned to his past
experiences, he talked about his father, an overbearing, domineering man whose
authority could not be questioned. Gradually the interviewer could see that

the employee's dissatisfaction was rooted somewhere in his attitude toward authority, developed during early childhood. He tended to hate anyone in a position of authority in the same way he hated his father.

The investigators began to realize that, to understand what was involved in an employee's complaint, it was often necessary to understand the background of the employee and his personal situation. The complaint in itself might be primarily a symptom of a personal situation which needed to be explored.

As a result of this insight, the interviewers for a while tended to concentrate on the personal situation of employees, particularly on their early home background, applying the concepts of the psychopathologists. As a result, a number of very interesting case studies were developed. This, however, turned out to be rather a dead one. Very few Hawthorne employees were extreme cases of psychoneurosis, for whom this delving into early family life would have a therapeutic value; and, indeed, the interviewers were not professionally equipped for this type of therapy.

In their interest in personal situations of the employees who complained, and in the unusual cases which had been discovered, the investigators had tended to ignore some of the uniform threads which had run through the interviews. When they started to interview supervisors, however, certain characteristics were so uniform that they forced themselves to the attention of the investigators, and turned their attention to the social relationships among people in the working group.

The interviewing of supervisors was done by two representatives of the Harvard Business School. What particularly struck the interviewers was the mass of comments about social distinctions; in differences between supervisory ranks, between office and shop, length of service, men and women, etc.

Distinctions between Different Supervisory Ranks

Social distance was not the same between any two consecutive levels. The most marked cleavage was between foreman and general foreman (department chief and division chief were the corresponding office titles).

Distinctions between Office and Shop

1. Status in the company was not determined by rank alone; it also depended on the type of work. Certain jobs carried more social prestige than others. On the whole, an office worker had a higher social status than a shop worker.
2. This distinction carried through the first few ranks of supervision. A shop group chief or section chief had little or no more prestige than a non-supervisor in the office.

Distinctions of Seniority or Sex

1. All other things equal, two group chiefs in the same shop were not considered equal in status unless they had the same length of service and are of the same sex.
2. Occupations performed by men had a higher social status than those performed by women.
3. Employees with long service had a higher status than employees with short service.

None of these distinctions were particularly essential to the manufacture of telephones; they arose because the company was not only a manufacturer of telephones but a human organization in which people were trying to satisfy their hopes and desires.

And, of course, there were characteristics of their working environment which reflected these distinctions. The private office of the assistant superintendent certainly set him off from lower ranks of supervision. There were variations in the accommodations of shop and office supervisors (the latter, for instance, had private lockers and were supplied with towels). There were distinctions in pay treatment and payment for absences between shop and office people.

While workers and supervisors of various ranks and conditions felt these differences in social distance, there were many cross-currents of common feeling binding them together. The lowest worker and highest executive may feel the same about length of service. Supervisor and subordinate in the shop may feel the same way about office workers.

Some of these distinctions did not have the same meaning at each level. The distinction between office and shop status, for instance, did not seem to be felt very much by assistant superintendents.

The supervisors' comments about company policies in promotion, rate of pay, about other levels of supervision, and about relations with employees emphasized very strongly the supervisors' feelings about social status in the working situation and pointed up the social significance of the factors affecting them. This tended to illuminate the interviews with non-supervisory employees, in which much information could be found to indicate the importance of social relationship in all levels of employees.

An overall concept of employee satisfaction or dissatisfaction (whether supervisor or non-supervisor) is illustrated in the diagram on p. 296.

This diagram illustrates that the worker—whether supervisor or individual—has a certain status determined by his place in the social organization of the company. The effect of changes in working conditions, hours, rates of pay, etc., may be predicted according to their effect on the various factors which determine this status. The extent to which the employee finds satisfaction in his work depends on how his status corresponds with the social demands he makes

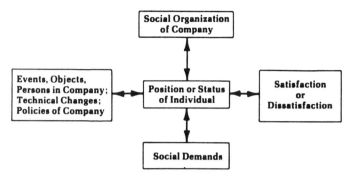

Figure 2. Worker's status determined by his place in social organization of his company.

of his work, which in turn is dependent not so much on his relation to the company as his relation to society in general. All these factors are interrelated—changes in any are likely to change all the others, to the extent that the employee feels the change.

The effect of all this on the investigators was to turn them to a study of social relationships on the job. They thought they should observe directly the behavior of employees on the job with specific attention to the kinds of things reported in the interviewing program. They were interested in how some of the feelings and attitudes mentioned in the interviews affected work activities, in the actions of groups in maintaining group standards, in the effect of group standards on working efficiency, and the like. The project they established was known as the Bank Wiring Observation Room.

BANK WIRING OBSERVATION ROOM, 1931-1932

The purposes of the Bank Wiring Observation Room were:

1. To develop a method of studying group behavior which would supplement interviewing with actual observations of behavior in the working group.
2. To obtain more exact information about social groups within the company by making an intensive study of one group under normal shop conditions.

In the group to be chosen there would be no changes in the work situation except that the group would be in a separate room. An observer would be stationed in the room to record production and make notes on all the activities, but he would never give orders or instructions, never make critical comments, never appear too eager to get into the group's conversations or to be too interested in their behavior.

There was also an interviewer who talked to the men off the job. His function was to gain insight into the men's attitudes, thoughts, and feelings. The interviewer rarely appeared in the observation room, since it was thought that the men might talk more freely to someone not familiar with their activities on the job.

The group selected for this experiment consisted of 9 wiremen, 3 solderers, and 2 inspectors working on banks of equipment used in step-by-step central office equipment. The job consisted of setting up the banks side-by-side on frames, wiring the corresponding terminals from bank to bank, soldering the connections, and inspecting, with a test set, for short circuits or breaks in the wire. One solderman soldered the work of three wiremen; the inspection work was shared by two inspectors.

Output Behavior in the Bank Wiring Observation Room

The most obvious fact about the output of the Bank Wiring Room was that each worker was restricting his output, and that none of them was reporting his output correctly to the group chief for his individual record. The total for the week would check with total week's production, but the daily reports would indicate a steady, level output regardless of the actual work done.

Beliefs Related to Output Behavior

Interviews with 32 operators (including those in the observation room and others in the regular department) showed that their idea of a day's output had little to do with the criteria set up by the wage incentive engineers. Only two of them stated correctly that they were expected to make the "bogey," which was 914 connections per hour, 7,312 for an 8-hour day. Twenty men said that the wiring of two equipments (6,000 or 6,600 connections on selectors or connectors respectively) was the expected day's work. Some of them said this represented 100% efficiency.

It was clear that the official bogey had little to do with their production. They had a standard of their own (6,000 connections a day) set well below the bogey, and well below what they could have done. The standard was set at this point because of certain beliefs and fears. They were afraid that if they did increase their output appreciably, something would happen. The rate would be cut, the bogey would be raised, someone might be laid off, the slower men might get bawled out. Practically none of them believed that if they increased their output their earnings would increase and nothing else would happen.

(As it happened, they had recently gone from a 48-hour week to a 44-hour week. At the time of the change, their supervisor had assured them that if they maintained the same output they would receive the same pay in spite of the decrease in hours. This actually occurred, and none of the men could understand it, in spite of repeated explanations.)

Just as they believed their output should not go above a certain level, they believed it should not fall too far short of that level. Consequently, their output curves, based on their own reports, were very nearly level.

They kept track of their output very closely without ever writing anything down. One day the interviewer asked a wireman what time it was. The wireman added up the number of levels he had wired and told him the time within 2 minutes.

Although almost all agreed on what constituted a fair day's work, and all maintained a level output record, they did not all turn out the same amount of work. Four of them were close to their standard, four fell far short, and one consistently exceeded it.

Why did this happen? The reasons were pretty well bound up with the social relations of the workers—so these will be described next.

Relations with Supervision

The workers' relations with the group chief centered on certain main activities.

1. Daywork Claims

    The operators often found it necessary to make excessive day-work claims in order to justify their reporting low output for the day. The group chief knew that many of the claims were unjustified, but signed off just the same, rarely questioning them.

2. Job Trading

    Soldermen and wiremen frequently traded jobs. The group chief presumably had the duty of forbidding this, because it was expected that each man could work faster if he remained on the job. The group chief made little attempt to stop the job trading.

3. Discipline

    The group chief was responsible for preventing horseplay and excessive talking and joking, and for enforcing company rules. In practice, he overlooked disobedience of some of the rules because he agreed with the operators that they were unimportant. He considered that his main job was to get an acceptable day's work out of the workers, and in this he succeeded.

The group chief was very highly regarded by the workers, because he had in effect aligned himself with them and accepted their code of conduct. He conformed to the workers' feelings of how a group chief should act. This group chief, toward the end of the study, was demoted as a result of the general reduction in force, and his place was taken by a group chief who tried to exercise stricter discipline. This resulted in no change in the workers' activities; they simply concealed from him many things which they frankly expressed to the first group chief. They obeyed the stricter group chief no better than they had the more lenient one.

Toward the section chief the operators' attitude was much the same as toward the group chief. They recognized a somewhat greater authority, but did not always obey him and frequently argued with him.

Toward the assistant foreman and foreman, however, the operators exhibited quite different attitudes. They never disobeyed or argued, and were restrained in their behavior when he was present. The foreman and assistant foreman operated strictly in accordance with the logic of management; they insisted on the rules of the game as specified by management. As far as they knew, the game was being played according to these rules. The output records indicated that this was so. The operators behaved correctly when they were present and their subordinate supervisors did not inform them otherwise.

Function of Control in the Observation Room

If the function of supervisory control was (1) to transmit orders downward and (2) to transmit upward information about what was happening down the line, it is obvious that neither was happening in the expected fashion. The operators were not acting as management expected, and knowledge of this was not passing upward to higher management. The reason for this was that the operators did not respond in the expected way to the incentives provided for them. If they had worked in accordance with the logics of the wage incentive plan, there would have been no job trading, excessive daywork or restriction of output. Instead the employees were making demands of the group chiefs which he could not deny without becoming disliked. So he and the section chief in effect became part of the group which they supervised. Having taken that position, they felt it necessary to conceal from the foreman everything which was contrary to the logic of management. The departmental performance records were therefore distorted, and the foreman was ignorant of much that was going on.

Relation between Employees

The five occupational groups were found to have varied status in the eyes of the employees. From highest to lowest they were:

> Inspectors
> Connector Wiremen
> Selector Wiremen
> Soldermen
> Truckers

The inspectors, who reported to a separate branch, had the highest status. They were somewhat better educated than the other employees, and were paid on an hourly basis (not incentive). They never traded jobs or went for lunches. They wore ties at work, and wore jackets when they came for interviews, as compared with the wiremen and solderers, who came in shirtsleeves or sweaters.

Wiremen working on connectors had somewhat higher status than those working on selectors. There was no difference in the skill involved, but it happened that new men usually started on the selectors, which were at the back of the room and moved "up" to connectors as vacancies occurred. Sometimes there was an increase in hourly rate, but it was considered a promotion even when no increase was involved.

The position of wireman was considered somewhat superior to that of solderman. Beginners usually started as solderman and moved up to wiring, usually with an increase in hourly rate. The social superiority of wiremen was demonstrated in the fact that job trading was always requested by the wiremen and the soldermen almost always traded without protest. It was always a solderman who went out to get lunches for the group.

Both the wiremen and soldermen demonstrated their superiority to the trucker who served the observation room. They made fun of him, poked his arm when he was stamping numbers on the equipment, tickled his ribs while he was lifting equipment onto the truck. There was no personal feeling involved; they acted this way with any trucker who came into the room.

The Informal Group in Social Activities

During the lulls in activity the men matched coins, played cards, had baseball pools and chipped in to buy candy. In these activities two groups were formed— the first 5 wiremen, solderman 1 and Inspector 1 who worked at the front of the room, formed one group. The other four wiremen and solderman 4 formed another group at the back of the room. One solderman and one inspector did not participate at all. The two groups were almost completely exclusive of each other; all the gambling games occurred in one group, and all the "binging" (hitting another person on the upper arm with the fist), in the other. Both groups chipped in to buy candy at the club store, but they bought different kinds and neither shared with the other.

Participation in Job Trading

Participation in job trading emphasized the superior status of the connector wiremen. The selector wiremen traded jobs only with their own solderman, while the connector wiremen traded jobs to some extent with all three soldermen; they apparently felt free to do this, but the selector wiremen did not.

Participation in Helping

All the men helped each other from time to time, although this was frowned upon by management. This activity was not confined within work groups; it seemed to draw the whole group together rather than separate it into parts.

Friendships and Antagonisms

A chart of the work and play activities and the indications of friendship and antagonism that appeared in the group gives a picture of the existence of two chief groups in the organization. A group toward the front of the room, which we may call Clique A, consisted of an inspector, three wireman and one solderman.

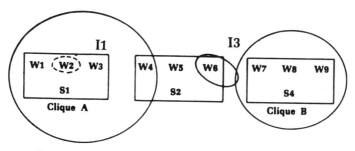

Figure 3. Clique membership—bank wiring observation room.

The diagram indicates membership in the cliques. W2 is a special case, since he participated in games with Clique A, but that was all. He did not talk much with the others and seemed to be somewhat insecure in the group. Wireman 6 participated in some activites of Clique B, but was not entirely accepted. I3, W5 and S2 were not included in either Clique.

A number of suggestions have been made as to why these cliques developed as they did. None, however, are completely satisfactory. Certain characteristics, however, are reasonably clear. One is that Clique A was considered superior to Clique B. Their output was higher, they talked about more serious subjects, got involved in less horseplay. Some of the prestige even carried over to Solderman 1, who had a somewhat higher status than the other soldermen as a result of his association with the "group in front."

The Individual's Behavior and His Position in the Group

It appears that the individual's behavior with respect to an informal code of conduct influenced his acceptance in the group. For example, Inspector 1 was welcome in Group A because he did not assume higher status. He often told the wiremen about defects, and even repaired them himself, instead of reporting them. He participated in their activities as an equal, not a superior.

Solderman 1 was accepted because he subordinated himself to the wiremen, as a solderman should. Wireman 2 was not a full-fledged member because he ignored the group's standards of output, consistently turning out and reporting more output than they believed proper.

Wireman 5 was excluded from both groups because he had a tendency to criticize other workers in the presence of bosses.

Wireman 6 belonged with Group A with respect to his output (higher than Group B but not above the group standard) but he horsed around too much to suit Group A, and he had a tendency to try to assert leadership over the entire group, which they did not accept.

The entire group of men had certain ideas or sentiments as to the way a worker should conduct himself. They were:

1. You should not turn out too much work; if you do, you are a "rate-buster."
2. You should not turn out too little work; if you do, you are a "chiseler."
3. You should not tell a superior anything to the detriment of a fellow worker; if you do, you are a "squealer."
4. You should not try to maintain social distance or act important; if you are an inspector, for example, you should not act like one.

The individual's position in the group was largely, though not entirely, determined by the extent to which his behavior was in line with those sentiments.

The members of Clique A, the people who held the most favored position in the room, followed these rules of behavior in all respects. Members of Clique B followed rules 1, 3 and 4. They slipped somewhat with respect to Rule 2; their output was rather low. They made up for this by a greater insistence on the other rules. Squealing, for instance, was particularly abhorrent to them, because more of their actions were wrong from the standpoint of management, and they hated any show of superiority because they apparently felt that they were in a subordinate position to Group A.

The Group's Methods of Control

The methods used by the group to bring pressure on the individual and control his conduct was neither gentle nor subtle. They included sarcasm, name-calling, "binging" and ridicule. They ostracized persons whose behavior was against their interests.

They protected themselves against interference by bringing into line those outsiders—such as supervisors and inspectors—who were in a position to interfere in their affairs. When one inspector got out of line, they caused him to be transferred. They would finish a large number of equipments at once, then charge daywork because they had to wait for him to inspect the equipments. They dropped solder and screws in his test set so that it short-circuited. Pretending to help him, they would pull the plugs on his test set out just far enough so that it wouldn't work. They goaded him until he finally blew up and made exaggerated statements about the group's behavior to his supervisors. The Bank Wiring section chief and foreman supported their people, and the inspector was transferred.

The group protected themselves against management by keeping their output records level and uniform. In this way they felt that they were protecting themselves against changes.

Why the Group Felt a Need to Protect Themselves

To understand why this group felt a need to protect itself, it was necessary to understand the position of the group in the company structure. Three major groups had an important effect on the worker and his job: management, supervisors and technologists—or perhaps supervisors and technical specialists as the visible representatives of abstract management. The technical specialists— engineers, cost accountants, rate setters—are employed by management, in part at least, to improve processes and methods. They tend to be experimentally-minded. They look at the worker with a critical eye, thinking of ways in which his job can be improved.

To the worker, however, his job, the way he does it, and his relation with other workers, are not objective matters. They are full of social significance. Changes in them affect his status, and may upset his feelings of self-importance.

Frequently plans to improve efficiency do not take the worker's feelings into account. The worker is frequently called upon to adjust himself to changes about which he has not been consulted; and from his position at the bottom level of the organization, he cannot be expected to feel the same way about the changes as do those who are planning them. Many of these changes tend to subordinate the worker still further in the company's social structure.

This attitude was reflected in the response of the group to supervision. Most of the problems of the supervisors were in getting the workers to conform to the rules of the technical organization. The worker's conduct was considered right or wrong in so far as it followed those rules; the supervisor was judged according to his success in enforcing those rules. These rules were considered to be economically advantageous to the worker; but to the worker they were merely annoying—they seemed to be merely ways of showing authority over him.

For example, the rule about not helping each other to wire was intended to promote efficiency and therefore increase the earnings of the worker. To the wiremen it was just an arbitrary rule. They liked to help each other. It was a way of expressing their solidarity, their group spirit, and they felt sure that it did not slow them down—it gave them a lift.

To sum up, in the Bank Wiring Observation Room there had grown up an informal organization that controlled the behavior of its members for the sake of protecting itself against technical and supervisory interference. The group was banded together to resist change or threat of change. They felt the need of resistance because of their position in the company structure and their relation with other groups in the company.

SIGNIFICANCE OF THE HAWTHORNE EXPERIMENTS FOR THE SUPERVISOR

Now, we've been talking about some events that took place at Hawthorne between 1927 and 1932. If you read *Management and The Worker*, however, where in many cases you will find verbatim reports of what workers said, you will find that people felt and thought and talked about the same as they do now.

What is the significance of all this for the supervisor today?

The Individual

First, the interviewing program demonstrated very clearly that complaints cannot always be taken at face value. Complaints are often symptoms of underlying problems or preoccupations which employees cannot recognize without help or cannot state except to a person who, they feel, will understand. What can the supervisor do about this? He can listen more and talk less. He can try to

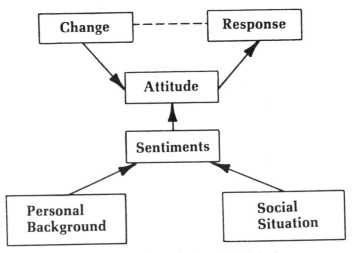

Figure 4. Related factors in determining behavior.

understand. He can try to behave in such a way that employees will want to talk to him.

Second, a point clearly demonstrated in the illumination experiments, the Relay Assembly Test Room, and the Bank Wiring Room is that an individual's behavior can rarely be predicted in terms of a simple cause and effect relationship. Rather, the individual's response is usually determined by a complex system of related factors which must be considered as a whole before predicting behavior.

The Company Social Structure

The interviewing program, particularly the interviews with supervisors, brought out the significance of the social relationships throughout the company, and the importance to the employee of the symbols of prestige and status connected with his job. Employees, for instance, were much more concerned with wage differentials as symbols of status than with absolute amounts of wages. There were other obvious symbols of prestige—double pedestal desks, different types of calendar pads, name in the telephone directory, etc. Symbols of status are of great importance to the individual, and activity which threatens to change them will usually provoke a defensive response.

The Informal Group

The Bank Wiring Observation Room demonstrated the workings of an informal group, the various levels of membership in the group, the unofficial code under which it operated, and its methods of enforcing that code. Its reason for existence was shown to be the resistence to change. On the other hand there was a group in the Relay Assembly Test Room which demonstrated that under certain conditions a group will not be affected adversely by change. The differences in attitudes between these groups are full of significance for those who are interested in the effects of supervisory action and attitudes.

Influence on Change in Individual and Group Behavior

People get adjusted to things as they are, or at least to a kind of balance or equilibrium such that the minor variations which constantly occur are accepted and compensated for. When changes are made that upset the equilibrium, we have an employee relations problem. Changes put into effect without regard for the sentiments and beliefs of individuals and groups are frequently interpreted as lowering the individual or group in the company structure.

To make changes, therefore, with the least possible violation of the sentiments of the group requires that the supervisor understand what those sentiments are and what they are based on. He must understand the position of the people in the informal organization and must know what symbols in the working environment are significant to those positions. To achieve that understanding, the supervisor must listen to his employees, must behave in such a way that his employees will trust him and speak more frankly to him; and he must be alert in his observation of the working relationships which develop around him.

INDEX

Alienation: misfit victims, 23

American industry: at a turning point, 47

Attitudes and motivation: defined, 12; drive or incentive theory, 12; expectancy theory as base for research on work motivation, 12; problem of individual differences, 12

Austria: successful in using participative methods, 45

Automated machines: led to increased split in individual and organizational goals, 100

Bank Wiring Room: led to discovery of worker peer groups, 80; not involved in 'whole task' principle, 124; Theory Y refuted by workers' behavior, 85; workers behaved in anti-organizational, anti-managerial manner, 85; workers did not respond logically to management's incentive system, 80; workers developed group structure, 80; sabotaged management control system, 80; under-utilized human resources, 25

Behavioral scientists: assume that work itself is inviolate, 100; group meeting his primary tool, 76; groups his most powerful and beloved tool, 76; people with influence and power are skeptical of, 34

Bimodal: working population, 22

Blues: blue collar blues, 21; managerial blues, 21; professional blues, 21; white collar blues, 21

Career development: planned to defeat under-utilization, 28; management assumes responsibility for, 28

Co-determination: participative methods, 45

Contextual factors: developed by Hawthorne Studies, 129; employment security, 129

Contingency theory: defined, 28; of organizations, 87

Design of supervision: at Kalmar and Topeka, 116

Drive or incentive theory: defined, 12

Dynamic compound job fitting: defined, 28

Emotions: identifying emotional problems, 198; psychological function of work, 195; transference, 199; transference in the work situation, 200

Employee participation: provides added satisfaction to those involved, 38

Employee security: contextual effect of Hawthorne Studies, 129

Employee selection: identified with employee testing, 10; used as an abbreviation for a variety of predictor variables, 10; for promotion, 10

Environmental design: characteristics impact on the way people work, 15; individual differences in perception, 14

Expectancy theories: as base for contemporary research on work motivation, 12

Typologies: as a method to classify occupations, 8; developed for intellectual, personality and urban ecology problems, 8; future research in, 10

Uncertainty: as a unifying concept in study of work, 20; defined, 20; work organizations fail to reduce, 26

Underutilization of human resources: Bank Wiring Room, 25; behavioral scientists share blame for, 26; consequences of, 25; dynamic compound job-fitting, 28; increased in last fifty years, 25; misfit victims, 24; need to plan career development, 28; organizations fail to reduce uncertainty of, 26; personnel specialists at fault, 26; solutions to, 25; underutilization error preferred in practice, 28

Volvo: elimination of assembly line and program of participating work groups increase productivity, 37; Kalmar auto plant, 116; new Virginia plant designed with participative management, 36; work restructuring experiments began in 1960's, 120

Whole task principle: not derived from Hawthorne Studies, 124; or work design, 124

Women: rising role in American society, 71

Work complaints: muted by problems of the economy, 21

Work design: must offer stimulation, challenge and lift to employee morale, 48; whole task principle, 124

Work ethic: changing in America, 71

Work organization: viewed as social system in Hawthorne Studies, 121

Work redesign: can help individuals care about their work and competence, 102; can result in re-humanizing people, 102; changed jobs sometimes diminished, 104; changes behavior of person, 100; changes planned on basis of diagnosis, 112; changes tend to stay, 101; changing job changes relationship of person and his work, 99; contingency plans made beforehand to deal with problems, 113; forces opportunities for other organizational changes, 101; ingredients for effective implementation, 110, 114; little planning or diagnosis in actual job redesigns, 105; managed with bureaucratic practices, 109; managerial staffs, unions rarely getting education in theory, strategy and tactics of, 108; people do the tasks given them, 100; projects rarely systematically evaluated, 107; raises possibility of bringing individual and organizational goals back together, 100; responsible individuals move towards difficult problems, 110; theory-based diagnosis of job starts before change is made, 111; what can go wrong, 103; why it should survive, 99; work itself does not change, 103; work system around redesigned job rarely assessed for readiness, 106

Work restructuring: at Kalmar and Topeka, 116; defined, 117; Volvo experiments began in 1960's, 120

Worker councils: participative methods, 45

Workers: most productive ones are the most dissatisfied, 35; prepared to risk economic penalties, 34

Working population: thought of as bimodal, 22

Young employees: have different notion of success, 36; morale is low and productivity minimal, 36

Yugoslavia: successfully uses participative work methods, 45